ANXIOUS CHINA

T0385455

The publisher and the University of California Press Foundation gratefully acknowledge the generous support of the Sue Tsao Endowment Fund in Chinese Studies.

ANXIOUS CHINA

INNER REVOLUTION AND POLITICS
OF PSYCHOTHERAPY

Li Zhang

UNIVERSITY OF CALIFORNIA PRESS

University of California Press
Oakland, California

Calligraphy credit: Zhang Wenxun 张文勋

Library of Congress Cataloging-in-Publication Data

Names: Zhang, Li, 1965 May- author.
Title: Anxious China : inner revolution and politics of
    psychotherapy / Li Zhang.
Description: Oakland, California : University of California
    Press, [2020] | Includes bibliographical references and
    index.
Identifiers: LCCN 2019059515 (print) | LCCN 2019059516
    (ebook) | ISBN 9780520344181 (cloth) | ISBN 9780520344198
    (paperback) | ISBN 9780520975392 (ebook)
Subjects: LCSH: Psychotherapy—China. | Psychotherapy—
    Political aspects—China.
Classification: LCC RC451.C6 Z43 2020 (print) |
    LCC RC451.C6 (ebook) | DDC 362.19689/1400951—dc23
LC record available at https://lccn.loc.gov/2019059515
LC ebook record available at https://lccn.loc.gov/2019059516

29   28   27   26   25   24   23   22   21   20
10   9   8   7   6   5   4   3   2   1

For my late mother, Li Lanping 李兰平

CONTENTS

ILLUSTRATIONS

ACKNOWLEDGMENTS

My research would not have been possible without the generous help of many psychotherapists, their clients, and other people in Kunming who shared with me their stories, struggles, pains, hopes, and dreams. My deepest gratitude goes to them for their generosity, insights, and trust. Among them, I would like to mention three specifically to whom I am most indebted (with their permission to use their real names). Mr. Cao Xinshan and Mr. Liu Chengzhe, two seasoned psychotherapists in Kunming with very different counseling orientations allowed me to follow them and their practice over the past ten years. I attended countless workshops, lectures, and informal training sessions they offered and sat in on many of their counseling sessions described in this book. We also had numerous conversations on a broad range of issues when I returned to Kunming every summer beginning in 2010. The initial ideas for this project were sparked by a casual conversation with Ms. Zhao Baifan—my childhood friend, who later became a psychotherapist. She introduced me to Kunming's counseling world and granted me access to several therapy sessions in the early stage of my research. I have learned tremendously from them and am grateful for the hours and hours they spent with me, for their patient guidance, and for their unfailing friendship.

Many thanks to my wonderful colleagues and friends for their valuable comments and stimulating conversations during the long process of research and writing: Emily Baum, Nicholas Bartlett, John Borneman, Amy Borovoy, Susanne Brandtstädter, Paul Brodwin, Howard Chiang, Lily Chumley, Jocelyn Chua, Anne-Christine Trémon, Elizabeth Davis, Yue Dong, Shanshan

Du, Joe Dumit, Matthew Erie, Sara Friedman, Karl Gerth, Cristiana Giordano, Byron Good, Susan Greenhalgh, Chris Hann, Huang Hsuan-Ying, Sandra Hyde, Matthew Kohrman, Zev Luria, Tomas Matza, Lenore Manderson, Zhiying Ma, Keir Martin, Rima Praspaliauskiene, Sonya Pritzker, Eugene Raikhel, Steve Sangren, Louisa Schein, Natasha Schull, Dorothy Solinger, Peter van der Veer, Robert Weller, Yunxiang Yan, Jie Yang, Roberta Zavoretti, Mei Zhan, Everett Zhang, Yi Zhou, and many more. I especially appreciate Junko Kitanaka and Aihwa Ong for engaging my draft introduction deeply and for pushing me to think comparatively. From conceiving of this project to developing my NSF grant proposal to selecting the cover image, I have had many inspiring and delightful conversations with Joe Dumit. I am grateful for his insights and friendship. I am sure that all of those mentioned here (and any I may have missed) can see the marks they left on my writing. I am especially grateful for my longtime friend Hong Chun Zhang, who kindly granted permission for me to use one of her amazing art works for the cover of this book. I fell in love with this haunting yet beautiful image the minute I saw it, as it nicely captures the mood of what this book seeks to convey.

I also benefited greatly from the engaging discussions with the faculty and students at the following institutions where I was invited to present earlier versions of some chapters: Boston University (Anthropology), Brown University (Watson Institute), Columbia University (Weatherhead Institute for East Asian Studies), Cornell University (East Asian Studies), Duke University (Asia/Pacific Center and Anthropology), Emory University (Anthropology and Women's Studies, and East Asian Studies), Harvard University (Anthropology), Pomona College (Pacific Basin Institute), Princeton University (Anthropology and East Asian Studies), Stanford University (Anthropology and East Asian Institute), Tulane University (Murphy Institute), University of California at Los Angeles (Anthropology and Center for China Studies), University of Washington at Seattle (Jackson School of International Studies) Australian National University, Uppsala University, Max Planck Institute for Social Anthropology, Max Planck Institute for the Study of Religious and Ethnic Diversity, Cologne University, Vrije Universiteit Amsterdam, Peking University, Fudan University, and Yunnan University among others.

My research was supported by a fellowship from the John Simon Guggenheim Memorial Foundation, a three-year grant from the Cultural Anthropology Section of the National Science Foundation, and several UC Davis Faculty Research and Travel Grants. Much of the writing was done while

I was on sabbatical leave granted by my home institution (UC Davis). I thank these foundations and institutions for their generous support.

It was delightful to work with the University of California Press. I am very grateful to my superb editor, Reed Malcom, for his wise guidance, care, and enthusiasm for this project, and to Archna Patel for her first-rate professional assistance in the process. My thanks also go to Gary Hamel who carefully copyedited my entire manuscript. I sincerely thank the two reviewers (one of them, Ayo Wahlberg, revealed his name later) who read my manuscript so carefully and provided incisive and useful suggestions that helped make this a better book.

Portions of several chapters in a somewhat different form appeared in the following articles and book chapters: "Bentuhua: Culturing Psychotherapy in Postsocialist China," *Culture, Medicine, and Psychiatry* (2014) 38 (2): 283–305. "Cultivating the Therapeutic Self in China," *Medical Anthropology* (2018) 37 (1): 45–58. "The Rise of Therapeutic Governing in Postsocialist China," *Medical Anthropology* (2016) 36 (1): 6–18. "Cultivating Happiness: Psychotherapy, Spirituality, and Well-Being in a Transforming Urban China," in *Handbook of Religion and the Asian City*, edited by Peter van der Veer (University of California Press), 315–32.

I want to thank my families across the Pacific Ocean for their sustained love, understanding, and support. I am so fortunate to share my life with two amazing human beings—my husband Mark and our daughter Emily—who are always there for me with their unconditional love and unceasing curiosity for life. Their presence reminds me every day what really matters in this world. They are the joy and anchor of my life. I am also grateful to Mark for reading every chapter I wrote with care and for providing thoughtful editorial suggestions, as he did for all my previous books. In China, my ninety-three-year-old father has always been an inspiration for me. He never ceases to explore intellectually and never hesitates to live life to its fullest. His joyful spirit, grace, and wisdom are a constant source of strength and consolation to me. Living physically so far away from my natal family for almost thirty years is not easy. I miss them so much every day and am grateful to my sister, Xiaoping, for kindly taking good care of our aging parents in my absence and for supporting me in reaching my dreams.

My profound gratitude also goes to two very special people—Mr. Zev Luria and Dr. Rick Trautner, my therapists who have provided me with the finest care and incredible support, and accompanied me on my long healing journey in search of clarity, equanimity, and resilience. Over the past eight years, I also participated in numerous insightful workshops and retreats that combined spirituality, meditation, mindfulness, and psychology offered by Jack Kornfield, James Baraz, Thich Nhat Hanh, and Lee Lipp among others in person or online. This deeply personal healing experience has no doubt enriched my understanding of the inner struggles and spirits of the people who appear in this book.

I dedicate this book to my late mother, Li Lanping, 李兰平, with forever love and fond memories. She passed away while I was doing fieldwork in Kunming six years ago. Like many other Chinese people of her generation, she endured varying degrees of anxiety for decades but did not have the language to express her anguish until her later years. Perhaps, my mom's particular experience uncannily propelled me to pursue the topic of this book in the first place.

Introduction

An uneasy feeling crept into my heart as I stared at WeChat on my cell phone. It was an evening in October 2014. It had been two months since I'd last spoken to my childhood best friend, Hongnan, who lived in my hometown Kunming. We had known each other for over forty years, since middle school, and would usually video-chat at least once a month on the popular Chinese communication portal. Recently, I had tried to contact her several times, leaving many voice messages, but I had gotten no answer back. I had grown worried and finally called her house phone. After five rings, someone answered, but I did not recognize the voice.

"This is Li calling from America. I am looking for my friend Hongnan. Is this her house?" After a long pause, the person said slowly: "I am Hongnan. Li, sorry for being out of touch." I could tell instantly that something was wrong, as her voice was strangely weak and almost shaky. "Are you alright? You do not sound like yourself," I carefully asked. After another long pause, she replied with some hesitation: "I am not well. . . . I've got depression and anxiety. It is pretty severe. I have not been able to go outside the house for a week."

I was utterly shocked because this was a woman who had always seemed to be cheerful, dynamic, and strong. And she was a part-time psychotherapist herself; in fact, it was she who had introduced me to the Chinese counseling domain. "I do not know what the trigger was. It happened suddenly after I came back from a family vacation to Dubai. I did not enjoy the trip at all. It was hot, stressful, and pointless." She mentioned that her husband's parents had joined them on the trip and that she had been taking care of them a lot while her husband and son ran off to scenic places. After coming home, she started to have frequent bouts of insomnia, and her mind was often racing out of control, most of the time preoccupied by negative thoughts and a sense of dread.

"I have stayed in bed for several days because I have neither the energy nor courage to get up and go to work. I feel like I am falling into a deep, dark hole. I can see light above but have no desire or strength to climb out. Even worse, I fear that people around me might find out what I am going through. So I just want to hide. The most difficult thing is that I cannot tell anyone. They do not understand and will laugh at me. I lied to my colleagues that I had food poisoning and thus could not come to work."

I tried my best to comfort her: "You know I am always here for you. You can call me anytime—day or night—if you want to talk to someone. And you must get help! Does your husband know?" She said: "Yes, he does, but you know he is a businessman and does not know much about mental health. He told me to just toughen up and cheer up, since in his view there is nothing for me to worry about." I heard her sobbing on the other end. I comforted her some more and promised to call every other day. She said she would see a psychiatrist, since she could not hold up any longer. Just before we hung up, she pleaded, "You must remember not to tell my aging mother, because she will not understand either and will only think I am crazy. I do not want her to worry about me."

At that moment, even several thousand miles away I could feel the doubly heavy weight she was carrying—the struggle with her own inner distress and the attempt to conceal her emotional pain from colleagues, friends, and family. I was saddened to realize that even a therapist could not overcome the social stigma attached to emotional disorders.

Hongnan was not alone; many of the people I met during my eight years of research in southwestern China were suffering from different forms of psychological distress in a rapidly changing society.[1] Feeling anxious, depressed, restless, confused, unfulfilled, or simply unhappy, they were yearning for some kind of professional help to escape their emotional torment and live a happier and fulfilling life.

––––––

The breathless pace of economic reform in China has brought about profound ruptures not only in its socioeconomic structures but also its people's inner landscape.[2] According to some reports, the National Center for Mental Health quoted a startling figure of roughly one hundred million Chinese suffering from different kinds of mental illness (Moore 2009). Among these people, some sixteen million are believed to be severely affected by their conditions, and another estimated two hundred fifty million need psychological services.[3] Even though many middle-class urbanites have accumulated considerable material wealth and live in private "paradises" of gated communities (Zhang 2010), they have begun to realize that such gains do not necessarily endow them with a deeper sense of fulfillment and happiness. Faced with increasing market-driven competition, rapid social changes, and pressure to become successful, more and more people who feel unsettled and lost are turning to psychological counseling, rather than relying on families and friends, to grapple with their problems and distress (see Frammolino 2004).[4] In this context, a new therapeutic language of personal emotions, self-fulfillment, and self-mastery, along with a medicalized language of managing anxiety (*jiaoluzheng*), depression (*yiyuzheng*), and stress (*yali*) is being introduced to Chinese society. As one reporter puts it, "This is a radical shift in a nation where focus on the individual was discouraged by both socialist ideology and traditional culture" (Lawrence 2008).[5]

This book is an ethnographic account of a new kind of revolution unfolding in postsocialist China: a bottom-up popular psychotherapy and counseling movement that is reconfiguring the self, family dynamics, affects, social relationships, and the mode of governing.[6] I term this phenomenon the "inner revolution" (*neixin de geming*) to highlight its transformative potential, even though it is still in the early stage of development and not a full-blown revolution.[7] Unlike other kinds of revolution—the "Cultural Revolution," the "consumer revolution" (Davis 1999), the "housing revolution" (Zhang 2010), or the massive land-use transformation (Hsing 2012), this inner revolution engenders relatively quiet yet profound changes from within, and it is spreading rapidly with far-reaching impact beyond the individual and clinical space. It is thus simultaneously personal and political, intimate and social, subtle and powerful.

Since the early 1990s, a "psy fever" (*xinli re*) or "psycho-bloom" (Huang 2014; Kleinman 2010; Yang 2018) has been sweeping Chinese cities. This new phenomenon consists of a broad range of practices including the teaching and learning of psychology, group and individual counseling, self-help, cultivating happiness, and other mental health activities, geared not only for middle-class urbanites but also for marginalized social groups such as laid-off workers (see

Yang 2013a, 2013b). Members of the younger generations are interested in learning how to recast themselves as new and happier persons through psychological techniques or self-help methods.[8] A lucrative counseling industry is flourishing: Numerous books and magazines on mental health and counseling have been published; there is a burgeoning regime of private counseling centers, training workshops, and websites on psychological well-being and service; international experts are invited to lecture to large crowds of Chinese who are eager to learn how to escape emotional pain and attain the good life (see Zhang 2014). This therapeutic turn forms a stark contrast to the time under Mao's regime when Western psychology and psychotherapy were largely nonexistent and were considered a useless and harmful bourgeois invention. As one anthropologist has observed, "'the psychological' (*xinli*) has recently become an indispensable dimension of individual and interpersonal experience in urban China" (Huang 2014: 183). Further, psychological counseling in China is not limited to the reshaping of the individual and family spheres but also extends to the remaking of organizational and governmental practices. In the midst of this thriving therapeutic culture, a host of work units (*danwei*) such as schools, enterprises, the police, and the military are increasingly keen to incorporate modern psychological techniques into their personnel management as a possible solution to many rising challenges.

How do we explain this significant shift in the way people manage their well-being, endure distress, and recast selfhood when family bonds and social ties become increasingly fragile in postsocialist times? How can it be that a popular psy-fever has taken hold in China at this particular historical moment? In this book, I set out to examine the causes and ramifications of this expanding therapeutic culture. I explore some of the key existential concerns and challenges that spawn the troubling affective condition of urban middle-class people and their struggle to grapple with the enormous pressures and social ruptures experienced while living through massive societal transformation.[9]

Among various forms of mood disorders, anxiety (*jiaolu* 焦虑), broadly construed in both medical and social terms, has become an indicator for the *pulse* of contemporary Chinese society.[10] Over the past two decades of research, it has come to my attention that people of different social strata are experiencing not only medically defined anxiety, but also widespread social anxiety for a variety of reasons.[11] *Fu zao* (restless), *bu an* (disturbed), *hai pa* (fearful), *dan xin* (worrisome), *kong xu* (empty or unfulfilled), and *meiyou yiyi* (purposeless) are just some of the local expressions used by my interlocutors to describe their state of mind. Perhaps, one can say that we are all living in the age of global anxiety today, as some Western writers have noted, and that this is not just a medical condition but also a sociological condition (Williams 2017).[12] But I want to argue further that this sense of edginess, apprehension, and perceived rifts is particularly palpable in contemporary China because this society has been undergoing four decades of profound structural and cultural transformations. This is not to say that anxiety is the only mood of the nation or that Chinese people do not experience other moments such as joy, excitement, and tranquility. What I suggest is that anxiety has emerged as a potent signifier for the general affective condition shared by a great number of Chinese. Further, what's unique about the Chinese context is that it is different from other forms of anxiety in many parts of the globe where people are anxious not only because they are going through major social change but also because they face a gloomy future ahead, such as the case of Japan after the collapse of its economy in the 1990s (see Kitanaka 2012). In China, many people are feeling anxious and stressed out rather than optimistic despite the rapid rise and expansion of the economy.[13]

It is in this particular milieu that I examine how a new psychotherapeutic culture takes root, thrives, and transforms across a wide range of social and political domains in China. My account goes beyond a medical approach that would label this state of being as a "disorder" or "pathology." Instead, I use the notion of "anxiety" as a unique lens to look into the subjective experiences of a subset of the Chinese population in order to understand how larger social conditions shape their individual lives. Therefore, my ethnographic gaze travels from the clinical space of psychological treatment to much broader social spaces, such as family, school, and workplace.

The main argument of this book is threefold: First, psychotherapy—originating from the West—took hold and spread so quickly in urban China today largely because it is regarded as a potential answer to the myriad social and personal problems that need to be addressed. This new field comes with what I would call "a double aura" of making scientific claims and promising magical effects at the same time. A key step in this process is what I term *culturing effort* or what Chinese people call *bentuhua* 本土化. Chinese psy practitioners strive to make globally circulated psychotherapy not only comprehensible to their clients but also suitable for their cultural sensibilities so as to engender meaningful changes. Thus, bentuhua is not a mere intellectual or technical exercise of localizing global psy knowledge; rather, this practice is part and parcel of the broad effort to tackle a host of difficult issues facing Chinese individuals, families, and organizations today. Bentuhua, literally meaning "turning into native soil," is one of the key concepts I examine in this research. While bentuhua is similar to the notion "indigenization," it carries much richer connotations because it implies a sense of thriving and enriching by going beyond the original vitality of a thing. As I will show in chapter 2, among the many branches of psychotherapy, Chinese therapists have embraced several for their potential compatibility with local social conditions and Chinese cultural tradition: the Satir Model of family therapy, cognitive behavioral therapy, and Jungian-inspired sandplay therapy. My analysis uncovers why this is the case and how specific bentuhua practices take place and speak to an emerging "psychological complex" in China over the past decades.

Second, the impact of psychotherapeutic technologies as they are deployed in China goes far beyond the clinical sphere of treating mental illness and extends into other domains—personhood, family, sociality, and governing. In recent years, a new notion, "governing through psychological science," has been promoted by Chinese authorities as a preferred modality for self-management and organizations' personnel management (see Zhang 2020).[14] It is against the backdrop of a particular socialist legacy, known as "political thought work" (*zhengzhi sixiang gongzuo* 政治思想工作), or governing through ideology based on persuasion, that a new form of therapeutic governing based on "kindly care" (*guan ai* 关爱) becomes appealing to Chinese workers, students, soldiers, and others. I suggest that an emerging "therapeutic self" is not a simple retreat to the private self or a shift toward individualism; rather, it indicates a complex rearticulation with one's social nexus through incorporating psychotherapeutic techniques. In this process, a new form of therapeutic sociality—that is both private and public, intimate and social, healing and political—is emerging.[15] Several chapters of this book are devoted to illuminating how such multi-level reconfigurations take place and the ramifications of depoliticizing psychotherapy in the name of science.

Third, there exists a tendency to psychologize a host of social and economic problems derived from structural changes in China. Psychotherapy is often used as a political tool to naturalize certain hegemonic ideologies through working on the individual psyche. This trend is highly problematic but not unique to China. Many scholars have shown how psychology and psychotherapy are deployed to promote a certain form of selfhood or illusion of empowerment when in fact all it does is disempower people by shifting their attention from social and political realms to individual psyches (Herman 1995; Duncan 2018). But at the same time, my observations suggest that psychological intervention can also provide some relief and hope to those who struggle with their emotional crisis or long to live a better life in an anxious time. Thus, I propose to treat this therapeutic turn seriously and uncover its deep contradictions by carefully discerning its promises and shortfalls, claims and unintended consequences from different perspectives. Further, the extensive application of psychological knowledge and counseling practice in China blurs the boundaries between the inner psyche and the outer world, the mental sphere and the social domain, emotions and politics. This complex situation compels us to think beyond dichotomies in order to better grasp the imbrication of affects, politics, and sociality.

PANIC ENCOUNTERS

I was born and raised in China. I spent my first eighteen years in Kunming and then seven years as a college and graduate student at Peking University in Beijing. Over the past twenty years, I have conducted extensive ethnographic research on migration, housing, consumption, and middle-class culture in and beyond these two cities. Fieldwork encounters through everyday living remain vital to my research, as they keep surprising me and touching me in infinite ways. For this project, the "being-there" (Borneman and Hammoudi 2009) experience is even more unpredictable and intimate.

In August of 2013, my mom passed away at age eighty-four after a long-term illness. A week after the funeral, which I took charge of for my entire family in Kunming, I had a full-blown panic attack. It was around noon just before lunch time, I suddenly felt a wave of dizziness and nausea. I was sweating and short of breath, while my heart was racing fast. I ran into the bathroom and threw up. I closed the door behind me in order to hide from my family. At that time, I was about three years into my research on psychotherapy. By then I had read a great deal on mental health and knew what was happening to me: I was having a panic attack. But knowing it rationally did not help much with my visceral reaction. I was caught off guard and thought I was going to die.

I heard my father and sister calling me from the dining room: "It is time to eat. What are you doing there?" I regained a bit of composure and said: "I think I got a flu or maybe food poisoning. Just eat without me." Five minutes later, I came out and went straight into my bedroom to lie down. My anxiety was slowly receding, but my heart rate was still at 110. For the following several days, I had frequent nightmares and flashbacks of my mom's body going into the cremation chamber and coming out as a pile of white bones. And I kept lying to my eighty-seven-year-old dad that I just got a bad stomach flu because I did not know how to begin to explain to him. I managed to talk to my sister, who also suffered from some anxiety a year ago.

After returning to California a week later, I went to see my physician. He said that I had a "situational panic attack" probably caused by the trauma of my mom's death and the stress of handling the funeral. He thought it would go away gradually and prescribed thirty pills of Ativan (also known as lorazepam) in case I had more episodes.[16] But the condition did not go away; instead, it morphed into a prolonged general anxiety disorder. I was feeling edgy and vulnerable most of the time, and every day was a struggle. So I started to see a psychotherapist weekly to tackle my issues. It turned out that my mom's death was only the trigger. I thus embarked on a long expedition to explore my own psyche, my upbringing, and my family relations, especially my years of complicated relationship with my mom, who had lost her mother at eight and suffered from anxiety disorder for decades without a proper diagnosis and treatment.[17]

My own unexpected encounter with a panic attack during the fieldwork and the subsequent firsthand engagement with psychotherapy as a client have given me a very different perspective on my research. It has also opened up a rare opportunity for me to connect with my informants in a more personal and empathetic way. I was no longer a neutral, rational, and distant researcher who was only interested in gathering data or who tried to imagine other people's emotional agony. Because of my own struggle with psychological turmoil for several years, I could feel their pain beyond words more easily. When I opened myself up during fieldwork, most people I met would put off their guard immediately and willingly share with me their problems, concerns, and emotional battles. Our interaction became an intimate, dialogic conversation, rather than a one-way path. The rapport we built together based on affective bonds was stronger and deeper than any I had ever been able to foster before. In some ways, doing this research and writing this book has become a personal journey for me to make sense of my own psyche and understand what psychotherapy can do to help people, as well as its limits.

It is widely believed that large numbers of Chinese are suffering from psychological and emotional problems but have not been diagnosed or treated.

Since depression and anxiety disorders were simply unknown categories in China until the 1990s (see Lee 2011), these people tended to somatize their illness or seek traditional Chinese medicine and other coping methods (Kleinman 1986; Zhang 2007). And there is still a heavy social stigma attached to mental and psychological problems. The common reaction from people in distress (including my friend Hongnan and myself as I described earlier) is to hide their sufferings from family and friends out of feeling shame. This situation makes it extremely difficult to estimate mental illness rates in China.[18]

Mental health facilities are alarmingly inadequate throughout China. Take Kunming as an example: For a city of more than six million residents, it has only two psychiatric hospitals with a total of about eight hundred in-patient beds treating only severe cases of psychosis. The four major general hospitals have their own psychiatric wards, but the scale of operation is very limited. They mostly target schizophrenia patients and rely predominantly on the use of psychotropic drugs. In recent years, out-patient clinics at these hospitals have begun to treat patients with mood disorders, such as depression, anxiety, stress, attention deficit disorder (ADD), obsessive-compulsive disorder (OCD) and so on. But the treatment is largely based on the use of a class of antidepressants known as selective serotonin reuptake inhibitors (SSRIs).[19] Talk therapy in the hospital setting is kept at minimum. This means that people who wish to engage in talk therapy usually have to seek private practices outside the hospital, and the quality of such services varies hugely. Psychological counseling is an emerging field in China without sufficient oversight. Acquiring the counselor certificate to open a private practice does not require much training.[20] Many therapists are woefully unprepared and lack the knowledge and skill to help their clients in distress. Thus, for a long time, the reputation of private counseling as a profession suffered; most people who need help prefer to participate in group-based counseling training workshops led by well-known, respected "masters."

During the summers from 2010 to 2018, for a total of eighteen months, I conducted extensive ethnographic research in the city of Kunming, the capital of Yunnan Province. Over the past three decades, Kunming has grown from a relatively poor and small city in China's southwestern borderland into a bustling regional hub of tourism, commerce, and international trade. The current estimated population is more than six million residents plus over a million migrants. Since most research on China's mental health and counseling have been carried out in large metropolises such as Beijing, Shanghai, and

Guangzhou, I intentionally want to focus on a mid-sized city that has not received enough attention and may better represent the experiences of ordinary Chinese cities. Like other Chinese cities, Kunming has undergone profound economic reform and urban restructuring since 1978, but the pace of change is a bit slower than Beijing and major coastal cities. Because it is relatively far away from China's political center, it gets a bit less state scrutiny. Another reason to choose Kunming is because this city holds a special place in the history of contemporary psy fever. It is regarded by many Chinese therapists as the cradle of the current counseling movement because the first Advanced Sino-German Psychotherapy Symposium was held there in 1988.

There are also personal considerations for selecting Kunming as my fieldwork site. This city is my hometown, where I grew up and did extensive research on housing, city planning, and middle-class living for my second book, *In Search of Paradise*. I have maintained close ties with friends and families who provided many crucial contacts and the context for my fieldwork. Yet coming home as an anthropologist to explore the mental and psychological landscape of the city along with my own roots and family medical history was a deeply emotional experience and sometimes made me feel vulnerable. I have gradually learned to accept and cherish this sense of openness and vulnerability, which made my ethnographic encounter even more meaningful and enjoyable.

I was fortunate to obtain a formal affiliation with the Yunnan Provincial Health Education Institute's counseling center. Through an old friend, I came to know the head of a private counseling firm (SoulSpa) and became an affiliated and trusted member. I enjoyed open access to the firm's activities and collaborated with the director on several international cooperation ventures including acquiring the authorization to establish the first training center of the Satir Model in southwest China. At the same time, I also got to know and maintained close ties with a popular internship center, which I will call Xinlin, that offered newly licensed psychotherapists advanced training. These three sites became my main bases for participant observation, making contacts, and getting access to private counseling sessions. I was able to participate in numerous counseling training workshops and other activities they offered, ranging from sandplay therapy, hypnosis, art therapy, Satir family therapy, cognitive behavioral therapy, and mindfulness practice. In 2014, I received a certificate on sandplay therapy after a week of intensive training at Xinlin—one of the most memorable parts of my fieldwork.

My ethnographic account is drawn primarily from my extensive participant observation at these psychotherapy workshops and private counseling offices, as well as from thirty-six interviews with Chinese therapists, their clients, counseling trainees, enterprise managers, workers, and police officers who participated in the various training workshops I attended. Most of the informants were aged between twenty-two and forty-eight. Interviews were central to my research but they were far less formal this time than those I conducted for my previous projects.[21] I prefer to use the word *conversation* to describe these interviews, as they were dialogic and open-ended. I used either Kunming dialect or Mandarin, depending on which one made my interlocutors more comfortable. The majority of my conversations lasted from one to two hours each and were digitally recorded and transcribed later.

Obtaining permissions to sit in on private counseling was far more difficult than I had originally imagined. It was a delicate matter based on trust and largely depended on the relationship between the therapist and the clients. I was allowed to observe about five individual and eleven family therapy sessions and was introduced as a Kunming native and a professor from an American university who studied mental health. The fact that I came from this region and spoke the local dialect seemed to ease some of the clients' concerns. Occasionally, out of the respect for my "expert" status, some clients wanted to have a second opinion from me, even though I told them that I was not qualified to give them any advice. Sitting in these sessions was eye opening, intense, and at times difficult and poignant, since the clients talked about very private and sometimes traumatic matters and often burst into tears. I tried to take some notes and shared my sympathy, but sometimes I simply felt out of place and awkward.

There are three major conceptual issues central to the rise of the new therapeutic ethos: the relationship between culture and psychotherapy, changing technologies of the self, and the intersection between emerging therapeutic interventions and postsocialist governing. In what follows, I will briefly outline the theoretical debates that animate my inquiry into these issues and how my study extends and challenges some of the claims made by other researchers.

BENTUHUA IN PSYCHOTHERAPEUTIC ENCOUNTERS

Psychotherapy is itself a cultural product originally born out of the Euro-American historical context. To make it work in contemporary Chinese society, engaging in the process of bentuhua—adapting it to fit the local context—is essential. The relationship between culture and medicine has long been a central issue in medical and psychological anthropology. Countless researchers have demonstrated that disease and illness categories are not universal, fixed, or self-evident; rather they are culturally constituted and fluid in their meanings (Good et al. 2008; Kleinman 1991, 2000; Kleinman and Good 1985; Lock 1995; Phillips 1998; Sargent and Johnson 1996; Young 1982). In particular, culture plays a crucial role in how mental illness is recognized, understood, and treated, and how the therapeutic process is shaped (see Biehl 2005; Crapanzano 1981; Csordas and Kleinman 1990; Giordano 2008; Luhrmann 2000; Martin 2007; Mezzich et al. 1999; Santiago-Irizarry 2001). For example, Arthur Kleinman and Byron Good (1985) have argued that depression itself is a cultural category rather than a universal disease, as it is experienced, recognized, and made meaningful differently in culturally and historically specific contexts. Kleinman's study of neurasthenia and depression in Chinese society (1986) shows how a seemingly universal category known as "depression" is experienced and transformed into a culturally specific disorder known as "neurasthenia." Janis Jenkins also points out that "culture is critical in nearly every aspect of schizophrenic illness experience" (1998: 357). It is thus essential for anthropological studies of mental illness to integrate the clinical approach with careful social and cultural considerations (Jenkins, Kleinman, and Good 1991).

Literature on transcultural psychiatry (Cheng, Cheung, and Chen 1993; Kirmayer 2005, 2007; Phillips 1998; Qian et al. 2002; Tseng 1999; Zhang et al. 2002) has clearly revealed how different cultural notions and social expectations affect the diagnosis and treatment of mental illness and shape the therapeutic relationship in diverse contexts. These studies provide useful analyses of the general patterns of how culture affects diagnosis and treatment in mental distress, but also address how tensions embedded in psychiatric and psychological intervention may or may not work themselves out in specific therapeutic situations (see also Duncan 2018; Giordano 2014; Matza 2018).

In this book, I ask the following questions: What is the role of culture in adopting, translating, and transforming psychotherapy in China? How is "cultural difference" understood and negotiated by Chinese therapists in their practices? What kind of therapeutic relationship is emerging in the specific Chinese context? But first I need to unpack what I mean by "culture" and what it means to deploy this notion critically. Yanhua Zhang (2007) points out that there is still a tendency in some studies to treat culture as an abstract, bounded entity or simply as non-Western "local knowledge" in contrast with Western normative biomedical knowledge. Yet, psychotherapy itself is also deeply cultured, since it is built on a distinct set of Euro-American theories and values regarding personhood, selfhood, and social norms (see Caplan 1998). More recent literature offers a nuanced view of culture, seeing it as a set of shifting, historically situated practices, rather than a closed system or a set of bounded ideas (Chang et al. 2005, Good et al. 2008, Kirmayer 2005; Raikhel 2016; Skultans 2004).

Drawing upon these insights, I regard "culture" as a changing set of beliefs, norms, and practices, which is in constant dialogue with regional, national, and global forces. Therefore, to speak of "Chinese culture" or "local culture" is to keep in mind how it intersects with multiple regimes of knowledge and value, rather than simply juxtaposing them. In my research, I paid close attention to how therapists and clients negotiated different orientations with regard to cultural norms, values, and practices, and decided on what was most suitable in a given social milieu. While Chinese therapists often need to modify Western-originated diagnostic categories and therapeutic models and align them with local notions of selfhood, sociality, and efficacy, one cannot assume a fixed, clear-cut boundary between the so-called "Western" and "Chinese" cultures. Both the therapist and the client are constantly exposed to new global therapeutic ideas and practices, but at the same time they are embedded in and shaped by Chinese cultural conditions. Thus, it is important to grasp what constitutes "cultural sensibility" in a given social milieu (Wang and Zhen 2005) as Chinese practitioners navigate through diverging and converging cultural spheres.

In his book *Crazy Like Us: The Globalization of the American Psyche*, Ethan Watters argues that globalization homogenizes not only the material world, but also the way mental illness is expressed and treated throughout the world. He depicts a disturbing trend of the Americanization of madness and emotional disorders, which is erasing "the diversity of different cultural understandings of mental health and illness" (Watters 2010: 7). In so doing, he argues that we may lose precious knowledge that can help improve the human psychological condition, and thus "we erase this diversity at our own peril" (2010: 7). While his alarming account reflects in part what is taking place in global encounters of psychiatry and psychology, Watters may have oversimplified the story by downplaying another important and fascinating process within this prevailing trend of homogenizing the psyche, namely, the constant friction, rearticulation, and contingency in global encounters (see also Rofel 2007; Tsing 2004). In other words, the homogenizing tendency is never a smooth and complete one; rather, it is contested and transformed at different locales in uneven ways.

Based on my research, I suggest that a complex, *dialogic* process is taking place as Chinese practitioners embrace, select, and rework different strands of psychological knowledge and therapeutic practices imported from North America, Europe, and Japan. I use the term *dialogic* in Bakhtin's sense (1981) to emphasize the mutually constitutive nature of knowledge production as a relational and dynamic process, in which the previous work and the present one are constantly altering each other's meaning. The cultural encounter I explore here is not a simple triumph of Western therapeutic interventions over Chinese cultural values, norms, and healing, but rather a process of constant dialogue and rearticulation between multiple forms of knowledge, practice, and ethics (i.e., socialist ideologies, Daoist and Confucian ethics, traditional Chinese medicine, and Western psychological techniques). Understanding this dialogic process will shed new light on how a set of global therapeutic reasoning and techniques articulates with situated cultural elements and practices to reshape a given social terrain.

Building on the study of "global assemblage" (Collier and Ong 2005), my research examines ethnographically what the interaction between Western psychotherapeutic notions and methods and situated Chinese beliefs and healing practices produce in the process of translation and rearticulation.[22] For example, the notion of "somatization"—the manifestation of mental and psychological illness in somatic problems—is often seen by some as "a basic feature of the construction of illness in Chinese culture" (Kleinman 1980: 146).[23] Yet, this view has been challenged by later research for presupposing "an essentialist distinction between mind and body, psyche and soma, and thus psychiatric and general medical diseases" (Zhang 2007: 33). In the Chinese cultural tradition, the concept of psyche does not exist as a separate domain; rather, the heart is seen as the grounding space for cognition, emotion, and morality. For this reason, psychology was initially translated into Chinese as *xinling xue* 心灵学, "the study of the heart" (Larson 2009: 36). It is through the heart (*xin*) that the body and the mind are mutually embedded (see Yang 2015). Further, from traditional Chinese medicine's perspective, "qi flow transcends the divisions that psychiatrists make between emotions, the mind, and the body" (Scheid 2013: 7; see also Zhan 2009). As I will show, Chinese therapists do not discredit somatic claims, but at the same time they also encourage their clients to explore their distress in a way beyond somatic expressions. In sum, they seek to consider the complex *mind-body-society nexus* in order to go beyond the dualistic Western biomedical epistemology on which modern psychotherapy pivots. I argue that attending to this nexus as a whole is a crucial part of the bentuhua process.[24]

It is here that I find the notion of *translation* particularly useful in grasping the complexity of global circuits of psychotherapy. Broadly understood as what Lydia Liu calls "a troupe of epistemological crossing" (1995), cultural translation is a formative process in which new knowledges, identities, and meanings are produced (see also Giordano 2014; Zhan 2009). Theorists like Walter Benjamin remind us that translation is never just a matter of finding equivalences between two linguistic systems; rather, it is inevitably a process of alterity, in which the original is also transformed (1969).[25] In other words, translation is a dialogic process of what some have called "living translation" involving constant negotiation and embodied practices (see Pritzker 2011). In critiquing the concept of "cultural translation," Talal Asad also calls our attention to the unequal power relations deeply embedded in the process of "cultural translation." One of the key conditions of power is "the authority of ethnographers to uncover the implicit meanings of subordinate societies" (Asad 1986: 163).[26] Benjamin's and Asad's insights are vital to the culturing process I seek to understand. What Chinese psychologists and therapists are facing today is how to translate a powerful yet unfamiliar knowledge regime, which claims to be scientific, advanced, and universal, for a Chinese audience that is at once in awe of and dubious about it. This book, in part, is an attempt to unravel such ongoing experimental processes of bentuhua during cultural encounter in the therapeutic setting.

THERAPEUTIC SELF

Why is the "self" (*wo* or *ziwo*) granted extraordinary salience among the Chinese middle-class today? What specific projects of self-development and self-care are emerging in the wake of popular psy education, training, and counseling? What kinds of self-care and self-management are fashioned at the crossroads of new psychological knowledges and sociality? These are the questions I explore in this book, especially in chapter 5. Existing research shows that therapeutic intervention has a significant impact on the conceptions of personhood and selfhood, identity formation, and the politics of citizenship (see Dumit 2003; Jenkins and Barrett 2004; Kirmayer and Raikhel 2009; Pandolfo 2000; Petryna 2003). In particular, recent studies on Russia indicate that psychological work has become an important part of a larger project to refashion postsocialist subjectivities and class formation (see Matza 2018, 2012; Raikhel 2016). Thus, I am intrigued by how the relationship between therapy and selfhood is reshaped in contemporary China. By *therapeutic self*, I mean a mode of self created with the aid of psychotherapeutic engagements (through private counseling, group training, or self-study).

The question of selfhood and self-cultivation has a long genealogy in Chinese history. There are important continuities and discontinuities in the way the self is conceived and nurtured over time. In ancient Chinese, there were two words roughly equivalent to the word "self": *yu* 余 or *wu* 吾. The use of *wu* or *yu* suggests that the concept of self already existed a long time ago, but it was a socially embedded self. Further, there were two forms of self: *dawo* 大我 (big self) and *xiaowo* 小我 (small self). In Confucianism, the concern with self-improvement was a key element, manifested in the notion *xiushen* 修身, which meant cultivating one's moral character through embodiment. This notion includes both the body and the soul, indicating the self as an object that can be worked on and improved over time.[27] Yet, the making of an ethical self is not isolated or abstract, but is embedded in multiple social layers and manifested through bodily conduct. I should point out that the Confucian discourses on self-cultivation had a clear class and gender dimension because this moral project was meant primarily for elite men.

At the dawn of the twentieth century, propelled by the May Fourth Movement, Chinese youth and intellectuals embraced the idea of individualism and challenged traditional Chinese cultural values. But their struggles for modern notions of self, love, and family were met with strong antagonism (Lee 2010). Under Maoist socialism, the concern for selfhood was largely eclipsed by the concern for collective well-being and the party-state's projects. This did not mean that the self or individuality ceased to exist; rather the exploration of selfhood was largely folded into revolutionary causes, collective production, and nation building. In particular, women were pressed to step out of the domestic domain to "hold up half of the sky" and erase their feminine attributes to become "iron girls" in the new socialist order (Honig 2000).

In the post-Mao era, serious inquiries of the self first reemerged in the realm of literature and literary criticism, and then spread more widely into society. But at times when political climate was tight, such renewed interests were seen as a problematic result of Westernization and thus were kept in check by the state. Since the 1990s, the question of the self has resurged as part of the new waves of popular psy fever and the revitalization of Confucian ethics. This time the emphasis is placed on understanding and mastering the self through what is deemed as "modern" and "scientific" psychological techniques, and the possibility of combining the new methods with traditional cultural practices. In short, self-cultivation has become more of a technical matter involving psychological methods and expert intervention. It is in this sense that I borrow Michel Foucault's notion of "technologies of the self" to refer to practices that "permit individuals to effect by their own means or with the help of others a certain number of operations on their own bodies and souls, thoughts, conduct, and way of being, so as to transform themselves in order to attain a certain state of happiness, purity, wisdom, perfection, or immortality" (1988: 18). Such technologies to enhance the self are very much historically and culturally conditioned, including a broad range of practices in order to attain a desired state of being at a given time and place. In this study, I focus on social and political ramifications of recent integration of global psychotherapeutic techniques with the existing means for self-care and self-improvement among Chinese middle-classes.

My analysis is informed by Nikolas Rose's study (1985, 1996) of what he calls "the psychological complex," through which psychological, social, and political domains intersect and mutually shape one another. Like Rose, I am also interested in tracing the conditions under which psy practices become a plausible and desired way of managing the self. Expanding Foucault's (2006) argument about the generalization of psychiatric power beyond the mental illness domain, Rose demonstrates how psychotherapies can offer a technical means to reform the self and promote a mode of governance premised on self-management. Yet, as he shows, "the self" is not pre-given; instead, it is formed through social recognition. Thus, self-cultivation is a changing process involving the negotiation with social expectations, duties, and norms (Rose 1990: 218). In China, this negotiation is further complicated by at least three sets of expectations, norms, and ethics: traditional, socialist, and neoliberal. All of them are in constant interaction with one another and together shape the making and remaking of the self in relation to others. Thus, what intrigues me most is how the micro-process of therapeutic self-work actually takes place in a specific cultural context and how it is deeply embedded in China's historical, cultural, and political nexus.[28]

The reconfigurations of selfhood and the search for self-actualization in China, however, should not be read as the rise of an individualistic self against a collectively oriented self. It has been acknowledged that Chinese notions of personhood are deeply embedded in larger social relationships including the family, kin, neighborhoods, and work units (Pellow 1996; Tu 1985; Yan 1996; Yang 1994). The production of personhood is realized in a relational process by creating and maintaining social ties as well as cultivating socially acceptable behaviors. Over the past two decades, even though this socially embedded selfhood has been undergoing profound transformations (Yan 2010; Liu 2002), it would be a mistake to assume that recent changes indicate a move toward a discrete self. Ethnographic evidence suggests that Chinese people's search for *ziwo* and personal actualization is still very much entangled with social obligations, socialist ethics, and certain cultural values (Rofel 2007; Zhang 2010; Engebretsen 2009; Yang 2015).[29] In China, the way "psychologization" takes place is distinctly embedded in the familial and other social processes. As anthropologist Andrew Kipnis (2012) has rightly argued, the "rise" of individualism today is more of a psychological problematic than a social fact. For him, the psyche is not a socially isolated site but a domain where conflicting feelings, expectations, and discourse manifest.

Some scholars have adopted another notion, "the divided self," to describe the fragmented and complex nature of the self for Chinese today (Kleinman et al. 2011). I propose to move beyond this divide by unraveling the constant articulation and rearticulation of the self and the social. As Nikolas Rose has reminded us, "Our contemporary regime of the self is not 'antisocial.' It construes the 'relationships' of the self with lovers, family, children, friends, and colleagues as central both to personal happiness and social efficacy" (1996: 159). To illustrate how self-work in a Chinese therapeutic setting is simultaneously individual and social, I will unravel a dual process of what I call "disentangling" and "re-embedding" (see chapter 5). *Disentangling* refers to the effort to detach one's self temporarily and mentally from the familial and social nexus in which one is deeply embedded in everyday life so as to create a space for contemplation. Re-embedding refers to the subsequent effort to return to the social once certain therapeutic self-work is done. I argue that these two processes can form a useful analytical framework for better understanding the remaking of the middle-class self and sociality in contemporary China.

In writing about the postrevolutionary self (*moi*) in France, Jan Goldstein argues that by "granting the self extraordinary cultural salience and providing a new criterion for ranking people" (2005: 11), a new principle of structuring bourgeois society was established to replace the old social order. The rise of psychological science centered on the making of a unitary self, *moi*, was a critical component in the making of a new French society. Likewise, in urban China today, the ability to examine and manage one's self is also becoming a new criterion for assessing a person's worth (if not a structuring principle) in a society influenced by an emerging therapeutic culture. But self-worth (*ziwo jiazhi*) is not an individual matter; it is closely intertwined with one's family and societal obligations. This is particularly the case in the context of a sharp decline of government welfare support for its citizens and the fast increase of aging parents who need family care. Given the one-child family structure over the past several decades, one's obligation to parents and grandparents has doubled.

THERAPEUTIC GOVERNING

The third key concept I develop in this book is "therapeutic governing." The impact of psychotherapeutics further extends into organizational life, modes of governing, and other public realms. In his book *The Rise of the Therapeutic State* (1991), political scientist Andrew Polsky analyzes a particular approach that the modern welfare state takes to normalize the marginalized social groups by subjecting them to the help of experts or "social technicians"—clinicians, psychologists, and social workers. The basic assumption is that these people cannot govern their own lives or adjust to the demands of increasingly stressful everyday life and thus need expert help in order to gain "self-sufficiency, healthy relationships, and positive self-esteem" (1991: 3). It is believed that with the right and sufficient help and guidance, these malfunctional people will be able to overcome their personal deficiencies and deal with pressure and adversity better. In other words, the problem of poverty and marginality, according to this approach, can be alleviated (if not solved) by effective instruction, counseling, and supervision of the experts. Thus, a therapeutic state is able to impose various kinds of medical and psychological intervention on marginal citizens through legal implements.

Psychiatrist Thomas Szasz (2001a) depicted an even more dystopic image of the therapeutic state encroaching deeply into civic life including the health and the soul of the people. For him, "the therapeutic state is about tyranny, not therapy" (2001: 516), and it is a type of "total state" that extends its control to the entire society (not just the poor and the marginal). Thus, he uses the term *pharmacracy* to describe and lament what American society has become when health trumps liberty (2001b). In both Polsky's and Szasz's critique of the moral foundation of psychiatry, the state is regarded as a coercive Leviathan using public health and therapeutic tools to achieve its own goal of control at the expense of citizens' will to choose or govern their own lives. For them, the merging of the therapeutic sector and the state is highly problematic and dangerous.

Rather than offering a black-and-white depiction of a therapeutic state, some anthropologists and researchers have adopted a much more nuanced approach, treating the relationship between state power, capitalism, and psychology/psychiatry as deeply fraught yet complicated (see Illouz 2007; Duncan 2018; Giordano 2014; Yang 2015). To unpack such complexity, I invoke a different concept, "therapeutic governing," in my analysis. By *governing* I do not mean to refer narrowly to government policies and actions only. Instead, I use it to include practices, procedures, and ideas of both state and non-state authorities that attempt to shape, regulate, and manage the conduct of individuals and social groups (see Rose 1990). As Nikolas Rose points out, "modern systems of rule have depended upon a complex set of relations between state and non-state authorities, upon infrastructural powers, upon networks of power, upon the activities of authorities who do not form part of the formal or informal state apparatus" (Rose 1999: 15). Speaking of "governing" does not mean to examine governmental objectives and activities in a top-down manner; rather, it allows us to explore a broader spectrum of rule and tactics involving regimes of knowledge, expertise, and values to produce governable subjects. More important, it opens up the space for grasping how and why certain tactics of governing flourish and are embraced by some citizens while other forms meet resistance or subversion. Through the analytics of "governing," we can better understand what forms of authority assume a prominent role in a specific historical and cultural context.[30]

Moreover, "therapeutic governing" involves the embracing of what James Nolan calls "therapeutic ethos"—namely, "the ideas, practices, and language of the therapeutic enterprise" (1998: 1)—so as to improve the management of the work force and help individuals cope with life in a rapidly changing society. Nolan suggests that this widespread cultural ethos or moral order has largely taken precedence over the traditional mode of salvation through religious frameworks (see also Rieff 1966). It is in this sense, he argues, that the psychologists and psychiatrists become "a new priestly class" exercising substan-tial aggregate influence on Western societies (Nolan 1998: 7). This new elite, equipped with psychological knowledge and emotivist language, has assumed the role of an authority for "secular spiritual guide" (see also Ehrenreich 1983). My research shows that it is in this kind of cultural milieu that "therapeutic governing" is gaining traction and recasting postsocialist politics.

————

This book is organized into seven chapters. Chapter 1 traces historical devel-opments of psychology and mental health care in modern and contemporary China and provides the background on the rise of the "psy fever" that led to the inner revolution. Chapters 2 to 4 take a closer look at how Chinese thera-pists and clients reconfigure therapeutic practices and therapeutic relationship in response to the particular social and cultural conditions and specific prob-lematics facing them in life. My focus of inquiry is not on importation process but rather the dialogic encounter between global knowledge and local situa-tion, which gives rise to a set of practices and relationships with distinct Chinese characteristics. Chapters 5 and 6 address how middle-class urbanites cultivate new forms of self and family dynamics through the notion of happi-ness and therapeutic tools. They do so not by retreating to a private self but by creating a novel psycho-sociality so as to better manage their family and social life. Moving beyond concerns of the self and family, chapter 7 examines how certain therapeutic techniques are appropriated by individuals and orga-nizations in the wider social and political setting to revamp postsocialist governing at a time when socialist thought work has lost its effectiveness. The epilogue highlights some of the most recent developments in state intervention in the health and well-being of the population and reflects on the implication of the expanding medical gaze in Chinese society.

If anxiety can be seen as a general symptom of a society in distress (cf. Kitanaka 2012), the aim of this book is to offer a glimpse of how individuals, families, organizations, and government agencies in China grapple with this condition, and how multiple forces have given rise to the "inner revolution" beyond mental health concerns. It is my hope that the stories presented here will not only convey the anxiety, doubts, confusion, and pain of the people who shared their life experiences with me, but also their aspirations, hopes, and resilient spirits in their search for the good life in the midst of a massive societal transformation.

CHAPTER I

Psy Fever

A "psy fever" (*xinli re* 心理热) has been sweeping Chinese cities since the 1990s. This popular wave signals a widely shared desire and aspiration among middle-class Chinese searching for therapeutic fixes and self-help techniques in order to attain the good life. This chapter begins with a brief review of psychological and mental health practices in modern China with a particular focus on several key developments (official, popular, and professional) in the People's Republic of China (PRC) highlighting both drastic changes and continuities in this domain. While my account concerns urban China in general, special attention is given to the city of Kunming's unique history because it was the site of the inaugural program of the Sino-German Psychotherapy Symposium, through which many leading contemporary Chinese psychotherapists were trained. My purpose in tracing the historical roots and developmental disruptions of mental health as a professional endeavor in China is to contextualize the current "psy fever" and better understand the forces that drive this popular trend. My account also shows how psychology and mental health care has long been conditioned by the sociopolitical climate throughout Chinese history.

EARLY DEVELOPMENT AND DISRUPTION

Many Chinese scholars have claimed that psychology per se as we know it today did not previously exist in China, but rather the so-called "study of the heart" (*xinxue* 心学) or psychological thoughts and reflexive discourses was embedded in other fields such as philosophy, folk medicine, and education. For instance, Gao Juefu 高觉敷, a famous Chinese psychologist, wrote in the preface of his renowned book *Zhongguo xinlixue shi* (The history of Chinese psychology): "Psychology as a scientific discipline was introduced to China from the West. It is true that we did not have psychology as such, but we had psychological thoughts." (Gao 1985). Gao made a careful distinction between psychology as a systematic discipline and "psychological thoughts." His book was an attempt to trace the development of a rich field of ideas in this area through Chinese history, even though he did not believe that psychology in the form of a modern science existed in China. About twenty years later, another leading Chinese psychologist, Li Shaokun 李绍崑, published *Zhongguo de xinlixuejie* (China's psychology world) in 2007, which illustrated core psychological ideas in the writings of several prominent Chinese thinkers such as Laozi 老子, Kongzi 孔子, Mozi 墨子, Dong Zhongshu 董仲舒, Huineng 慧能, and Zhuxi 朱熹. Dr. Li got his doctoral degree in psychology from an American university and was well versed in this discipline. He had already published two important volumes on American and European psychology before turning to Chinese psychological history; thus, he was able to offer some interesting comparisons. He too argued that there was a wealth of psychological thought in Chinese philosophy and religion although it was not presented in the kind of language found in Western psychology. Both Gao and Li offered abundant evidence on Chinese psychological theory that could be connected with and interpreted by modern psychology.

Western missionaries first brought Euro-American psychological ideas and practices into Chinese port cities and implemented them in their teaching programs in the nineteenth century (Gao 2013). Meanwhile, some medical missionaries created a few mental asylums in China. Most Chinese, however, shied away from these institutions, as they saw such places as dangerous, violent, and only for lunatics.[1] The first mental hospital, named "Refuge for the Insane," was opened in Guangdong in 1898 (Szto 2014). It was spearheaded by an American Presbyterian medical missionary, John G. Kerr, MD, who was appalled when he saw how the mentally ill were treated in China at that time. They were "usually confined by their families in a dark room of the house, essentially neglected. If left to wander in the streets, they were often mocked and laughed at, and sometimes stoned" (Blum and Fee 2008: 1593).[2] He wanted to treat the mentally ill as patients and human beings, not as prisoners or animals, providing them with humane care and using persuasion instead of coercion. Kerr later became the president of the Medical Missionary Association of China and was able to secure support for the hospital from the association and gradually expanded its operation to five hundred beds. The hospital was eventually closed down in 1937 due to the breakout of the Sino-Japanese War.

At the turn of the twentieth century, modern psychology writings from the United States and Japan were introduced into China as a result of the expanding overseas educational exchange. Some Chinese scholars were able to study abroad and were fascinated by psychological works, which they believed could benefit Chinese society. Two key figures made important initial efforts in introducing this new field to Chinese readers. The first was Yan Yongjing 颜永京, who had studied in Ohio as part of his missionary education. Yan translated Joseph Haven's *Mental Philosophy: Including the Intellect, Sensibilities, and Will* into Chinese in 1889. He did not use the term *xinli xue* 心理学, but coined the term *xin ling xue* 心灵学 (the study of the heart/spirit) to highlight the importance of understanding the heart in Chinese culture. The heart commands a central place in traditional Chinese medicine and is viewed as the source of emotions, affects, and bodily sensations (Yang 2015). This focus on the heart, not just the mind, has had a profound influence on the holistic development of psychology in China, as I will discuss in later chapters. The other person was a prominent Chinese culture master, Wang Guowei 王国维, who had studied in Japan for some years before returning to China. Psychology was not Wang's main focus of research, but he translated the Danish writer Harold Hoggding's *Outline of Psychology* into Chinese as *Xinlixue gailun* in 1907.[3] He was one of the first few who used the term *xinlixue* to emphasize "li 理" (principle) in order to highlight the scientific quality of psychology. These two translated works by Yan and Wang are generally regarded as the first Chinese translations of Western psychology books and early attempts to introduce this discipline to Chinese readers. The use of *xin ling xue* did not take hold while *xin li xue* eventually became the standard expression used in China.

In the several early decades of the twentieth century, a group of Chinese psychologists went to study at American universities. After obtaining their training, they returned to China in the attempt to institutionalize psychology as a discipline. This period witnessed a relatively open and free intellectual milieu. Peking University—China's eminent higher education institution—established the first psychological laboratory in 1917. It was strongly supported by the then university president, Cai Yuanpei 蔡元培, a leading liberal educator, who had studied psychology with Wilhelm Wundt at the University of Leipzig in Germany from 1908 to 1911. Cai was keenly interested in experimental psychology and wanted his university to be the pioneer in implementing this scientific program in China. The laboratory eventually became Peking University's Department of Psychology. In the South, the first psychology department was created at Nanjing Advanced Normal University in 1920, co-led by Professor Lu Zhiwei 陆志伟, who received his PhD in psychology from the University of Chicago, and Professor Chen Heqin 陈鹤琴, who studied education and child psychology at Columbia University. In the following years, several other major Chinese universities such as Qinghua, Fudan, Yanjing, Tianjing, Xiamen, and Guangzhou also launched their psychology departments and began to train students. Psychology gradually made its way into the college academic curriculum.

As a critical mass of interest in psychology in the Chinese academy was emerging, the Chinese Association of Psychology, the first professional organization of this kind, was formed in 1921. It began to publish the first Chinese professional journal in this discipline, *Psychology*. However, after only a few years its activities were suspended, as the Sino-Japanese War started (Li and Guan 1987). Overall, this early period of development was largely institution building and remained within the academic circle. It was very much shaped by the possibilities and constraints provided by the larger political climate and international relations. As Gao has noted, "sociopolitical changes made the import of psychology into China possible," adding that "psychology as a social apparatus can be used for achieving disparate political ends" (2013: 293). This situation continued to be the case for the fate of psychology in the years to come.

Modest growth in the adoption of modern psychology and psychiatry took place in the 1950s and the 1960s. The PRC government was skeptical about this field because it was seen as a bourgeois product, but it initially permitted limited research and teaching in this domain. As Chen (2003) noted, mental health under socialism was largely linked to the notion of mental hygiene and public health. The goal of mental health was thus to develop the minds and well-being of the population. In the city, new programs advocating mental hygiene education and rudimentary treatment were established; in the countryside, barefoot doctors received very basic training to diagnose and treat mental illness (Chen 2003: 129).

At the institutional level, psychology was considered a branch of philosophy, so the two departments merged at most universities (Han and Zhang

2007). During the official campaign to learn from the Soviet Union, Ivan Pavlov's theory of reflexology permeated the teaching of medicine, physiology, and psychology in Chinese academia (Pai 1989) because it was largely regarded as scientific and suitable for Chinese society, as opposed to "bourgeois" Euro-American theories. Many Chinese intellectuals in a number of disciplines studied Pavlov's work, and psychoanalysis was abandoned, redirecting early Chinese psychological research to a physiological basis (Gao 2015). However, Zhipeng Gao's extensive research demonstrates that Pavlovian behavioral theory did not eventually dominate the discipline of psychology, as this theory itself was soon viewed by Chinese researchers as reactionary and bourgeois. Pavlov's influence in psychology waned, even though it continued to be viewed as orthodox in medicine and physiology. Due to the restrictive political climate, even though psychological research and teaching existed in the early PRC, its influence was largely constrained during this period.

During the Cultural Revolution (1966–1976), psychology and psychiatry suffered a colossal setback. Mental illness was regarded by the party-state as a result of wrong political thinking that could be corrected through forced reeducation labor camps (Chang et al. 2005). There was a popular saying at that time: "Who needs the psychologist if one has the party?" The study of the mind was regarded as against Marxist historical materialism and hostile to the revolutionary project. On the eve of the Cultural Revolution, Yao Wenyuan 姚文元 (a member of the ultra-left leadership later known as "the Gang of Four") published an official newspaper essay openly condemning psychological experiments as pseudoscience. Soon research and teaching of psychology and psychiatry were suspended. Universities were ordered to close down their psychology departments, and the faculty were reassigned to other departments. Some were violently attacked by the Red Guard, and some even committed suicide, as they could not tolerate the extreme public humiliation and societal torment. Psychiatric hospitals were taken over by the local worker-peasant-soldier revolutionary committee. Patients were forced to participate in political criticism sessions rather than receive medical and psychological treatment. Limited biomedical-based psychiatric interventions and behavioral modification techniques were available for prison-hospital uses and were often deployed as a means of political control and punishment.[4] While the Chinese adoption of the Soviet model retained some aspects of "penal psychiatry," it also allowed the possibility of rehabilitation to transform the mentally ill into productive citizens (Chen 2003: 129).

In general, mental illness in China was largely associated with the notion of "madness," which encompassed various forms of psychosis and insanity, and thus was heavily stigmatized. Those labeled as *fengzi* 疯子 ("crazy/mad people") became outcasts scorned and abandoned by society. They were either locked up by their family or left to wander the streets. Some were given anti-schizophrenia drugs (such as Clozapine) and tranquilizers, or were subjected to electroshock therapy that often caused pain and serious physical and mental side effects.

Mood disorders, of course, existed under Mao, but they were often seen as a result of one's personality flaws or weak will. Such diagnostic categories as depression, anxiety, and bipolar disorder simply did not exist at that time in China. Mental health problems were largely misdiagnosed and untreated. For this reason and due to heavy social stigma, it is very difficult to gauge the rates of mental illness in socialist times. Some recent researches suggest that rates of schizophrenia and other mental disorders markedly increased during the Cultural Revolution compared with before and after the period (Liu and Zheng 2016). One main cause was attributed to the excessive political violence, humiliation, and abusive experience many officials and intellectuals had to face in everyday life.

Another common trend during this period was for mental distress to manifest in somatic ways, as medical anthropologist Arthur Kleinman has famously argued (Kleinman 1986). According to Kleinman, "somatization is the substitution of somatic preoccupation for dysphoric affect in the form of complains of physical symptoms and even illness" (Kleinman 1980: 149). This adaptive strategy, Kleinman suggests, is often due to heavy stigmatization of mental illness and unavailability of psychotherapy. Since there was no language readily available for people to describe their psychologically derived problems, they tended to locate their illness in physical maladies. During the 1960s through 1980s, a condition known as "neurasthenia" (*shenjing shuairuo* 神经衰弱)—a vague umbrella term covering a range of psychosomatic symptoms—became a paramount category in diagnosing and treating those who suffered from problems such as insomnia, exhaustion, headache, low energy, sadness, anxiety, lack of appetite and so on. Neurasthenia was first popularized by an American neurologist, George Miller Beard, in the 1870s, as the exhaustion of the central nervous system due to an increasingly competitive environment and the stress of urban living. Beard saw this troubling phenomenon as a price of modern civilization, and he attempted to link the soma and psyche together (Caplan 1998). In China, this diagnosis was particularly widespread among intellectuals and students, or those who were labeled as doing "excessive mental labor" (*naoli laodong* 脑力劳动). It was widely believed that mental workers were more prone to develop neurasthenia than manual workers because they used their nervous system too much. For example, my father, who was a university professor of Chinese literature, and many of his colleagues were diagnosed with neurasthenia. Given the intensity of political turmoil and the stress brought by endless class struggle during the Cultural Revolution, it was no surprise to see many people (especially victimized intellectuals) fall ill and experience what we would perceive as sever anxiety and depression. Neurasthenia was treated as a medical condition and thus was political and socially acceptable at that time. Some used this diagnosis as a way to partially shield themselves from participating in required and often fierce involvement in political struggles. With a doctor's note, one could stay home for several days and avoid nerve-wracking political events temporarily.

Still, many people with psychological distress suffered silently. They were seen as weak, bad-tempered, or simply odd. Some of the severely distraught who could not get any medical help committed suicide. When I was a child, I heard about three suicide cases at my father's university—a former chancellor who drowned himself in a pond, a professor's wife who overdosed on sleeping pills, and a staff member who jumped off a building. People whispered about them with pity or contempt. They were never linked to possible mental illness, and their deaths were interpreted as the result of feeble willpower, flawed personality, or in some cases an act of political protest.

To alleviate their pain and suffering, it was common for people to seek traditional Chinese medicine and *qigong* 气功 practice or get consolation from family members and friends (Chen 2003; Palmer 2007). Patients diagnosed with neurasthenia were also referred for herbal treatment and asked to engage in some kind of physical exercises (such as running or playing sports). A common belief was that one's mood was intrinsically linked to bodily condition and the *qi* circulation, a view quite opposite to the mind/body dichotomy of the West. The liver *qi* stagnation was believed to be associated with *yuzheng* 郁症, which caused a number of physical and emotional discomforts (Zhang Yanghua 2007). Herbal medicines and acupuncture were used to improve the qi flow and therefore enhance the mood. In my home province, a rare kind of root vegetable called *tianma* 天麻 (often pricy and cooked in chicken or rib soups) was and is still used by families to calm nerves (*an shen* 安神) and improve sleep quality. I remember when I was in elementary school I had frequent headaches and disturbing dreams. My concerned parents would feed me the precious tianma chicken broth they had saved. I am not sure if it helped, but I drank a lot of it and felt cared for and loved.

In those days, Western-style psychotherapy or counseling was unheard of. Talking in the form of what Chinese called *tanxin* 谈心 (a heart-to-heart conversation about private matters) usually took place only among family members, very close friends, or colleagues. A good friend was expected to spend time listening to one's troubles—often interpersonal conflicts and family dilemmas, and provide socially acceptable suggestions and rudimentary consolation. Tanxin provided some relief, although it was not intended as medical therapy. One of my distinct childhood memories was the frequent and lengthy visits of Mr. Yuan—my father's colleague and next-door neighbor. He was in his forties and had recently gotten divorced. His teenage son lived with him. A heavy smoker, Yuan looked tired and sad most of the time. He liked to visit my father and talked about his problems and worries. Sometimes he just sat in our living room in silence while smoking cigarettes one after another. My father was too polite to imply that it was time to end the visit after three long hours. My mother used to get annoyed by such repeated occurrences and the unbearable smoke that quickly permeated our small one-bedroom apartment. But my kind father would explain to us that his lonely friend suffered from neurasthenia and needed his support. So, this went on for several years until the man married again. At that time, we of course had no idea what depression was. Looking back today, Yuan seemed to have displayed all the classic symptoms—sadness, insomnia, loss of interests and vitality. Even though we dreaded his visits then, I am glad to realize that my father might have inadvertently played the role of a lay therapist and helped this man enormously during his darkest time.

After the death of Mao and the end of the "Gang of Four" rule in the late 1970s, the political climate began to relax, and the Chinese academy began to open up to the outside world. Psychology as an academic unit was first restored at five universities in the 1980s—Peking University, Beijing Normal University, East China Normal University, South China Normal University, and South-West China Normal University. As this list shows, psychology was then considered pertinent to training teachers, and that is why it was first reinstated at the four major normal universities for teachers. The growth of psychology departments has been steady over the years: there were a total of 20 by 2000, but the number reached 187 by 2007. Initially, professors who were brought back to teach were vigilant in terms of what they could teach and research, given the painful memory of their fate in the recent past. But gradually they began to explore different branches of Western psychology, while many younger generations of scholars studied or visited abroad. Interestingly, cognitive psychology arose as a prominent field in particular (Han and Zhang 2007).

In 1986, with the growing professional interest and popular demand in mental health, the Chinese Psychological Health Association—the first national level of organization in this field, was created, signaling the beginning of a new era for psychological research and professional practice after two decades of devastation. Since then, numerous professional societies and organizations have been emerging and forming ties with the international community.

INNER REVOLUTION

Mental health awareness among the Chinese public began to rise in the late 1980s. While the state played an important role in facilitating this wakening, the phenomenon should not be viewed as a top-down government initiative. Mental health awareness development and the resulting "psy fever" was a gradual and bottom-up process. Here I will first highlight a few key moments involving the government's and health professionals' efforts to promote and regulate this emerging field and then turn to highlight several popular activities initiated by grassroots actors. I call this phenomenon a new "revolution" because this is the word used by some people I met to describe the psy fever scene in view of its large scale and depth across different social domains.

First, it is worth noting that in 2000 the Chinese government formally observed "World Mental Health Day" (October 10), sponsored by the World Health Organization (WHO), which signaled its recognition of mental health as a significant social and public health problem in China. It has since then led to several nationwide campaigns to raise public awareness of mental health issues. Another significant official step was taken by the Health Ministry by issuing the "Guidelines Regarding How to Further Strengthen Mental Health Work" in 2004, which instructed local government health agencies to pay closer attention to identifying and treating mental distress and promote mental health care. These policy changes set the necessary political condition for expanding public mental health work in society.

Second, in 2005 the state-run Central Chinese Television Station (CCTV) launched a late-night show called *Xinli fangtan* 心理访谈 (Psychological consultations), which became very popular among urban middle-class viewers. The viewing rate doubled in a year, and it became one of the most competitive late-night shows in China. The program features a twenty-minute counseling session that a client (or a couple or a family) has with a therapist and a skilled female host, and the dialogue covers a broad range of personal and family issues. This program was created by a CCTV host, A Guo 阿果, with the aim of fostering a happy life by opening the heart and listening to the story. Many famous Chinese psychotherapists, including Dr. Li Zixun 李子勋, Dr. Yang Fengchi 杨凤池, and Zhou Zhen 周振, appeared on the show as the therapist. They listened to the client attentively; analyzed the problems presented; and offered advice on how to improve quality of life, reduce conflicts, and enhance family harmony. The show focused on what are seen as "psychological" disorders, rather than so-called "mental" disorders, as the former have been de-medicalized and thus are socially acceptable in China, as opposed to mental illness, even though the boundaries between the two are often blurred in reality. During the first year of the show, various relationship problems related to marriage, family, school, and workplace were the primary focus. Intergenerational divide (*daigou* 代沟) and conflict were especially prominent. The TV host and the psy expert sought to normalize these problems as being social, not medical, in nature. Rather than stigmatizing, they expressed deep empathy and full acceptance toward help seekers.

The show was eye-opening, unlike anything Chinese viewers had ever seen before. Sharing intimate personal and family problems, struggles, and emotional ups and downs in front of a large viewing public was deemed courageous if not almost unthinkable at that time. Most sessions were highly emotional, involving tears, personal confession, and ultimate redemption. Since ordinary Chinese were new to talk therapy, this national television program played a critical role in popularizing counseling and reducing the stigmas attached to psychological disorders. The producer once made a famous statement: "We hope that viewers will realize this: Everyone can have psychological problems, just as everyone can catch a cold. It is very normal and no need to worry. What is important is to learn how to reduce psychological pressure and move out of the dilemma through proper psychological guidance and modification." To normalize emotion-related troubles in this context is to destigmatize them. Some of my friends told me that through watching this TV program they realized that they were struggling with similar psychological distress and it was acceptable and necessary to seek professional help. They first watched it secretly because they did not want others to know about it. As more and more people heard about the weekly show, however, they felt more comfortable talking about the episodes with friends and families. More important, they discovered a new language to express their moods, confusion, and discomfort without a sense of shame.

Popular demands for psychological help have been increasing steadily among the urban middle classes since the 1990s. Researchers suggest that this rising need is closely linked to recent profound socioeconomic transformations and the socioeconomic uncertainty people are experiencing (see Qian et al. 2002).[5] In order to meet this demand and regulate the newly emerging counseling field, the Chinese state launched a national examination program in July 2002 to certify qualified counselors. This program was overseen by the Ministry of Labor and Social Security, instead of the Health Ministry, for various reasons, one of which, as speculated by some, was that it would not have to meet stringent medical training requirements. "Psychological counselor" (xinli zixunshi) was recognized as a new profession with three levels. The certificate for the highest level ("rank one") was never put into practice because few people could qualify; only ranks two and three were obtainable. The exam, offered twice a year in May and November, was largely built on a model of what I call "the speedy assembly line." Young urbanites of diverse backgrounds could easily finish the required training courses in two to three months, pass the exam, and obtain their counseling certificates. In Chinese terms, this very low level of requirements is called menkan di 门槛低. For example, to qualify for level three of the counseling exam, one only needed an associate's degree (daxue zhuanke) in a relevant field or a vocational school degree (zhong zhuan) plus more than ten years' work experience in any related fields. Level two was a bit more vigorous, requiring a bachelor's degree plus eight years or more of relevant work experience or higher degrees in medical or psychology-related fields. But what was counted as a "relevant field" was often very vague and could include many areas not related to medicine, psychology, or health service.

In Kunming when I was doing fieldwork, there were a few dozen prep centers helping students pass the certification exam. Three were most well known and run respectively by Yunnan Normal University, Yunnan Provincial Human Resource Development Center, and Kunming Saibaiwei Vocational

School. They had been around for almost twenty years by 2018. A typical program offered classes on the following six topics covered by the national exam: basic psychology, developmental psychology, social psychology, psychological measurement, criminal psychology, and counseling psychology. I visited and participated in some of their training classes and activities over the past eight years, and also had the opportunity to talk to their instructors and students about their motivations, dreams, and challenges. The majority of the students were in their twenties and thirties, and there were more women than men (roughly a 3:1 ratio). They usually held a full-time job elsewhere but hoped to get the training and certificate either for self-help or as insurance in the job market should it one day be needed.

Through a friend's introduction to the head of the training center at the Yunnan Normal University, I was permitted to sit in on its classes. The center was located in an old building off the main campus. I purchased the text books and arrived at the classroom one morning in 2014. There were about forty students there. The teaching was largely based on standardized text books designed for the qualification exam. Limited mock counseling sessions (typically two days) were also offered toward the end of the training program. In the practice session, students took turns acting as the therapist and the client in front of the class to talk about whatever issues they were struggling with and received commentaries on the performance from the instructor and their peers. The "therapist" was asked to reflect on the experience of acting in this role. Most students valued such practice opportunities but also felt overwhelmed when they played the therapist's role. They needed to learn how to greet and make a client feel comfortable. They had to pay attention to their own verbal language as well as body language. The majority of them felt poorly prepared and realized that they would need far more hours of practice time and mentorship. Perhaps the most difficult part was when the "client" became emotional and started to shed tears. The "therapist" who was often too shaken to respond with calm and support would turn to the instructor for help.

Like others, this program also offered a one-day internship (shixi) at a local hospital's psychiatric ward, but in truth it was more of an observation only. I had an opportunity to join the class on their visit to a mental health center affiliated with a mid-sized local hospital. The students were curious and a bit nervous, since some of them had never been to a mental treatment facility. We followed the section chief, Dr. Huang, into the psychiatric ward and watched him reviewing the cases of two current patients. He then brought in one of them, a young man in his twenties, who suffered from hallucinations, insomnia, and severe mood swings. Suddenly being placed in front of a large group of strangers, this young man was a bit scared and looked confused. "Relax. These are just student interns with me. Just answer my questions as best as you can. We are trying to help you," said the doctor to him. He nodded and sat down at the long rectangular table in the center of the room. Students were not allowed to ask him questions directly but only observed the doctor-patient dialogue and interaction. Dr. Huang asked the young man how he was doing that day and whether he remembered why he was brought to the hospital. He said he was better but still had trouble sleeping; however, he did not remember why he was there or how he got there. After the patient left, Dr. Huang told us that this patient was from the countryside and was brought in by his family after repeated episodes of hearing voices and seeing things that did not exist. We were given the opportunity to ask the doctor questions and express our views. Most students were engrossed in the case and trying to figure out the causes of the illness even though the information they had was very limited. Such experience is extremely valuable, as it is often the first time the students have encountered mentally ill patients face-to-face, but one day's shixi is simply inadequate.

Despite the state's effort to ensure that a set of basic standards are met by issuing in 2005 the National Vocational Standards for Psychological Counselors, students coming out of such certification programs tend to have inadequate counseling experience and are poorly prepared for practice in real life. My fieldwork suggests that it is not difficult to pass the exam if one is good at memorization and that the vast majority of the certified students have no clue how to apply the basic knowledge they have learned to actual practice. By 2008 over one hundred thousand people had received their certificates, but curiously, less than 15 percent of them went into practice (Lawrence 2008).[6] Why do we see such a low rate of practice? The reason is not merely because most of these certified people do not meet the basic level of competence to engage in practice, but more importantly, because large numbers of them actually hold a regular job and seek such training primarily as a form of self-care and self-development. Some hope to use what they learn to enhance their social relationships and their regular work as teachers, police officers, health workers, civil servants, and so on. The broad social application beyond the clinical setting is a distinct feature of how psychological training is embraced by Chinese people, which I discuss in greater detail in chapter 6.

Meanwhile, a popular psy-industry began to flourish throughout Chinese cities in the late 1990s. It has become a lucrative business catering to anxious parents and young professionals who are worried about their well-being, family life, and self-growth. Numerous books on psychological theories, counseling, and self-help written by foreign writers are translated into Chinese and sold on the market. Translation is the immediate source of how global psy knowledge circulates into China. For example, David Burns's *Feeling Good: The New Mood Therapy*, Tal Ben-Shahar's *Happier: Learn the Secrets to Daily Joy and Lasting Fulfillment*, and Virginia Satir's series of books on family therapy are among the bestsellers. There has also been a surge in the publication of psychology and self-help books by native-born Chinese therapists and psychologists. Li Zixun, Zhu Jianjun, Shen Heyong, Zhao Xudong, and Qian Mingyi are just a few well-known writers. Some of them are professors with a doctoral degree in psychology or psychiatry based in China's leading universities; some are self-fashioned practitioners who have received advanced counseling training. Many of them have visited North America, Europe, or Japan as exchange scholars and are well versed in current psychotherapy practices and theories.

Among popular psy-related writings, two are worth noting. The first is a two-volume fiction titled *Nu xinlishi* (The female psychological counselor), written by a prolific, award-winning female writer, Bi Shumin 毕淑敏, who had been a medical doctor and studied psychotherapy. Published in 2007 the book became an instant success due to its captivating story of how a young woman, He Dun, struggled to become a psychological counselor without much academic background or professional guidance. The novel contains diverse exotic tales told by He's clients, focusing on problems such as emotional crisis, twisted love, depression, suicide attempts, anxiety, hallucination, fear, and confusion. This work, which reveals intimate personal details, secret emotions, and encounters with the psychological world, was the first of its kind presented to the Chinese reading public. It offered a rare glimpse of the emerging, yet mysterious world of counseling and the ethical dilemmas facing therapists and their clients in such intimate encounters. Chinese readers loved the revelations of the deep inner feelings and painful emotional battles of the fictional characters, something they could not easily find in other publications.

Another book that enabled tens of thousands of Chinese to get to know what psychological counseling is about is Yue Xiaodong's 岳小东 *Dengtian de ganjue* (Feeling like in heaven: My counseling experiences at Harvard

University, 2004). Dr. Yue is a Chinese psychologist who received his doctoral degree in psychology from Harvard University in 1993. While he was a student intern at Harvard's counseling service center, he encountered many successful students who at the same time suffered from various kinds of disabling psychological problems. He presented ten compelling cases (all under pseudonyms) of Harvard students struggling with mental distress and emotional pain, even though they were deemed by society as the smartest, most accomplished, and luckiest. After each case, he also offered a brief analysis from his point of view and introduced some basic psychological concepts and counseling techniques. The reason why so many Chinese readers (mostly young, urban, middle-class) loved this book is that they were fascinated by the unique and unlikely setting—Harvard—where these vivid stories about mental health challenges took place.

Yue's book was timely for China. Many scholars have documented the enormous pressure the younger generation of Chinese born after 1990 faces, in part due to the heightened familial and societal expectations on these children (many are "singletons" or "little emperors" in the family) to succeed and attain the so-called "high quality" (*suzhi* 素质). (See Fong 2006; Xu 2017; Kipnis 2011; Greenhalgh and Winckler 2005; Anagnost 2004 for example).[7] Over the past two decades, suicide had become a leading cause of death among Chinese college students. Suicide rates in this group had been climbing up steadily from 27 reported cases in 2002 to 130 in 2006 (Li 2012). Stress-induced depression and anxiety among the younger generation are a major concern of Chinese educators and parents today, but psychological screening and intervention are still poorly implemented. Some students from prestigious high schools and universities could not handle the academic and family pressure to perform well yet were reluctant to seek professional help due to a sense of shame. They ended up committing suicide by jumping off a building or taking poison.[8] These tragic incidents were a wake-up call for those parents who pressured their kids to succeed academically at all costs. Some had dubbed these students—the only child in the family, who are placed on the top of the educational pyramid—as the "fragile elite" (Bregnbaek 2016). Yue's book helped raise public awareness and reduce the stigma attached to psychological distress and treatment. "If world-famous Harvard's students have mental health problems and need psychological help, so do our Chinese students. It should not be a shame," a mother said to me after reading the book.

Glossy magazines that promise readers the path to a happier, balanced, and successful life also emerged. The most popular one is *Xinli* 心理 (Psychologies), which specifically caters to urban middle-class women. It claims to provide scientific self-help techniques on how to improve one's emotional outlook and interpersonal relationships. It is beautifully produced with a colorful cover and a high price tag (20 yuan per issue). Frequently discussed hot topics are dating, marriage, family dynamics, intergenerational conflict, self-esteem, sexuality, happiness, and workplace relations through real-life stories, combined with psychological experts' analysis and advice. Its cover page frequently featured a beautiful young Western or Chinese women, and only in recent years did it occasionally show a male figure. One of my informants, a middle-aged, divorced college professor in Kunming, told me that she subscribed to the magazine and read every issue avidly. The insights she got were helpful in managing her relationship with both her disobedient son and her mother who was anxious and critical toward her. "It gives me some comfort to know that other people also have these difficult issues and I am not alone. Some of the articles make me begin to understand why I have such a turbulent time with my son. But I fear it is too late since he is twenty-three now. I wish I had known some psychology earlier," she sighed.

Psy fever emerged in the era of the internet, on which countless websites dedicated to teaching psychological well-being and counseling service have mushroomed. My quick search in the Chinese search engine, Baidu, resulted in numerous sites offering anonymous online counseling and advanced training workshops specializing in sandplay therapy (see figure 1), Satir family counseling, psychoanalysis, cognitive behavior therapy, parent-child communication, and many others. It is very hard to determine the quality of the providers simply based on online information, but people now have access to cheaper online courses and private counseling sessions that are more anonymous and flexible in scheduling. Busy professionals and students can obtain online counseling in the evening or on the weekend without risking being seen by friends and colleagues. This is particularly useful for first-time clients who simply want to experience what counseling is about in a short session. If they find it helpful, they are likely to see a therapist in person.

In the age of globalization, international psy experts from North America, Europe, Japan, and Hong Kong are frequently invited to speak at special training workshops in Chinese cities. Often touted as "masters" (*dashi* 大师) of a particular counseling approach by their local Chinese collaborators, they

FIGURE I. A school boy playing with sand during a sandplay therapy treatment. Photo by Cao Xinshan.

attract large crowds of several hundred to over a thousand zealous people. Even though the fees are high, ranging from 200 to 1,000 yuan per ticket, many are still eager to be enlightened. Among the array of topics presented, the most popular ones concern how to cultivate happiness, reduce emotional pain, and augment self-growth by using positive psychology.

New communication technologies also make it easier nowadays for transnational collaborations. To overcome physical distance, some organizations conduct training lessons via video-conferencing on Skype. For instance, the China American Psychoanalytic Alliance (CAPA), which was established in 2006 by an American analyst, Dr. Elise Snyder, began to run some of its psychotherapy training programs and psychoanalysis sessions via Skype for Chinese mental health professionals based in Beijing, Shanghai, Chengdu, Wuhan, and Xi'an (Snyder 2018). The online practice was coupled by occasional visits to China in order to supervise Chinese clinicians in person. I interviewed Dr. Snyder on the phone in 2009. At age seventy-five, she was extremely enthusiastic and dedicated to spreading psychoanalysis to China. She told me that while the Skype teaching was not ideal, it worked well with some technology help from an MIT student and a good Chinese translator. Given limited access to Western analysts among Chinese neophytes, she saw her team as pioneers bridging the needs of an Asian society with the global psychoanalytic world. She assured me that her goal was not to make money, as their fees were nominal, instead she firmly believed that a vast and rapidly changing country like China could benefit from psychoanalysis. It was this sense of mission that drove her and her colleagues to engage with China's emerging psychotherapy circle.

In recent years, Chinese psy academics and professionals have hoped not only to learn from the West but also to make China a new center for exchanging current theories and treatment practices while addressing pressing issues facing Chinese society. With the support of some provincial and city governments, a few major cities have hosted several large international psychology, psychotherapy, and psychiatry conferences to increase China's global exposure and status in this area. For example, the Chinese-German Congress on Psychotherapy held an international conference in Shanghai in 2007 focusing on the timely theme of "Changing Societies—Changing People: Psychotherapeutic Answers." In 2010, the Transcultural Psychiatry Section of the World Psychiatry Association and the Chinese Psychiatry Association cohosted an international conference in Shanghai, exploring the intersection of cultural diversity, social change, and mental health. Their foremost concerns are how culture articulates with mental health and how to create a "harmonious society" through psychological care. In 2015 and 2017, the Third and Fourth International Conferences of Positive Psychology and Well-Being took place respectively in Beijing and Hangzhou. Chinese practitioners sought to demonstrate that psychotherapy and counseling were not merely a private matter for a few privileged individuals but had broader relevance to the nation, especially at a time of profound societal change. To gain official support and wider societal recognition, they intentionally linked positive psychology with the new China Dream (*Zhongguo meng*) advocated by the Xi Jinping regime by showing that there was a congruence between personal, family, and national well-being and stability.

In the domain of psychological counseling, broadly speaking there are three "camps" of practitioners:

1. the academy-based (*xueyuan pai*): university psychology professors who tend to focus on theories although some of them come from a clinical background and also participate in counseling work;

2. the hospital-based (*yiyuan pai*): psychiatrists who focus on drug treatment and engage only in brief talk therapy;

3. the society-based (*shehui pai*): self-fashioned private counselors who come out of the short-term certification programs.[9]

The first two groups are relatively small yet have strong institutional backing. They tend to be elitist and look down upon the third group for lacking credentials and systematic training. My research focuses on the third group, although I also interviewed some university-based psychologists and hospital-based psychiatrists. Self-fashioned counselors are actually the major players in the Chinese psychotherapy domain because they see the majority of the clients. They in turn scorn the first two groups as being arm-chair therapists who have proper diplomas and know theories but lack real-life experiences.

Counseling fees have increased over the years and vary greatly from city to city and from counselor to counselor. Psychological counseling is usually not covered by any insurance plans in China, thus individuals and families have to pay out of their own pocket. When I began my fieldwork in 2009, the fees in Kunming for a therapist with a few years' experience normally ranged from 200 to 400 yuan per hour, but as of 2016 they had increased to 400–800 yuan. The more experienced therapists with a good reputation could charge as much as 1,000–1,500 yuan. In Beijing and Shanghai, one can expect even higher rates (adding 200–300 yuan). These prices are considered excessive by ordinary Chinese, since the average annual income per capita is only around 56,000 yuan in Kunming and 99,000 yuan in Beijing.[10]

The several main hospitals I visited in Kunming did not provide any psychotherapy services until the early 2010s. The Provincial Traditional Chinese Medicine Hospital first established a small counseling office with two staff members who were trained as TCM doctors but later got their counseling certificates through the national exam. Along with talk therapy, herbal medicines and bio-feedback were offered to patients. Then a few psychiatrists from the First and Second Affiliated Hospitals of Kunming Medical University obtained counseling training and started to offer talk therapy to their patients. But the dominant mode of treatment has been psychotropic drugs, especially the new generations of selective serotonin reuptake inhibitor (SSRI) antidepressants. The first SSRI drug that entered the Chinese market in the late 1990s and gained wide recognition was the so-called "wonder drug"— Prozac, produced by Eli Lilly Pharmaceutical Company, followed by Zoloft,

Paxil, Celexa, and others (Lee 2011). To attract more potential users, Prozac was cleverly translated as *baiyoujie* 百忧解, meaning "dissolving hundreds of worries." Even though the use of antidepressants has been increasing steadily, Chinese consumers are very cautious about taking psychotropic drugs due to their fear of potential side effects. To counter such resistance, drug companies sent out numerous small groups of contracted sales agents into residential communities to directly market the drugs.[11] I myself encountered these marketers several times during the 1990s in the community and surrounding areas where my parents lived. They provided colorful flyers and pamphlets and explained to the inquirers that this wonder pill would make them feel much happier and less worried. In those days, people could buy antidepressants, antibiotics, and other medicines in local drugstores without a doctor's prescription.

In sum, what we witness today in urban China is a combination of burgeoning interest in popular psychology and a desire to use psychotherapeutic techniques to improve oneself and enhance social relationships, not merely to treat mental illness. Psy fever has not only set off an "inner revolution" in China on the personal level, but has also profoundly changed social relationships through the guidance of "experts." Thus, this revolution is both inward and outward, private and social, at the same time. People are eager to learn and experiment in this new field to calm their restless hearts, yet there is also a sense of hastiness and superficiality in their looking for quick fixes. It is in this context that the "speedy assembly line" counseling training model thrives in Chinese cities. But the biggest challenge for mental health care in China today is still the shortage of qualified mental health professionals and trained psychological workers (Szymanski 2012). Finally, although this psy fever appears to be a spontaneous popular movement and is privatized and market driven, the reform state has also played an important role in endorsing and channeling the "fever" at every stage of the development after its initial cautious reaction to it. On the institutional level, nearly all urban schools and universities over the past two decades have been required to establish a psychological counseling office that offers basic mental health education and prevention work.

But why focus on Kunming? What is unique about this city in China's psy fever development? I will now turn to look at the specific social and political circumstances that led to the selection of Kunming as the first site of a serious engagement with Western psychotherapy in the early years.

"THE CRADLE OF PSYCHOTHERAPY"

Perhaps, Beijing, Shanghai, and Guangzhou can easily claim the status of being the centers of importing and practicing psychology and psychotherapy in China. Not only are these major urban universities (such as Peking University, Fudan University, Tongji University, and Zhongshan University) the leading institutions, with more developed infrastructures for training new generations of psychology students, but also these metropolises are under more direct global influence and their residents are eager to embrace new forms of help with their psychological and emotional issues. But during my fieldwork in Kunming, many local therapists and psy workers proudly claimed that this city was the true origin or "cradle" (*yaolan* 摇篮) of contemporary Chinese psychotherapy. Their claim was largely based on a significant event that can be traced back to 1988.

The initial revival of Chinese psychology and psychiatry after Mao was deeply influenced by its early encounter with German therapists.[12] It happened this way not by any systematic design or government effort, but through fortuitous personal experiences. In 1985, two German women, Margarete Haass-Wiesegart and Ann Kathrin Scheerer, who had both studied philosophy and history in China in the late 1970s, invited a small group of Chinese psychiatrists and psychologists to visit Germany. Both women were extremely interested in developing ties with Chinese psychologists and hoped to bring psychotherapy to China. At the same time, the Chinese delegation was eager to learn from their German colleagues. They visited several German institutions and were particularly impressed by Heidelberg University's psychoanalysis research and systematic family therapy center. The next year Haass-Wiesegart and Scheerer visited China and discussed the possibility of holding a psychotherapy symposium in Beijing. But China in the 1980s was just beginning to open up to the outside world and the political climate was still conservative. Very few people knew what psychotherapy was about and how it could be relevant to Chinese society. Foreigners were not permitted to visit any psychiatric hospitals because such places were considered too embarrassing and dark to be revealed to foreigners. Thus, few Chinese researchers were willing to take the risk of hosting a psychotherapy symposium with foreign experts let alone offering hospital field trips. In major metropolises such as Beijing and Shanghai, it was even more difficult to obtain government approval due to tighter political control, censorship, and potential media exposure.

Wan Wenpeng 万文鹏, however, who was part of the Chinese delegation to Germany, boldly took the lead and agreed to host the symposium in Kunming, despite his traumatic personal experience during the Cultural Revolution. Wan, who passed away in 2005, is now a legendary figure in China's psychotherapy and psychiatry world. He graduated from Wuhan Tongji Medical School in 1957 but was persecuted during the "Anti-Rightists Movement" and subsequently expelled to Kunming, then considered a remote borderland city. He became the only formally trained medical staff at the newly established provincial psychiatric hospital. He worked very hard and earned high respect from his colleagues. Later he assumed a leadership position in the hospital and was able to get necessary local government and institutional support to make the symposium happen.

In 1988, after careful preparation by Wan, some 130 people interested in psychotherapy traveled to Kunming from different Chinese cities to participate in the symposium at their own expense. The German side played the role of experts and instructors, while the Chinese side participated as students/learners (*xueyuan*). The first lecture was on the fundamentals of psychoanalysis, followed by lectures on Rogerian client-centered therapy and systemic family therapy. Two German professors, Helm Stierlin and Fritz Simon, taught systemic family therapy and left a deep impact on China's counseling world. This symposium was an eye-opening experience for the Chinese participants, as it was the first time they were exposed to Western therapy theories and treatment practice beyond reading the limited books available. What they found most intriguing was the dynamic interactions between German experts and Chinese students through small workshops (rather than large passive lectures). They also loved the person-to-person mentorship—a productive learning style new to them. In the beginning, some students were very reserved and reluctant to participate in role playing or putting themselves out there for analysis since this was just not the style of learning they had been used to. But gradually they opened up as trust grew among the participants. In the end, the Chinese students concluded that what impressed them most was learning how to engage in self-reflexivity practice during the simulated treatment process—something they felt seriously lacking in. In addition, watching actual counseling case studies conducted by the German therapists was invaluable, as it was practice oriented and broke through the mechanical mode of textbook-centered learning that dominated the Chinese education system.

One of the students, Dr. Zhao Xudong 赵旭东, a young psychiatrist from Kunming, was very active at the symposium and later emerged as a star of psychotherapy in China. He recalled his memorable experience of encountering family therapy at the symposium: "I was fascinated by their description of this approach. Although all the participants were confused by the innovative ideas and techniques at the beginning of the symposium, I was pleased to notice that this kind of Western psychotherapy was clearly applicable to Chinese cultures."[13] He later went on to study under the supervision of Professor Stierlin at Heidelberg University and wrote his dissertation on the "Introduction of Systemic Family Therapy into China as a Cultural Project." A decade later, Dr. Zhao became an acclaimed authority on family therapy in China, and rose to prominent positions as the president of the First Affiliated Hospital of Kunming Medical College, and as the vice president of the German-Chinese Academy of Psychotherapy.[14] He was able to use his social and political resources to promote psychotherapy and host an international conference again in Kunming on the theme of "Dialogues between the East and the West" in 2001. For the above reasons, Kunming holds a special place in the history of contemporary Chinese psychotherapy development.

To continue such fruitful exchange, the second and third German-Chinese Psychotherapy Symposiums were successfully held in Qingdao (1990) and Hangzhou (1994), which drew even larger numbers of Chinese counseling neophytes. After nearly a decade of groundwork, the Chinese-German Psychotherapy Academy was formally established to serve as the central platform for continued psy training and collaboration between the two countries. By this time, the national political milieu was very different from that of the 1980s. Local governments were more open to psychological research and counseling; foreign researchers could travel in China more easily. Psychological counseling was no longer a taboo but began to enter the urban household vernacular.

As I have shown, the Chinese path of professionalization was not smooth, and sometimes very haphazard. It was a few dedicated individuals whose efforts, curiosity, and passion ignited the nascent interest in this new field previously unknown to the Chinese population. In hindsight, Wan's audacious effort to host the first symposium in Kunming and Haass-Wiesegart's unwavering passion for introducing psychotherapy to China first opened the gate for Chinese practitioners to have a face-to-face encounter with the Western therapy world. Such early encounters and collaborations between Chinese and German psy professionals not only solidified a unique bond between the two groups but also paved the way for China's broader global engagement in this field later. The next three chapters delve into diverse and creative efforts by Chinese practitioners to transform Western-style counseling in order to address specific psychological problems in China's sociocultural context.

CHAPTER 2

Bentuhua

Culturing Psychotherapy

> I prefer to use Zi Xing 自性 (self-nature) to translate Jung's Self. Zin Xing originally was a special term of Buddhism primarily meaning (a) the heart of fufa (i.e. Buddhism); (b) the first truth, the cause of everything. In my theory about the psychology of Heart, Zi Xing ["heart-mind nature," or simply "heart-mind"] is better (because less freighted with other meanings) than other Chinese philosophical terms that have been advanced, such as Zi Wo 自我, Zi Ji 自己, and Zi Shen 自身, for what Jung meant by Self. Xing (heart-mind) combined with Zi (nature) brings the idea of "heart" and "life" together; it gives [a word picture] of the original psychological image [of what we are] which we carried from the very beginning of our life and [gave it] psychological meaning. (Shen Heyong, private letter)

The above passage is an excerpt from a renowned Chinese psychologist and analyst, Professor Shen Heyong, in his letter to Dr. Murray Stein (a Jungian psychoanalyst, past president of the International Association for Analytical Psychology) in a series of correspondences between them discussing Jungian psychology's deep connection with traditional Chinese culture. It was quoted in his article titled "C. G. Jung and China: A Continued Dialogue" (2009: 6). Here Shen is preoccupied by the translation of a key concept in Jung's writing—Self. He believes that the Chinese term *Zi Xing* 自性 conveys the meaning of Self much better than other terms because the heart has long been central to Chinese understanding of the working of embodied emotions. Dr. Shen has devoted his career to the mastering of Jungian theory and analytical psychology. It is not an overstatement to say that he brought Jung to China and popularized this therapeutic approach in the Chinese psychotherapy world. But more important, Dr. Shen is among the foremost thinkers who have spearheaded the movement of bridging the East and the West in psycho-therapeutic encounters. This excerpt and his article are a wonderful example that illustrates how Chinese psy practitioners attempt to unearth and create affinities between Western psychotherapy and Chinese cultural sensibilities.

Indeed, one of the main challenges facing Chinese psychotherapists is how to make global therapeutic models speak to Chinese social norms, cultural values, and individual desires (see Zhu 2008; Xu 2008; Yang, Huang, and Yang 2005). This process of creative "fitting" is called *bentuhua* 本土化, which can be roughly translated into English as "localization," "indigenization," or "culturing." However, it is important to point out that bentuhua is not merely a local indigenization of imported Western knowledges and practices; rather, it is a creative and dialogic course involving bricolage and innovation. Its ultimate goal is not importation or adaptation but transformation by paying heed to the particular local culture, history, and real societal problems. This is a bottom-up, generative undertaking rooted in a broader effort to make sense of and reduce various psychological distresses brought on by China's massive socioeconomic changes.

It has been widely recognized by Chinese practitioners that bentuhua is an extended and demanding process involving creative thinking, experiments, and one's deep understandings of both Western and Chinese cultural tradition and the present social condition.[1] As I discuss in the introduction, this cultural translation work is a key problematic that needs to be addressed in global psychology. In China, the ability to engage "bentuhua" in practice is regarded as a crucial step toward a successful counseling career. Yet, just how and what kinds of changes and reinventions are needed in this contingent process is unclear. And the answer largely depends on the specific psychological theories, therapeutic circumstances, and the training background of the practitioners.

In this chapter, I examine how Chinese psychotherapists selectively embrace and "culture" certain psychotherapy branches in order to address their clients' expectations, desires, and sensibilities.[2] I use the term *culturing* as a verb here to highlight the active bentuhua process of recasting talk therapy through culturally specific idioms and reasoning to address local conditions. Although a range of psychological theories and treatment models have been introduced to China, three approaches have gained most popularity in Kunming and are undergoing myriad alterations: Satir-based systematic family therapy, cognitive behavioral therapy (CBT), and Jungian psychology–inspired sandplay therapy. In addition, art therapy that combines different interpretive modes is also gaining some traction. Interestingly, Freudian theories and classic psychoanalysis are recognized as the foundation of contemporary psychology and counseling, but they are not commonly applied to actual counseling or advertised by Kunming therapists as their areas of expertise. During my fieldwork, I did not meet any therapist who asked their clients to lie on a couch during the session or come three times a week for intensive therapeutic work as the classic psychoanalysis usually demands.

What does bentuhua mean to Chinese therapists and how do they practice it? I hope to address this question through specific ethnographic accounts. Although my findings and analysis below are concentrated on several practitioners and their therapeutic encounters, these cases are carefully selected among over thirty therapists I interviewed or worked with. Their stories and narratives, I believe, can offer a more vivid account than quantitative numbers alone. I focus on these cases because they are among the most articulate, key informants who best represent the "culturing" psychotherapy effort in their own way. In my writing, I also try to weave in these therapists' interactions with their clients as much as possible.

THE SATIR MODEL AND THE CHINESE FAMILY

One of the therapy models that many Chinese practitioners embrace is the "Satir Model" developed by American psychotherapist, Virginia Satir (1916–1988). Even though Satir's influence has largely waned over the past three decades in the United States, her writings are rapidly gaining popularity in Chinese cities. Three of her books have been translated into Chinese and published in recent years: *The Satir Model Family Therapy and Beyond*, *The New Peoplemaking*, and *Satir Step by Step: A Guide to Creating Change in Families*. The Satir Institute of China originally established in Hong Kong in the 1990s has created several branch offices in Beijing, Guangzhou, and elsewhere. In 2010, the counseling firm I was affiliated with obtained permission from the Satir Institute of the Pacific to establish a regional center in Kunming.[3] These branches operate after the franchise model, offer fee-based training workshops, and engage in various branding activities to spread Satir therapy ideas. In chapter 4, I will detail the history and branding of the Satir Model as well as its implications. Here my focus is to show how Chinese people's emphasis on the family provides a fertile ground for the Satir Model to take root and how Chinese therapists "translate" and modify Satir's beliefs and techniques in their everyday practice.[4]

The core of Satir family therapy is to situate what appear to be the individual's problems into the larger family system, rather than isolating the troubles and solely focusing on a single person. Researchers and therapists I spoke to suggest that the strong preference for family-oriented therapy is clearly shaped by a long-standing Chinese cultural expectation of the self as a social self, strong obligation to one's family, and collective-oriented ethics (see Chang et al. 2005; Qian et al. 2002; Tseng 1999 for example). One prominent therapist in Kunming, Mr. Liu Zhen, whom I had been in touch for years, put it this way: "It is very hard to talk to my Chinese clients about the social and emotional problems they experience without talking about their interaction with family members, friends, and coworkers. Oftentimes, their problems are deeply entangled with the social world in which they are embedded. Their anxiety and depression are largely derived from the dysfunctional communication and interaction within the family." Liu was in his late forties when we met in 2012 and had been in private therapy practice for fifteen years. I have been following his practice since then and was given permission to sit in on several of his counseling sessions over the years. Although he saw clients of different demographic backgrounds, his specialty was in family dynamic and communication problems as well as troubling youth behaviors. In the mid-1990s, he enrolled in weekend preparation classes and was certified as a therapist through the national qualification program. He eventually decided to give up his secure university lecturer position envied by many others. "I was in the branch of doing students' political thought work that every university had. But I was bored and felt empty inside because the task was meaningless. Students were required to take my class but obviously had zero interest in its content. They would come and pretend to be listening but were actually reading on their smart phones or simply taking a nap," Liu explained to me. He soon opened his own counseling practice and started to accept clients based on word of mouth. Parent-child relationship was his area of expertise. His practice expanded steadily and so did his reputation in the city.

After gaining advanced training by attending specialized workshops and years of counseling experience, Liu concluded that the Satir model of family therapy was the most effective tool, particularly in working with children, youth, and married couples. He told me that many Chinese parents brought their children to counseling only when the problem was so severe that it had clearly interfered with the children's school performance and social life. Anxious parents, however, tended to think that they themselves were "normal" and it was only their children who were problematic. But after the first session, Liu could often trace the root cause of the problems to troubled family dynamics. Using the Satir Model, he would ask key family members to join the therapy sessions in order to change and improve the communication skills and the mode of interaction among family members. One of the techniques Liu used is called "family reconstruction," developed by Satir. It uses role playing to help clients gain new perspectives of how members can be related to one another in order to break the existing pathological pattern of family dynamics. This experiential component of the therapy is particularly attractive to his clients, who are skeptical about solely relying on verbal communications. Therapists who are drawn to the Satir Model suggest that since the Chinese notion of personhood is deeply rooted in family, kin, and social relationships, the Satir approach makes good sense in this context. After all, "personal" psychological problems are rarely derived individually; the family is usually the key milieu. Thus, a crucial step in family therapy is when parents begin to see their "children's problems" through the lens of the family, involving themselves.

One day I had the opportunity to observe a two-hour family counseling session conducted by Liu at his office. A migrant couple in their early forties from a rural county in Yunnan Province brought their seventeen-year-old son in. The chief complaint was their child's inability to socialize at school and the poor academic performance reflected in his grades. The father was a short man wearing a faded yellow T-shirt and dark blue jeans. He said that he came to help his wife describe their son's problems: "I am here to lay out the problem. They cannot say it clearly. My son is rebellious. He does not talk to us at all, nor does he listen to us. We need your expert help quickly!" He went on for about ten minutes, mostly providing more examples of his son's issues. The mother was a thin woman with short hair. Holding a worn handbag, she was largely quiet, looking timid and worried.

After listening to the preliminary report, Liu asked the parents to step out of the office because he wanted to talk to the son separately. The conversation, which lasted for about thirty minutes, was very difficult in the beginning because the teenager was reluctant to speak. He was a relatively tall boy wearing a pair of jeans and tennis shoes. With his head down, he said he was not used to talking about how he felt openly, and most of the time he was yelled at by parents and teachers. "What is your name? Could you please look at me?" said Liu gently. "I would like to hear your story from your point of view. I am here to help and listen," added Liu. "My name is Xiong Hai," he said quietly as he raised his head up. "Nobody really listens to me. I do not see my dad often. Maybe that is better because when he is around, he just scolds me or beats me up when he is angry at me." It appeared that the root cause of Xiong's "abnormal" behavior was the troubled father-son relationship. His father was a migrant worker who was largely absent in the family, as he had to follow temporary jobs from place to place. When he returned home for short periods of time, he was impatient with his son because he was not doing well at school. Over time, Xiong grew resentful toward his dad and simply refused to talk to him. "Mom is better, but she nags me all the time." He found communication with others also painfully difficult and preferred to withdraw socially.

Given this situation, Mr. Liu decided that it would be crucial for the three of them to return for follow-up counseling and work on their family dynamic. However, he encountered multiple layers of resistance. First, the father refused to participate, citing time constraints. While recognizing the importance of family members' participation in the healing process, Chinese men tend to be reluctant to do so. There is an unspoken assumption that the mother is the primary caregiver in the family and therefore it is sufficient to include her alone in the treatment of the child. In addition, some men find it difficult to express their feelings openly and see talk therapy as a feminine sphere that can potentially undermine their manhood. So, when Liu told the parents that they both needed to come back with their son a few more times, the father became apprehensive and said: "I cannot come back. I am very busy and will be out of town for the next few months. . . . Maybe my wife can come back one more time. Isn't she enough? I have to work and got no time for this." He said thank you and left right after.

Second, long-term counseling or multiple sessions are not affordable for most ordinary families even if they are willing to engage. No health insurance covers counseling service. For this working-class couple, 150 yuan per session (already a reduced rate due to their economic status) was not a small amount, given their monthly income was less than 3,000 yuan. Thus, when they came, their goal was to get an expert's evaluation and advice. They had not intended to return. In the end, Liu was able to convince the parents to at least let the son come back three more times at a heavily discounted rate of 50 yuan and offered to let him participate in group youth activities Liu was supervising for free. "Giving him an opportunity to interact with his peers outside the family and school setting may give him a fresh start to connect with others. Needless to say, I am very disappointed that his parents cannot participate in the counseling. But I cannot force them and have to start from somewhere," Liu said with a look of defeat. I later learned that Xiong's mother accompanied him back one more time and worked together on their communication skills. He started to make some progress at school and appeared less antisocial and rebellious.

This family's situation—troubled domestic dynamics and strong parental worries over their children's defiant (*nifan* 逆反) attitude and behavior—is quite common in China today. Indeed, *qinzi guanxi* 亲子关系 (parent-child relationship) has emerged as one of the chief concerns among those who seek psychotherapy. The generational gap (*daigou* 代沟) and conflict have been exacerbated by two factors: First, children and youth born in and after the 1990s are mostly the single child in their family. They tend to be spoiled and overprotected, and at the same time are under greater pressure to succeed academically and meet their parents' high expectations (Fong 2006; Kuan 2015). Childhood has become an intense period during which parents want to invest and intervene in order to insure a bright future for their kids. Children feel that they have largely lost control of their time and life; their social worth is measured by test scores only. Parents are anxious about their children's school performance and want to give them a competitive advantage by enrolling them in numerous prep classes and extracurricular activities. Thus, the clash of wills and heightened parental expectations leads to widespread stress and anxiety among both children and parents.

Second, the younger generation kids who grow up in the digital age are heavily influenced by social media and online culture. Their notions of selfhood and sociality are shaped by online peer activities and may differ greatly from those of their parents. Some of them are also addicted to the internet, which basically consumes their entire life.[5] Parents and teachers often feel that they are fighting a losing battle but do not know how to deal with this situation. Parenting is becoming even more challenging than ever before, and the need for expert's help is thus growing. Family therapy has emerged as a preferred modality of intervention for some as a way to deal with intensified psychological burdens.

In sum, while the Satir family therapy resonates well with how most Chinese people think about the role of the family in shaping a person, in practice it is not always easy to secure family participation due to time pressure, financial limits, and gendered understanding of parental responsibilities and emotional care. In the cases I observed, some clients and their family members were willing to change their initial expectations and come back for more sessions. Others could not do so or might engage in a limited fashion such as a mother-child therapy. This situation was not ideal and likely hindered therapeutic effectiveness, but even limited or modified treatment, in my view, was better than nothing. More important, the involved families felt that they had benefited from such brief encounters.

Liu once said to me semi-jokingly: "Maybe what I do is what we like to call 'Chinese characteristics.' I must be very creative and make do with what I have. My approach is basically guided and inspired by Satir's core beliefs and techniques, but I make a lot of modifications in practice all the time. In the physical absence of key family members, I and my client try to relate his or her problems to the larger family context in our conversation. One cannot be dogmatic about the Satir Model; it is a guiding framework only," he smiled. Given this reality, Chinese therapists often need to negotiate with their clients and make many compromises (including a watered-down approach) according to the specific circumstances.

COGNITIVE BEHAVIOR THERAPY AND SOCIALIST "THOUGHT WORK"

Another widely used approach is cognitive behavioral therapy (CBT), which was originally developed by two leading American psychologists, Albert Ellis (2001) and Aaron Beck (1993). The Beck Institute for Cognitive Behavior Therapy offers a concise definition: "CBT is a time-sensitive, structured, present-oriented psychotherapy directed toward solving current problems and teaching clients skills to modify dysfunctional thinking and behavior." As we can see from this definition, CBT is largely based on psycho-social intervention aimed at helping clients to develop sound coping strategies through reshaping their behavior and cognitive patterns. Further, unlike traditional Freudian psychoanalysis, which seeks to unearth early childhood traumas as the root causes of problems, CBT claims to be "time-sensitive" in that it focuses on the present and does not engage in prolonged treatment. Although the efficacy of CBT is still debatable in the international community, it has been widely viewed as an effective approach to treat emotional disorders and improve mental health.[6] Because CBT is relatively brief and produces observable results quickly, it is seen as a cost-effective and evidence-based method, and is thus much preferred by the health insurance industry in North America and beyond.

Recent reform of the medical system in China has moved away from the state-subsidized, virtually free service offered by work units (*danwei*) under socialism to a commercialized, hybrid system that draws financial contributions from the state, work units, and individuals. Psychological counseling, which is still a novel thing, is generally not covered by any insurance plan, thus individuals and families have to pay for this service out of their own pockets. Counseling fees vary greatly from place to place and have increased rapidly over the past ten years. In recent years, the normal range in Kunming is from 200 to 500 yuan per hour while the famous therapists in high demand can charge 800 to 1,000 yuan. These numbers are considered extremely high, given the average annual income per capita in this city is less than 15,000 yuan. Therefore, long-term treatment is not sustainable even for two-income middle-class families, let alone poor working-class families. For this reason, both Chinese therapists and clients prefer CBT and believe that it can produce quick results. Classic psychodynamic psychoanalysis, which normally requires a prolonged treatment period, has never gained traction in China.

In addition to financial considerations, there are also important cultural factors at work. Although CBT includes a variety of approaches and therapeutic techniques, its gist is to help patients recognize when and where their thinking processes go awry, and how to challenge the distorted thinking pattern in order to cultivate a more reasonable, positive schema. In short, CBT insists that it is possible to change the way people think and respond, and that such cognitive and affective shifts will result in desirable behavioral changes. This method is very similar to the long-standing notions of self-cultivation and self-improvement for social and political purposes. In particular, it shares a striking similarity with the principle and method of the socialist "thought work" (*sixiang gongzuo* 思想工作) carried out by the party-state in its grass-roots campaigns and other political endeavors.

Essentially, doing "thought work" under socialism is to alter the way people think about themselves and their relationship to the party-state by instilling a new set of values and ethics aligned with the goals of the party and revolutionary ideals. A definition on Baidu Baike (China's most popular search engine) states: "Thought work, also called thought education (*sixiang jiaoyu*), is the ideological influence imposed on the people by a class or political party in order to realize its political goals. It seeks to change people's thinking and guide their social behavior through policy and case explications as well as using one's own personal experience to persuade. . . ." Two things are worth noting about thought work: First is its strong ideological content; second is its external goal set by the ruling party. Every Chinese who grew up during the socialist decades was familiar with thought work and could not escape it at school or the workplace. "Thought work" can be done in groups through collective political study meetings, which are mostly dull, mechanistic, and tedious. But it can also be carried out in a more private fashion through face-to-face, heart-to-heart talking (*tanxin*) between a politically "enlightened" party member and a member of the masses. It is important to note that effective political "thought work" tends to take place in a more personal setting and has an affective dimension involving feelings, attitudes, and gestures of care.[7] Thus, it can be simultaneously political and personal, social and intimate.

Over time, doing "thought work" had become a widespread, everyday method of engendering change in a person beyond the political domain. Nowadays, it is common for someone to ask a friend or relative to help do thought work on another person, which may involve purely personal matters. In my family, for example, my sister for years asked me to do my nephew's thought work when she ran into a parenting block and could not be persuasive regarding his dating, school work, marriage planning, and so on. My mother used to do thought work on me in order to dissuade me from leaving China for America and living away from her and the family.

Although the content and ideological goals of "thought work" differ greatly from those of CBT treatment, one can identify some interesting parallels between the two interventions. I am not the first one who noticed this coincidence. Several therapists I interviewed first pointed out this interesting connection to me. Three of them had actually been in the profession of "doing thought work" at universities or state enterprises for years before turning into therapists. They all found CBT a good fit with the way Chinese people think about the relationship between thought and behavioral change. Even though their focus in CBT work today is no longer on political ideology or political persuasion but rather on promoting personal growth and tackling emotional problems and familial troubles, the communication skills they had learned from previous "thought work" can be applied to talk therapy. One female therapist explained the similarities and differences to me this way: "Working with numerous students in those years taught me how to be an attentive listener and be very patient, discerning, and caring. I have also seen firsthand how people's thought patterns can be altered under sound guidance and persistent influences. But for sure, I enjoy doing CBT work much more than doing socialist thought work because I feel that I am actually helping my clients and making a meaningful difference in their life." She then jokingly added, "perhaps people like me were the pioneers of psychological counseling even before this profession emerged in China." She also noted that listening and building trust was far more important than persuasion and reasoning.

A strong CBT supporter I met was Dr. Zhao Jin, a therapist well known for treating youth depression, anxiety, socialization difficulty, and problems with schooling. He received his doctoral degree in psychology from one of China's top universities in the early 1990s and became a professor at a well-respected provincial university in Kunming. In his spare time, he maintained his private counseling practice, which he had been doing for about fifteen years when I met him in 2010. Even though still young in his early forties, he was already a prominent figure in Kunming's counseling scene. I read some of his publications and checked his profile on the website. I had wanted to meet him for a long time, and finally a mutual friend introduced us via texting. It took me several phone calls to get hold of him. I explained to him my background and intention for an interview. He listened and finally agreed to meet me at his home in two days.

Zhao conducted therapy in his home office—a small room in a two-bedroom apartment on the university campus. When I arrived at his door, he greeted me and said that he was in the middle of a counseling session. I felt terrible and suggested that I would come back at another time. But he did not seem to mind and waved me into his living room, "Have a seat and just wait a bit. I will be done soon." He returned to his office with the door semi-open. I was uncomfortable sitting there because I could hear their conversation. He seemed to be finishing up the session with someone who appeared to be a high school student. He asked the client to go back home and practice a list of things they had discussed earlier and return to report to him in a week. I caught a glimpse of the young man when he left with a piece of paper in hand.

Apologizing for the delay, Zhao said, "This client is an add-on referred to me by a friend. The boy's parents are worried about his lack of motivation and school performance. I have too many clients these days and I am exhausted." "Why do you accept so many cases then?" I asked. "Well, because so many young folks have issues that their parents do not know how to deal with. They are anxious and find me by word of mouth. It is hard to reject them when your friends and acquaintances ask for help." Zhao, a short man, was wearing a pair of dark glasses and casual clothing. He was a few years younger than me but appeared to be self-possessed. He talked fast with a loud voice. Our conversation focused on his training background and therapeutic choices. He too saw important connections between thought work and psychological counseling in the Chinese context, although he emphasized several times the scientific foundation of the latter. "Psychotherapy is a science that is meant to help the clients to achieve their own goal and live a better life. We therapists have no interest in instilling any ideology or teaching ethics." He then explained to me why he preferred CBT in his practice: "I do not exclude any methods and theories that might be useful in treatment. But over the past ten years I have been more inclined to combine family therapy with cognitive behavior therapy. I focus on the problems in the present moment and show how the family can work together for positive changes without necessarily dwelling on one's childhood experiences. This choice has proven to be most effective and less mystifying. My clients can understand and take it well."

Trained in one of the best psychology departments in China, Dr. Zhao was well versed in a variety of psychology theories and counseling models. He firmly believed that a good therapist must be able to see what would work best in a given cultural context and adapt accordingly. His approach was eclectic, but he was particularly intrigued by Ellis's and Beck's work and its applicability to Chinese society. He noticed that his clients tended to lose patience if he asked them to explore their childhood or spend some time analyzing significant past events in their life. What they wanted to know, he maintained, was how to solve their current existential problems and how to correct their flawed way of thinking even though in reality the past and the present were so deeply intertwined. Thus, his therapeutic attention was on *here and now* and the style was more directive than he had originally intended.

Zhao further remarked that the appeal of CBT is in part derived from its action-oriented approach and tangible results, which his clients expected and appreciated. He looked at me and said with a smile: "You are Chinese. So you should know that Chinese people like to think they can *do something* in the treatment process, rather than just sitting here and talking with their therapist. Words alone cannot solve the problem. They want to know what they can do—exercising, eating nutritious food, getting up early, writing a journal, communicating better, meditating. . . . You name it." At this point, he was animated and using his fingers to list the activities he mentioned.

Among the long to-do list deployed in CBT therapy, some therapists have begun to incorporate meditation and mindfulness techniques into the treatment plan when appropriate and possible. They believe that this practice can help unify the body and the mind, while giving their clients one more concrete thing to do. This combined approach, they report, tends to generate better and faster results in enhancing mental and physical well-being. The application of mindfulness (originally borrowed from Buddhism) to clinical psychology and psychiatry, which I discuss in chapter 6 in greater detail, has gained enormous popularity in the West over the past twenty years. It has been widely used in stress reduction, cognitive therapy, dialectical behavior therapy, and Morita therapy. Here, I only want to point out that the appropriation of meditation by some CBT practitioners shows a pragmatic tendency to blend diverse methods and ideas among Chinese psy experts.

If the perceived linkage between CBT and thought work is rooted in more recent Chinese history (more specifically socialism), the cultural affinity between Jungian-based sandplay therapy and the Chinese cultural milieu can be traced even further back.

REARTICULATING JUNG THROUGH SANDPLAY THERAPY

There is a growing fascination among some Chinese scholars and therapists with Carl Jung and therapeutic techniques informed by him. In this section, I examine how Chinese practitioners rearticulate and advance the cultural affinity between traditional Chinese philosophy and religion and Jung-inspired psychological theories. I will also show how they seek to create new brands of psychotherapy through cultural fusion, especially with regard to sandplay therapy—a novel and popular method used in China.

A close reading of Carl Jung's writing, memoirs, and biography indicates that he had a long-standing interest in and was profoundly influenced by traditional Chinese philosophy and religion (and to some extent that of India as well). His works on collective unconscious, archetypal images, and symbols were partly shaped by his fascination with the *I Ching* 易经 (*The Book of Changes*) and *Taiyi jinhua zongzhi* 太乙金华宗旨.[8] In his memories, Jung depicted his obsession this way: "I would sit for hours on the ground beneath the hundred-year-old pear tree, the *I Ching* beside me, practicing the technique of referring the resultant oracles to one another in an interplay of questions and answers. All sorts of undeniably remarkable results emerged—meaningful connections with my own thought processes, which I could not explain to myself" (1961: 373). From time to time, he retreated to his secluded property, Bollingen Tower, on Lake Zurich to practice Daoist and Zen meditation. Inspired by a different way of viewing the world in terms of correlations of meanings rather than by the cause-effect model, Jung developed his theory of synchronicity to explore meaningful coincidences.[9] Another significant development Jung made in relation to Eastern culture is his understanding of Self or individuation (*zixinhua* 自心化) as symbolized by the four-layered mandala he drew. He saw "the mandala as a manifestation of the Self's intrinsic ability to hold and thus integrate the unconscious in an individual way" (Shen 2009: 9).

Jung's influence is clearly manifested in the use of sandplay therapy. Sandplay therapy (*shapan youxi zhiliao*), is a therapeutic method in which "the client is given the possibility, by means of figures and the arrangement of the sand in the area bounded by the sandbox, to set up a world corresponding to his or her inner state" (Kalff 1991). Through this free, creative play in a visible three-dimensional form, the therapist is said to be able to mobilize and access the unconscious processes of the client (especially the child). This therapy, originally developed in the 1950s–60s by Swiss therapist, Dora Kalff, intrigues some Chinese practitioners due to Kalff's close affinity with traditional Chinese culture and philosophy (see Shen and Gao 2004; Kalff 1980). Kalff was born in 1904 and studied Chinese language as a child. She became keenly engrossed in ancient Chinese culture, particularly Daoism, Chinese thinker Zhou Dunyi's 周敦颐 Taijitu philosophy (such as "Diagram of Ultimate Power"), and psychological thoughts found in the *I Ching*. She was also influenced by Tibetan Buddhism and Japanese Zen. Later, she became a devoted student of Carl Jung and studied analytical psychology for six years at the Jung Institute in Zurich. She also underwent personal analysis by Jung's wife Emma Jung. Her dream was to integrate Eastern and Western psychology in sandplay therapy.

Yet the deep connections among sandplay therapy, Carl Jung, and traditional Chinese culture are not always self-evident. The links had to be unearthed, highlighted, and re-created for the Chinese audience and beyond. This important task is primarily taken on by Professor Shen Heyong, a Jungian analyst and a central figure in the introduction of Jungian theory and sandplay therapy to China. He is now widely regarded as the authority on a fusion style therapy inspired by Jung yet rooted in the traditional Chinese culture. Shen received his doctoral degree under the mentorship of renowned Professor Gao Juefu in 1989 and then taught at several different universities in China, during which he traveled to the United States as a Fulbright scholar and to Switzerland for advanced training and scholarly exchange. In particular, his stay and research at the Jung Institute in Zurich (1999–2000) and the

Jung Analytical Institute in San Francisco (2000–2002) played a critical role in shaping his intellectual trajectory. Among his numerous publications, two are most influential: *Rongge yu fenxi xinlixue* (Jung and analytical psychology, Shen 2004) and *Shapan youxi: Lilun yu shijian* (Sandplay therapy: Theory and practice, Shen and Gao 2004). What is unique about his writing is that he is not interested in merely describing analytical psychology and sandplay theory as such, but seeks to make every effort to interpret their key concepts and approaches through the Chinese prism. In other words, these two books fundamentally aim to put analytical psychology and sandplay therapy in dialogue with Chinese culture. The key term Shen uses to describe this integration process is *zheng he* 整合 (integration).

In his extensive writing on sandplay, Shen highlights what he sees as deep connections between this therapeutic method, Jung, and the Chinese cultural ethos. In an article titled "C. G. Jung and China: A Continued Dialogue" (2009), Shen details the profound influence of a German sinologist and translator, Richard Wilhelm, on Jung, who later wrote an introduction for two important Chinese books translated by Wilhelm: *I Ching*, and *The Secret of the Golden Flower* (*Taiyi Jinhua Zongzhi*), a Taoist book on meditation and oracle techniques. Shen, who served as the president of the Institute of Analytical Psychology in China, was instrumental in organizing the first three international symposiums on "Analytical Psychology and Chinese Culture"— first of its kind on a large scale in China. Three central concepts, all derived from the traditional Chinese literature and aesthetics, were the focus of discussion: *lingxing* 灵性, *tiyan* 体验 and *yixiang* 意象. It is extremely hard to find an English equivalent term for *lingxing*, which roughly refers to "spirit" or "wisdom." It is something one can obtain not necessarily from formal and abstract learning but from personal bodily experience (*tiyan*) and mindful practice. Therefore, lingxing and tiyan are closely related and very much imbued with Zen Buddhist thinking (especially the notion *juewu* 觉悟 meaning "suddenly enlightened"). For Shen, tiyan is precisely what Western analytics lacks and what a culturally integrated approach can contribute to psychotherapy.

The other importance Chinese notion is *yixiang* (imagery), which literally means an object laden with meanings, as illustrated by Chinese ideographic and pictographic characters. Shen called them "readable archetypes." In his teaching, Shen trains his students how to grasp and interpret yixiang that emerge from sandplay, hypnosis, or art therapy by delving into Chinese religion, mythology, cosmology, and literature. In April 2009, on behalf of the International Psychoanalytical Association, Shen co-organized an international conference on "the Role of Yixiang in Psychotherapy" in Shanghai. Its goal was to identify sensible ways to bridge the yixiang theory, and Jungian psychology, with other psychotherapeutic techniques.

Drawing from Jung's theory on symbols and the unconscious, and Daoist and Buddhist thinking about the relationship among self, action, and perception, another therapist and writer, Zhu Jianjun, has branded his talk therapy as "imagery communication psychotherapy" (*Yixiang duihua*). The gist of his theory is that a dialogue with yixiang, rather than narratives, offers a better conduit of grasping Eastern psychological experiences. He claims that this method is a successful product of bentuhua in understanding culturally specific psychological experiences. By publishing his book in both Chinese and English, it is not difficult to see Zhu's intention to not only educate Chinese readers but also suggest how global psychotherapy can learn from the Chinese experience. Both Shen and Zhu feel strongly that China should not blindly apply Western therapeutic practices, but rather enrich and transform them in a meaningful way. In particular, Shen remarkably embodies the integration of knowledge through his frequent travels to distinct cultural spheres across China, Europe, and America.

Among the therapists I interviewed in Kunming, at least six of them followed Shen's interpretation of sandplay therapy and Zhu's yixiang dialogue method closely. Cai Jing is one of them, and his bentuhua attempt was most innovative and fruitful. Over the past several years of my fieldwork, I have been closely following Cai, a well-respected psychotherapist in Kunming. I have had extensive conservations with him and participated in several workshops led by him on sandplay therapy, hypnosis, and art therapy. He is the head of a counseling training center that offers specialized workshops for those who just passed the standardized test and obtained their counseling certificates. He also conducts private counseling sessions with his own clients. Cai impresses me most by his remarkable ability to blend elements of Daoism, Buddhism, traditional Chinese medicine, art, and Jungian psychology in his teaching and counseling practice. He believes deeply that it is imperative to develop an indigenized form of therapy in order to alleviate mental distress in Chinese society.

Cai is a Kunming native; he had done many different things before turning into a self-made therapist, including working in a factory for about ten years after graduating from high school. Then, under parental pressure, he took charge of the family business of selling women's nightgowns and bras. He was feeling very unhappy and confused about his future throughout the years. In his spare time, he studied *I Ching*, fortune telling, and traditional Chinese medicine, and was well versed in famous Daoist and Buddhist texts and classical Chinese literature. Cai recalled, "I drifted for years until one day I accidentally discovered psychology and counseling through a friend. I felt as if I finally found my calling and the path to enlightenment (a state of being Buddhism calls *wu* or *juewu*)." Against his parental wishes, he gave up running the family business in the late 1990s and devoted himself to full-time study and practice of psychological counseling.

When psychology and counseling entered contemporary China, diverse theoretical schools and therapy techniques were introduced. Chinese learners were exposed to them briefly during their initial training period. A few approaches (such as Satir family therapy, Jungian-inspired sandplay therapy, and a modified cognitive behavior therapy) gained traction quickly because they were regarded as more "fitting" for the Chinese social norms, values, and cultural expectations than other approaches (see Zhang 2014). During his encounter with psychotherapy, Cai discovered that Jungian analytical psychology and sandplay therapy were most appealing, as they allowed him to explore the new realm of Western therapeutics while simultaneously integrating the wisdom of Daoism, Buddhism, and other elements of traditional Chinese culture. In 2004, he enrolled in an advanced training workshop under the guidance of Professor Shen Heyong. Since then, Cai has consistently striven for an integrated therapeutic orientation in his teaching and practice. Several times he told me: "For me, all things should be considered, as long as they are useful for treatment. I see profound connections between the spirit of Chinese religion/philosophy and the core of Jungian theory. This is not surprising, because Carl Jung himself was deeply influenced by the writings of the *I Ching*, Daoism, and Buddhism."

I sat in many of Cai's training workshops and watched him invoking stories and symbols from ancient Chinese culture (figure 2). He was able to skillfully blend Jungian analytical psychology and sandplay theory with his creative interpretations that largely drew upon writings by Lao Zi and Zhuang Zi and Buddhist texts. Cai also used Jung's theory of archetypes and collective unconsciousness to interpret what he called "the deeper meanings" of the images and symbols that emerged in sandplay sessions and art therapy (Jung 1959).

FIGURE 2. A group of young interns with their mentor, Cai Jing, in a training workshop. Photo by author.

For example, he provided detailed readings of such images as fish, temple, river, pine tree, grass, Buddha, and Guanyin (the bodhisattva of compassion revered in Buddhism). These were all rich symbols in the Chinese cultural tradition that repeatedly appeared in his clients' and students' sandplay or hypnosis sessions. For instance, the image of a red carp that appeared in a female student's hypnosis was said to be imbued with her desire for autonomy and ease; another image of a tall, old pine tree was said to signify a state of mind marked by rootedness and steadiness. Cai gave us a long lecture of how fish and pine trees figured in various ancient Chinese literatures and the deep meanings attached to them. He stressed that the key was not to treat these images in isolation; instead a productive interpretation and healing hinged upon one's ability to read these images in a relational manner.

Cai's fusion approach was exemplified in a case he shared with me. During a long therapeutic process with a middle-aged woman named Qiuhua, Cai used a combined approach involving sandplay, hypnosis, and poetry therapy. The most unique feature about this case was that the therapist and the client engaged in extensive poetry writing as their primary form of communication.

Qiuhua was introduced to Cai by her older husband, who had taught Cai how to read the *I Ching* some years ago. At that time, she suffered from suicidal depression and severe anxiety yet refused to seek treatment. Because Cai was a family friend, she agreed to see him. Their sessions started with talk therapy combined with hypnosis. But soon Cai discovered that Qiuhua loved writing poetry to express her emotional turmoil and dreams. Since he also loved poetry, they quickly embraced this form of communication. For about two years, they engaged in extensive and deep poetry exchanges (sometimes including her husband, who is a writer) and accumulated over one hundred-twenty pages of writing. Reading their poetry, I was often amazed by their emotionality, poetic sensibility, and candidness.

With her permission, Cai shared with me a memoir she wrote at the end of the therapy, which nicely delineated her journey of inner conflicts. Qiuhua grew up in a family of three siblings. Her mother was caring, but her father had a terrible temper and beat them frequently. Coming from an impoverished background and feeling inferior in society, he sought physical violence to release his own anger and resentment. She remembered vividly the crying and sense of terror in the house, and how frightened and guilty her mother felt for not being able to protect her own children. When Qiuhua was eighteen, one day her father fell ill and died unexpectedly. The horror and abuse ended, but so did the financial support for the entire family.

Her mother was not prepared for this sudden loss and was in great distress. "Life came to a halt for Mom completely. Overnight I felt as if I had to grow up and began the era of taking care and accompanying my mom. That was my priority in life," recalled Qiuhua. Even though those were trying times and her mom worked really hard to raise the family, she was content to see her kids growing up. But at the same time, she grew hostile toward what she called "external invasion" into their family. She could not tolerate any of her kids dating or having a partner, viewing such an act as a sign of betrayal to her. Qiuhua's elder brother eventually got married and moved out. He only brought his wife back home to visit once. "Mom's life was totally subsumed by bitter complaints. My marriage sent her over the cliff. No matter how kind, patient, and filial my husband acted toward her, the return was always grumbling and criticism. The more successful he became in his career, the angrier she grew toward him," Qiuhua continued. Torn between her mother and husband, she felt as if she was drowning in a dark hole. She could not understand why her mother would act this way and hurt her so deeply.

It was at this moment that an exhausted and desperate Qiuhua met Cai. In multiple sandplay therapy sessions, they traced her emotional distress back to the chasm formed between her and her abusive father, her attempt to avoid pain, and the subsequent development of excessive mutual dependency with her mother. In some ways, Qiuhua had never fully grown up as an independent adult because her life was completely entangled with that of her mother. They had become each other's world. In her mother's mind, the sudden presence of Qiuhua's husband destroyed that unusually tight mother-daughter bond and thus the familial harmony. Then the situation got worse. Her mother became very ill from severe anemia and was hospitalized seven times for treatment, but due to her fear of contracting AIDS, she refused to receive blood transfusions and was generally anxious about any medical procedures. She fought with her children every time she went to the hospital, causing a lot of agony, and the only blood transfusion and care she would accept was from her own family members.

As her mother became older and weaker, Qiuhua decided to quit her full-time job as a successful journalist and devoted all her time taking care of her mother. The intense therapeutic work with Cai helped her look at the situation from a different perspective in order to cultivate a sense of compassion and loving kindness. The relationship made a miraculous turn: "Mom seemed too frail to fight and became calmer. She appreciated the fact that I quit my job and spent much more time with her. One day she surprised all of us saying to my husband that she felt most remorseful to him and asked for forgiveness. I know it was not easy for my mom to say something like this, and it meant a great deal to me and my husband. I also began to do a lot of soul searching to understand Mom's inner feelings, desire, and suffering better. Since my dad's death, she had devoted all her life to her kids, especially me. No wonder she felt abandoned when we got married. I sensed that the iceberg between us started to melt." In numerous poems she exchanged with Cai, Qiuhua expressed her sorrow, tenderness, and newfound joy in connecting with her mom and husband through countless subtle affective experiences of nature, dreams, and creative art.

The spirit of Buddhist wisdom and symbolism permeated her writing. The aura of *fo* 佛 (Buddha) or *guanyin* 观音 (the female bodhisattva) appeared frequently as a key symbol of compassion and gratitude through which their souls were transformed and enlightened. Here is a taste of her poetic journey mediated by Buddhism:

Buddha Is Here
In Zen's illumination
I begin to see your lotus-like dreams

Listening to the chanting
I hear your tireless humming

Aged old Mani praying stones
Suddenly your lips are turning warm

This loving-kindness
Warming up time
Warming up space
Warming up lands and rivers on earth

Your soul travels to mine irresistibly
Searching for mutual solace

Hand in hand
Bathed in the sacred lake
The two purified souls
In ultimate silent bliss

Notice that several Zen images are crucial for her healing and rebirth: Buddha, lotus, chanting, Mani stones, and enlightenment. "Scared lake" and "purified souls" both refer to the spiritual expedition toward awakening. As Cai reflected, "The true power of spiritual salvation is intrinsically compatible with the nature of psychotherapy." He acknowledged that this therapeutic encounter was very curative for both of them, and it contained certain powerful yet mysterious experiential elements that Western psychotherapy simply cannot replace. Moreover, he noted that serious transference took place in this process, as Qiuhua projected her yearning for deep emotional connection with her father (or the father she wished she had) onto Cai. Poetry not only provided a unique language to express her feelings but also functioned as an effective conduit through which the transference occurred. It was through this transference that an authentic healing relationship was established.

Qiuhua had always feared her father when growing up, but in the therapeutic process she gradually learned how to understand his pain and feel his love. One night she had a dream, in which her father appeared and had a heartfelt dialogue with her while escorting her through a long treacherous journey haunted by devils. For the first time, after twenty-eight years since his passing, she felt close to him, as if he was there watching out for her and giving her undivided attention and love. She woke up in tears and quickly wrote a poem, titled "Fatherly Love as Strong as Mountains."

(In father's voice)
I have been watching you from the distance
Always, always
My love has never ever departed
From your breath
From your love/hatred emotion
My prayers and armors have always been
Surrounding your dreams, your heart

Until today, I am finally emerging
In order to tell you that
You have never lacked
Or been left without father's love

(In her voice)
You can only watch me silently
Wrapping me up with your silky love
Today I can finally feel it and touch it

In this darkest night
You guide me through the forests
Away from the demons
Away from the beasts
Out of the gloomy abyss

Because of you
I am feeling so calm, so composed
Even while facing endless perils
No more panic
No more angst
For I am enveloped in your boundless love

Even though this realization of her father's love occurred in her dream, it signified a transformative moment and the power of her newfound deep connection with her long-lost father. The emotional bond gave her peace and confidence, melting away her anxiety and depression. This poetic expression can be read as a symbolic account of her audacity to fight the demons and find a path out of her emotional distress ("the abyss"). Finally, decades of fear and resentment, which had formed a knot in her heart, were gradually replaced by love, gratitude, and compassion.

Over the two years, Cai also incorporated her key family members (mother, husband, and brothers) in the therapy sessions, but the use of poetry was only between Qiuhua, her husband, and Cai. The treatment was successful: Qiuhua became less anxious and better connected with her family members. She was able to find joy in life and eventually returned to journalism.[10] In her own words, "having a true dialogue with Mr. Cai on a deep spiritual level through writing poetry saved my life."

In this case, we see that both the therapist and the client were interested in incorporating different therapeutic techniques in the treatment process and together they found the crucial dynamic that worked well—a fusion of poetry, Buddhism, and active imagination. This was truly a dialogic process in which each encounter was built on and shaped by the previous ones. Cai accentuated the notion of "whole well-being" and making deep emotional connectivity. He recognized no boundaries among philosophy, religion, art, and psychology— past or present, Chinese or Western. In addition, Cai often relied on the traditional Chinese medicine theory of the intrinsic relationship between the heart and the qi (known as *xinping qihe* 心平气和) to illuminate how one can adjust the mindset to reach a state free of anxiety and suffering—which is also the goal of modern psychology. We practiced the manipulation of qi to regulate emotions and find equanimity during workshops and were encouraged to integrate it into our everyday living. It was truly a joy to see him moving spontaneously between these cultural domains and drawing inspirations from diverse sources.

Not all therapists I met in Kunming, however, are interested in bentuhua work. Those who are younger and in the earlier stage of practice are more or less satisfied with understanding how their clients' problems and distress are generated in the social and family context in which they live. These practitioners are less eager to embrace the reworking of imported psychological theories and practices because they believe that the power of psychotherapy lies in its Western origin and scientific claim. Therefore, they tend to distance themselves from traditional Chinese culture by presenting their healing methods as novel and modern. Some clients are somewhat intrigued by the idea of integrating traditional cultural elements in therapy; others find it difficult to comprehend or irrelevant to their problems.

CREATIVE HEALING THROUGH ART THERAPY

The fourth approach that has become increasingly appealing to some Chinese therapists and clients today is art therapy (*huihua zhiliao*), which also requires a certain degree of bentuhua to make it work well. Art therapy, mostly through creative painting and drawing, has been adopted globally to treat depression, bipolar disorder, autism, schizophrenia, trauma, dementia, and other mental and emotional problems.[11] But this creative healing is a relatively new method in China, often used in combination with other therapeutic techniques, especially through construing the images and motifs that bear cultural significance. As a form of free and symbolic expression, it provides an invaluable medium through which the therapist and the client can communicate with one another effectively through nonverbal and verbal ways. The therapist often studies the art work carefully and interprets its meaning or generates a dialogue with the client. This process can also spur greater self-awareness and self-fulfillment leading to greater well-being.

Cai was a strong proponent of art therapy and strived to integrate it in his Jungian teaching and therapy in recent years. I sat in several of his workshops that introduced drawing and painting as a therapeutic modality. He usually gave students a broad prompt or theme such as "drawing a tree and a person in your memory," or "any scene with your family members in." After about twenty minutes, we would find a partner to talk about each other's work. Then Cai would ask a couple of students to share their drawings with the entire class. He would then engage in a dialogue with the creator and comment on the visual representation.

One day as I visited Cai, he took out a stack of paintings from his file cabinet and said, "You want to learn more about art therapy? Let me show you some work done by my clients recently. You will see how telling and powerful art can be in therapy!" I was thrilled, since we had talked about art therapy during our previous interviews, but it remained abstract. And I always wanted to see how he actually used it. We spent the next two hours looking through each of the fifteen pieces of art while he explained to me each client's background, problem, and therapeutic progress. The clients who created these works were mostly elementary or high school students and a couple of college students. He believed that this visual language (colors, lines, and patterns) was much richer than verbal communication alone, and that huihua is a potent mechanism through which one's unconsciousness is expressed through images and visual representation. The projection itself has healing effects and, at the same time, allows the therapist to access the client's inner feelings and conflicts. Let us look at two of them closely.

The drawing in figure 3 was done by Tianli, a twelve-year-old fifth grader who was brought in for help by his mother, whose complaint was that her son could not concentrate on anything or follow teachers' instructions at school, resulting in poor grades. She was afraid that her son was drifting aimlessly, and his life would be wasted (*fei diao*). Tianli received some psychological treatment for a couple of months but the therapist labeled Tianli as having a low IQ and concluded that he could not help any further. His mom was distraught and brought him to Cai, who was highly recommended by a friend, for another try. By the time of my conversation with Cai, Tianli had been treated for three months through a combination of art therapy and sandplay therapy. I learned that his parents were divorced when he was a toddler. His father suddenly became rich from real estate dealings and abandoned him and his mom. His mom was devastated and grew depressed. She attempted suicide twice but was discovered by her son, who rescued her in time. These were frightening experiences for young Tianli, who had a hard time comprehending why his mother would try to kill herself.

Cai pointed at the drawing and explained:

> I asked him to create a picture with the theme of house/tree/person (HTP) frequently used in psychological testing.[12] You can tell easily that this boy does not have a sense of security. Look at the tree he drew! It was so flimsy, almost not like a tree, and could break anytime. It is not rooted in the ground but extends into the sky. Moreover, the tree is not healthy at all because it only had a few leaves. Look at the house! It sits on a piece of leaf, which can break off and fall any moment. We can tell from his picture that his household lacks a strong supporting force or what we call yang qi 阳气 (masculine energy). Life for him is precarious and full of turbulence.

I noticed that the small house in the air seemed to consist of four figures. They appeared to be a mother and a father with two kids at the table—perhaps the dream of a complete and close family that he did not have. Like most Chinese children of his generation, Tianli was the only child. Perhaps, he wished that he had siblings. Cai continued: "This is a very smart boy. I do not think there

FIGURE 3. A drawing of a house on the tree by a young boy during his art therapy. Photo by Cao Xinshan.

is any problem with his intelligence. He was already ranked at a high level of playing *weiqi* [the ancient Chinese game go] and communicated with me nicely. What he suffered from was childhood trauma and insecurity. Therapy could give him a space to express his deep-seated fear, anxiety, and sadness from losing his dad and almost losing his mom." Through art, sandplay, and talk therapy over a period of three months, Tianli was making remarkable progress and became more communicative, cooperative, and motivated. His mom began to feel hopeful and was supportive of longer-term treatment.

Another piece of work was done by a middle-school-aged boy called Makun, who was asked by Cai to draw or paint something pertaining to the house/tree/

FIGURE 4. A drawing of scared trees by a young boy during his art therapy. Photo by Cao Xinshan.

person motif. He chose water painting but oddly his tree roots and trunks appeared to be on top of the leaves (figure 4). Most strikingly, I noticed four dark brown tree scars just above the roots. In psychotherapy, according to Cai, such scars or knots in a tree signified traumatic events, and the expression was often unconscious. Makun also came from a single-parent family. His mom was very concerned that he had developed an excessive dependency on her while having virtually no friends at school. At age thirteen, he still wanted to sleep with his mom in the same bed and sometimes walked around in the house semi-naked. Cai's interpretation was that due to the absence of the father—a male role model, his household lacked *yang qi*, and that this boy was confused about his own identity and could not grow past the infant stage. Cai strongly believed that the right balance between ying and yang, femininity and masculinity, caring and disciplining was crucial for the healthy upbringing of a child. Any lack in one element would be detrimental in Cai's eyes, yet the rate for one-parent families (*danqing jiating*), which would damage such balance, was soaring in China. While I do not necessarily agree with Cai's essentialist interpretation of gender and family dynamics, his view is widely shared among Chinese therapists.

As I have shown, art therapy, mostly in the form of painting and drawing, is used commonly in conjunction with other therapeutic methods. In Cai's case, it was deployed along with sandplay therapy to assess the client's psychological state of being and ignite conversations between the therapist and the client. Bentuhua efforts are manifested largely in the interpretation of the images and graphics by drawing from Chinese cultural motifs and semiotics. The two parties—therapist and client—jointly explore the client's inner feelings and lived experiences with the aim to solve his/her existential problems. Therapists find art therapy especially useful and powerful in working with children and teenagers. They can share children's art work and their own analysis with parents and find that it is much easier for Chinese parents to grasp their children's struggles through visual expressions than from abstract verbal reports.

REFLECTIONS

Psychotherapy, born in the Western context, often takes on a different life and form as it travels from place to place and across time (see Matza 2009; Raikhel 2016; Plotkin 2001; Borovoy 2012). People around the globe thereby experience it very differently, and transform psychotherapy to tackle specific pressing challenges facing a society and its local expressions of distress. During these cross-boundary encounters, cultural and historical tensions embedded in psychotherapeutic practices are likely to become more pronounced. Researchers have shown that this is the case for how Western psychotherapeutic (psychiatric as well) knowledges and techniques are appropriated in other Asian societies such as Japan, Korea, Taiwan, Hong Kong, Vietnam, Thailand, India and beyond (see, for example Borovoy 2012; Ozawa-de Silva 2010; Cohn 1998; Chua 2014). Contemporary Chinese psychotherapists are facing a similar dilemma: On the one hand, a great deal of the appeal and the perceived power of psychological counseling is derived from its Western origin and claim to scientific knowledge; on the other hand, these psychological theories and therapeutic techniques often do not necessarily fit the ways most people conceive of personhood, sociality, sensibility, and efficacy in healing processes in China. Therefore, it is vital for practitioners to engage psychotherapy creatively by incorporating culturally specific concerns and techniques and in turn transform the therapeutic culture itself.

Most Chinese therapists need to negotiate multiple transformations during the bentuhua process. They themselves must first undergo an epistemological shift in order to grasp psychotherapy knowledge and then reshape it according to the particular cultural and social context. They do so by embracing those therapeutic models that are more congruent with Chinese cultural sensibilities and ethics and by recasting them through the Chinese cultural repertoire. Several features are central to their consideration and effort to render psychotherapy a distinct cultural form: the strong orientation toward one's family and social nexus, legacies of socialist thought work, healing techniques borrowed from Zen Buddhism and Daoism, and interpretation methods based on communication with images and symbols beyond words. Further, Chinese therapists must respect and rework the expectations of their clients, who have little prior exposure to professional psychological interventions.

The tensions between inward-looking and outward-looking, Western and Chinese cultural orientations, collaborative and authoritative treatment styles, however, will continue to exist and evolve in the years to come. In the long run, I am hopeful that these tensions will prove to be productive because they also present a rare opportunity for Chinese practitioners to craft a culturally and historically embedded form (*zhenghe* 整合) of counseling practices. This integrated approach will have the potential to transcend the binary epistemological divide in thinking about body-mind experiences, and narrative versus nonnarrative modes of talking cure, and provide a better way to address many old and new problems facing Chinese families, organizations, and individuals. The culturing of psychotherapy, however, is not limited to the realm of psy knowledge, theory, and counseling technique, but extends to the cultivation of specific therapeutic relationships, which I will examine more closely next.

CHAPTER 3

Therapeutic Relationships with Chinese Characteristics?

Establishing a solid and healthy therapeutic relationship is usually regarded as the first key step toward an effective treatment. Some see it as the very foundation for healing, without which well-crafted methods and techniques would become meaningless. But what counts as "good," "desirable," or "suitable" is not universal or fixed. According to some influential Western books on counseling techniques translated into Chinese, an ideal therapeutic relationship is marked by the following qualities: respect, warm-heartedness, openness, equality, and mutual trust. A therapist's capacity to be empathetic (*gong qing* 共情) is said to be crucial for establishing such a trust relationship based on partnership. And further, the role of the therapist is to encourage the client to take risks and engage in a deep, self-reflexive exploration.

Most writings by Chinese psychologists and counselors are heavily influenced by the American psychologist Carl Rogers for his humanistic approach to therapy (see Qian 1994). For example, the national qualification exam textbook cites and elaborates on the following elements from Rogers's client-centered therapy for how to establish a sound counseling relationship: respect, warmth, authenticity, empathy, and positive regard (Rogers 1951). It instructs therapists to be sensitive to specific cultural contexts and individual situations, and to use their "cultural sensibility" to judge what is most appropriate for a specific case.[1] In this and other similar writings, however, the question of power and authority in therapeutic settings is rarely addressed. There is little discussion on how the unequal power relationship between the therapist and the client is shaped by social, economic, and cultural factors, or how to grapple with this unsettling situation.

During my fieldwork, I found that most Chinese therapists could easily cite the principles of a desirable therapeutic relationship based on what they learned from the textbooks. But when I observed their counseling sessions and probed the issue further, the situation became complicated and full of contradictions. Overall, talk therapy as conducted in China is fairly *directive* and largely based on an *authoritative* figure. Despite the effort to create a more relaxed and open environment, therapists find it hard to alter the overwhelming expectations of their clients for an external authority and for direction. As a prominent Chinese psychologist Qian Minyi explains, "Chinese people are socialized to heed the direction of elders, authorities, and professionals. Since therapists are the 'experts,' it is expected that they will direct the treatment and provide resolution of the problem" (Qian et al. 2002: 59). This expectation is at odds with Carl Rogers's *nondirective* approach that proposes minimum intervention by the therapist.

A fundamental belief in Rogers's theory is that people are by nature inclined toward growth and healing and thus are capable of finding their own answers to their problems. He states clearly: "Do we respect his capacity and his right to self-direction, or do we basically believe that his life would be best guided by us?" For Rogers, the role of a skilled therapist is to help the clients unearth this capacity, not to give out directions or do the work for them. But there exists a big gap between the ideal and the reality in China, as one cannot overlook the specific cultural context in which talk therapy takes place. Not everyone agrees that self-direction is vital in therapeutic adventure. While some therapists lean more toward a nondirective approach, others are more comfortable with combining both directive and nondirective approaches. In general, I noticed that a true client-centered model based on liberal individualism does not work well in the Chinese cultural milieu. Rather, a certain degree of dependency seems to be desirable from both sides. In what follows, I will describe and elaborate on three distinct features of Chinese therapeutic relations—fast and practical, authoritative, and using a familial proxy. By calling these "Chinese characteristics," I do not mean to suggest that they are unique to China and cannot be found elsewhere. I am aware that these features exist in most talk therapy to varying degrees, but they are especially pronounced in the Chinese setting for a number of reasons, which I will explain.

FAST AND PRACTICAL

The counseling cases I observed indicate that Chinese clients are usually eager to find out what the problems are and how to fix them. Frequently the first question they ask is: "What is wrong with me?" or "What is wrong with my child?" What they desperately want first is a straightforward diagnosis. The next question they tend to ask is: "Is the problem mental or psychological?" Chinese clients tend to differentiate what they call "mental problems" from "psychological problems," by which they mean the former is a more serious, psychiatric disorder and thus harder to treat, while the latter is socially induced and more remediable.[2] When such clients come to therapy, they anticipate a quick and up-front diagnosis and expect a linear progression in treatment. But psychological work takes time and often does not follow a straight line of progress. In short, it is often messy and there is no fast cure. This situation can create confusion, anxiety, and dissatisfaction among the clients and their family members.

The first counseling case I encountered during my fieldwork was in July 2006 at the Yunnan Health Education Institute's newly established psychological counseling center. My therapist friend, Huang Ying, had worked at the institute for almost twenty years. She had just received her therapy license after attending intensive prep classes and taking the national exam. This center is one of the very early counseling services that emerged in Kunming. Because of its official platform (under the name of a government health institute), it has quickly gained public trust, and the fees are very reasonable (about half of private counseling charges at that time). Ms. Huang was also invited to write for a weekly special column on psychological education in the city's most popular newspaper, *Spring City Evening Daily*, and thus enjoyed a fine reputation as a knowledgeable and trusted psy expert. Soon she gained a large readership and many of her clients came to her after reading her column.

Knowing that I was interested in counseling and conducting research in this area, Huang called me one day: "Hey, Li! I have a session coming up this afternoon. A mother and her daughter have traveled far from the Shangri-La region and agreed to let you sit in the session. They thought more experts are better. Do you want to come?" I was of course thrilled and said yes immediately, but I was both very curious and a bit nervous. I was still in the preliminary stage of my fieldwork and I had never seen a real counseling session, even though I had read a number of books about it. "See you at two o'clock here. I told them that you are my friend and a professor from America. If they ask for your opinions, feel free to chime in," she added. "Well, but I am not qualified . . ." but before I could finish my sentence, she had already hung up.

I took a cab and arrived at her office early. Huang greeted me and said, "Please go ahead and look around by yourself while I am finishing some paperwork." The center was just a small office adjacent to other administrative offices in the institute. It had two black sofa chairs facing each other and a small tea table in between, on which sat a small box of tissues. The room had the typical kind of office fluorescent lighting, making the space feel a bit cold and impersonal. There was nothing special to this office except for a rectangular sandbox table and two bookshelves full of sandplay objects—the only indicators that this was a counseling space. I took some pictures and sat down to review my notes.

At two o'clock, I heard three knocks on the door. Huang opened the door and introduced us. The mother with braided hair looked to be in her forties and appeared very concerned. Her hands were clutching her brown purse tightly. The seventeen-year-old daughter, Shuyu, looked distraught and apathetic, avoiding direct eye contact with us. After briefly introducing their family background, the mother started to tell us about her daughter's problems: "Teachers, this child is in trouble. Ever since she entered high school, she became rebellious and would not take any advice from us parents or others. She was overly sensitive, irritable, and liked to get hung up on trivial things. She asked 'why' just about everything and could not get along with her classmates. Her grades plummeted. And she was always worried about what other people might think about her. 'Why did they say that to me?' 'Why did they look at me that way?'"

It was common for Chinese people to refer to counselors as "teachers" to show their respect. The mother did not seem to mind my note-taking and looked at me from time to time as she talked. The girl was looking down most of the time. I realized how skinny and sad Shuyu was. Huang tried to engage a conversation with her by asking a few simple questions. She was not interested and only murmured a few words: "It seems that I can never return to the old days." That was all she said and then she dropped her head down in silence. Huang signaled to the mother to go out of the office with her. So I followed them into the hallway. She told the mother that she needed some private time with the girl and asked the mother to wait in another office for thirty minutes.

"OK, Teacher Huang! But can you tell me whether her problems are psychological or psychiatric in nature? Is it biologically derived?" asked the worried mother.

"I really cannot tell yet. I need to first make her feel comfortable to open up with me and find out what makes her so distressed. My first goal is not to diagnose but to establish communication with her," replied Huang.

"Sure, but still based on your brief observation so far, do you think her problem is treatable with counseling? Or will she need medications?" Her eyes were almost tearful.

"Maybe I can tell you a bit more after I talk to her. So just be patient. I know it is hard for you as a parent to see your daughter suffering. But try not to worry too much. We will help her." Huang patted her arm gently.

"OK, as you know it is not easy for us. We come from far away—several hours by bus. I need to know what is wrong with her and how to help her, especially her school performance and social life."

Huang and I nodded and then returned to the girl. "Shuyu, we are here to listen to you. You can feel free to open up your heart and tell us about the things that you do not want to tell your parents. It is my duty to protect your privacy," said Huang softly. "You mentioned earlier that you cannot return to the old days. What do you mean?"

After some hesitation, Shuyu said timidly: "During my freshman year in high school, I had to have a surgery to remove some bone cysts and thus stayed home for the year to recover. Ever since then, I have become irritable and lost interests in things. When I returned to school a year later, I was not happy (bu kaixin) and could not help my repetitive mode of thinking. People thought I was eccentric and stubborn, and stayed away from me. I had no friends."

"Can you give me a couple of concrete examples of what upset you?"

"Mmm, I do not know. I am just upset most of the time. Maybe I am just looking for trouble myself. I am so easily obsessed with trivial things." She used a Chinese expression, zuan niujiaojian 钻牛角尖 ("drilling into the narrow end of the cow horn"), which refers to a pathological behavior by which a person is stubbornly fixated on small issues and cannot be persuaded by common sense or reasoning. This phrase appeared several times in her own and her mother's narratives. She also told us that she did not want to come to this session because she had no idea about what counseling would involve and felt guilty that her parents had to pay so much money for her problems, but her parents insisted.

"Can you find anyone around you who may understand you or just talk to you?"

"No, people think I am weird and shy away from me. They think I am antisocial. So I feel tense and lonely at school. At home, I argue with my mom all the time. Sometimes, we both end up crying together. Dad does not live with us most of the time because he works far away."

"So, again, what are the good old days you wish to return?" Huang pressed a bit.

"I suppose the days before the surgery, before I started to feel weird about myself, before everyone treated me like an outcast. But I do not know what happened to me. My mind is murky. Things are just different now," said Shuyu. This time she was actually looking at us.

Later we found out that the surgery was not a small operation but was quite painful, involving transplanting bone from one part of her body to her leg. It was not clear to us what medications were used during and after the procedure, which might have affected her mood. Even though Shuyu and her mother did not provide much detail, we got the impression that she was traumatized from that excruciating experience. She said that since then she had developed a strong fear toward medical procedures.

After talking with Shuyu, we met with her mother alone for fifteen minutes. She was restless and expecting a clear diagnosis. Before Huang had a chance to say something, she burst out with several questions, her eyes wide: "Did she say anything at all? What is her problem? Is there any hope to save her?"

"Well, we had a nice talk and she was cooperative. Although I cannot give you a simple diagnosis label, I know she is suffering from some kind of trauma. She will benefit from follow-up counseling sessions so that I can continue our conversation and find a way to help her. In my opinion, improving her communication with you, me, and perhaps her teachers is the first step. Above all, she needs understanding and support from you, not lecturing or more pressure. At this point, I do not think she needs psychiatric medications, but I would like to get to know her more." Huang assured the mother and hoped to schedule another appointment.

"But we do not have more time and money to come back. I was hoping for a diagnosis and advice today," said Shuyu's mother with disappointment.

Then she turned to me: "Teacher Zhang, since you come from America, you must also have some insights to share."

I felt awkward and said that I was not trained as a therapist and thus could not give any advice to clients. "What about your thoughts as a friend?" she pushed me.

I knew it would be unkind to dodge her further. After all, she had let me sit in the session and had shared some of her most intimate feelings. Huang looked at me and encouraged: "Please go ahead!" I thanked them for their trust and said that I believed further counseling was crucial, as Shuyu seemed to have displayed some classic posttraumatic symptoms, but she was willing to share her feelings during therapy—a precious opening for further exploration. I offered to pay for the next three sessions if they decided to come back. The mother had a resigned smile on her face: "That is very kind of you, but I will have to think about it and see if we can stay in Kunming longer." I realized that for them, the economic obstacle was not just the counseling fees, but also living expenses while away from home. For a working-class family, the total cost for long-distance transportation, lodging in the city, and counseling fees amounted to a big burden.

Huang told me later that Shuyu and her mother never returned or called. She was sad but not surprised, since this was a typical situation for many clients she had encountered. Some clients might come back for two or three more sessions, but they rarely exceeded five. I have always wondered how Shuyu is doing all these years and whether she has gotten more help.

As this case shows, therapists like Huang are under constant pressure to give a diagnosis during the first encounter. Chinese clients tend to regard psychotherapy as like other medical treatment they receive. The desire to look for a quick practical solution also hinders the prospect for engaging in a deeper exploration of one's psyche and personal history. Through one or two sessions, it is almost impossible for transference—a key element in psychotherapy—to develop. In psychotherapy, transference usually refers to an unconscious tendency in which clients assign their feelings (positive or negative) associated with significant persons in early life to the therapist. It is believed that transference can help clients understand and work out their emotions and thus facilitate the therapeutic process. But my observation indicates that transference is nearly absent in most Chinese therapy sessions, partly due to the lack of time.

THERAPEUTIC AUTHORITY

Rather than searching for an inner authority and cultivating self-reflexivity, most Chinese clients look for external authority in the therapist, who can offer judgment, approval, and guidance. Thus, the therapeutic process is not built on partnership, but on dependency. If they do not get what they expect, they become agitated and disappointed, or simply lose confidence in the therapist's healing ability in some cases. They prefer a paternalistic expert to guide, console, and take care of them. After all, in their view, the expertise and guidance from the therapist is part of what they pay for. Therefore, they not only willingly subject themselves to this therapeutic authority but actually demand it.[3] Such a prevalent attitude often makes it very difficult to practice client-centered therapy and hinders treatment effectiveness.

Ms. Zhou, a skilled psychological counselor in her mid-forties, once told me that negotiating the expectations for quick, directive therapy was a big challenge facing her in her years of practice: "Typically during the first visit I try to make my client feel comfortable and safe, and also gather basic information to get to know the person and his or her emotional troubles. But at the end of the first visit, they already want to know what specific action they should take. They feel that it is my responsibility to offer my knowledge and advice, which they have just paid for. Otherwise, they feel that I owe them something or I am just a sham who has no idea about how to help them."

I had followed Zhou for three years and was impressed by her ability to make help-seekers open up even in some quite difficult cases, yet it was not easy for her to temper clients' desires to seek immediate enlightenment and solutions. Such desires tend to steer the focus of the therapy toward an external, authoritative figure, rather than gear it toward the client's own inner experiences and insights. One day, she lamented to me: "I repeatedly tell my clients that psychological work is interactive and requires their participation. As Rogers said, the client is the center. The therapist is only there to accompany and listen. They have to do the work; we are there like a mirror to reflect on their thinking from time to time. But the clients demand a clear diagnosis and explicit directions for *what they can do* to improve their situation. They want a list of orders to follow."

Very much influenced by Carl Rogers, Zhou believed in the client's capacity for self-healing. But oftentimes this capacity was hidden or needed to be cultivated. A main task of a therapist, as Zhou understood it, was to help the client to discover and develop this capability. But some clients did not agree. For example, she recalled one of her encounters with a rich business man. His teenage son became disobedient and was not doing well in high school, yet they had a lot of trouble communicating with each other. He was very frustrated about the situation, but said that he had no time to deal with his son. One day he came to see Zhou and offered her five thousand yuan up front to take care of his son's problem: "Keep this money as the counseling fee. I will bring my son here once a week to work with you. My work is too busy and I am a divorced single parent. So I hope you can help me take care of my boy. Surely with your knowledge and expertise, you can solve my problem!"

Basically this wealthy man wanted Zhou to act as a counselor and a mother at the same time for his son, and thought he could outsource his problem to an expert who would be indebted to him should she accept the money. He believed that money could buy an expert's healing power and regarded the therapeutic relationship as a business contract. When Zhou declined the money, he was in disbelief: "Why? This is easy money for you. Hmm, is it too little? I could give you more if you can solve my problem." Zhou eventually agreed to work with his son but would receive the normal payment session by session. She asked for his occasional participation in the counseling, but he said that it was not possible given his busy work schedule. Zhou shook her head and said to me: "I was not sure if I should cry or laugh at that moment. You know, healing is not something you can buy. Also, this man does not understand that the problem is not just his son's, but rather it involves the entire family, especially him as the father. I need parental participation for effective family therapy."

At Zhou's counseling center, I also met a thirty-four-year-old woman, Meiyue, who came to seek advice on her marriage troubles and emotional anguish. She was very talkative and stated her goal in the beginning: "I come today because I want to understand myself better and get out of the mess I am in. I do not want to harm myself emotionally, but it is so hard to stop. I have talked extensively about my problems with my parents, friends, and even strangers to get their perspectives. But I am still confused. Today I want to get an expert's opinion about my situation and a possible way out." Meiyue allowed me to sit in on the session and hoped I could offer some insights about her dilemma. As we sat down and I took my pen and notebook out, she began to tell us her love story and heartbreaks:

> I met my current boyfriend at my workplace. He said that he had broken up with his girlfriend after a two-year-long relationship, but later I found out they were not completely done. She showed up at my apartment one day screaming and cursing at me with a knife in hand. I was so angry and scared but soon later I found out that I was pregnant! Even worse was that it was an ectopic pregnancy, painful

and potentially dangerous. My boyfriend was not happy or sympathetic about the situation. I knew he did not have any money and could not help paying for my hospital stay. But I could not leave him since I had no family support and would be left completely alone. I was miserable and took a lot of medicines but the situation did not improve. . . .

On New Year's Day, he left me alone at home for three days. I was terrified, disappointed, and did not know what to do. I do not understand why I chose him in the first place. If I were not pregnant, I would probably have left him. But when he came back, I forgave him again. We decided to go to the hospital for surgery. I did not want to tell my parents, so I borrowed money from some friends.

Only two weeks after my hospitalization, I managed to find a job as an assistant to a CEO of a small private company. Even though I was still very weak physically, I had to pretend I was fine at work. I took the bus to work and spent two hours on the road every day. I had no choice, as I needed to pay back all the debts by myself. My boyfriend also got a low-paying office job for a while, but he quit after two months because he found it boring. He drifted around for a while from job to job. I wanted to encourage him to do something useful and suggested selling car insurance, but he was unconvinced.

I feel exhausted and hurt most of the time. One day it was stormy outside, I nearly had a mental breakdown and cried so hard for hours. Even though my parents do not like him at all and think he is unreliable and no good, I still have some feelings for him. You can say that he is irresponsible, but being with him at least eases some of my loneliness. So I am deeply torn and confused. What should I do? Break up or not?

Meiyue made it very clear that her goal for this therapy was to get guidance. She took out a piece of paper and asked us to help her make a list of reasons why she should break up and another list of why she should not. She was afraid to make the wrong decision and felt that an expert opinion would point her to the right path. Zhou and I sat there listening with sympathy but felt a bit taken aback by her strong desire for direction. She obviously had a very different idea about what psychological counseling was about. Zhou smiled patiently and asked her more background questions in order to get to know her better. While Meiyue was staring at the two columns for reasons, Zhou said, "It seems to me that the crux is to understand why despite all his shortcomings that caused you a lot of suffering, you still hesitate to leave him. What is the nature of your feeling toward him?" As they talked a bit more, it became more apparent that Meiyue had a deep fear of being left alone due to her early upbringing. Her father left the family when she was young, and it cast a long shadow in her life. Further, the difficult pregnancy made her feel even more vulnerable. Facing it alone emotionally would be very tough. As the two-hour session came to an end, she remained ambivalent: On the one hand, she was disappointed because she did not get a clear answer from the therapist about whether or not she should end the relationship; on the other, she felt a bit relieved that someone listened to her carefully and understood her conflicted feelings. She seemed to be inclined toward ending the relationship but still needed time to think it through.

One possible explanation for the tendency to seek external authority is that in both Western biomedicine and traditional Chinese medicine, doctors are generally seen by Chinese patients as the source of wisdom, trust, and power for healing (Farquhar 1996). They are in some ways revered for their restorative power and so must be obeyed in order for the patient to gain the desired cure. Thus, many people have adopted this familiar medical treatment model in the new talk therapy setting. As one client put it, "If my therapist cannot give me insights and instructions, why should I waste my money and time? I want real results in order to trust his or her ability. Respect, warmth, and empathy alone will not take my problems away." The measure of a good doctor, in many people's eyes, is the ability to diagnose, prescribe, and heal in a timely fashion. So a therapist is expected to do the same. But as we can see, the psychological domain is different and more complicated; it is harder to measure what can be counted as progress.

Another possible explanation is that the desire for direction and external authority may be seen as a lingering effect of people's habitual dependence on the state and their work units under socialism. This expectation somehow is transferred from the socioeconomic setting to the therapeutic domain. In this context, therapists' advocacy for self-exploration and self-reliance can be interpreted as a conscious or unconscious promotion for a neoliberal mode of the self, one that resonates with the Chinese government's recent call for individuals to become responsible for their own well-being and problems. With the withdrawal of previous state provisions of goods and services, it is not surprising to encounter resistance from some clients who still hope to be taken care of by others.

However, we must understand that the notion of authority also carries a different connotation in different cultural contexts. It does not necessarily entail negative or oppressive meanings for some social groups. As Borovoy points out in her study of Japanese psychiatrist Takeo Doi's critique of Freud and his effort to rehabilitate the notion of "dependency," authority and paternalism can be regarded as "potentially benevolent and socially necessary" (2012: 273). She argues: "Turning Freud's notion of freedom as rejection of authority on its head, Doi writes that it is Freud's inability to accept human passivity and dependence that lays the foundations for his harsh treatment. True authority attends to the needs of human dependency and is not corrupt" (2012: 273). The same argument can be made with regard to Rogers's client-centered theory. For those who take Doi's point seriously, there is still room for kindly authority and constructive dependency even in the client-centered approach. Given the particular understandings of authority and action-oriented attitudes, Chinese therapists are compelled to compromise by providing pragmatic advice on specific things that the clients can do to help generate quick, observable results, while offering space for self-exploration. They do not see the two orientations as mutually exclusive, but recognize the need to bridge and combine them.

Of course, not all Chinese clients rejected the opportunity of self-examination. A small number of them were willing to pay for multiple sessions and enjoyed the luxury of long-term therapy. One therapist told me that he had been working with two clients for over a year: One was a well-to-do entrepreneur who suffered from depression and anxiety; the other was a college student with depression whose fees were paid by his parents. They usually met once a week and talked about the problems facing them in an unstructured way. This therapist was happy to share his thoughts with me:

> When I first told them about Carl Rogers's style that I hoped to follow, they were both curious and a bit uncomfortable, but they were open enough to give it a try. As time goes by, they find working as a partner with me in this process empowering and refreshing since it is very different from any other relationships they have ever had before. I cannot say we are completely equal like friends, but they trust me enough to say whatever is on their mind and take the therapy as a journey on which we are traveling together. Thus, they refrain from asking for advice and solutions all the time. For me, it is also more enjoyable to work with them, but they belong to the minority.

I asked what made these two different from others? He said that he was not sure, perhaps having no financial or time pressure was a factor. It also depends on individual personality—having an open and curious mind was helpful.

Another therapist who used art therapy said that he did not have to preach to his clients about preferred therapeutic relationships directly; instead he was able to use drawing and painting as a medium to communicate with them in a subtle and interactive way that transcended the dichotomy between self-direction and dependency. "In art therapy, the client is the author, while the therapist is the interlocutor. The dynamic is much more natural and collaborative. I respect their creativity and train of thought, but I am also there to observe and guide them to go deeper and deeper, closer and closer to the place in the heart where they normally do not want to go." It was this kind of dialogic and careful approach that he sought and valued, rather than rigidly following any particular theory or school.

FAMILIAL PROXY

In China, if a patient is unable to see a doctor or therapist in person due to physical limits or fear of stigma, a family member can do so on behalf of the patient. This practice is common and acceptable in Chinese society, largely due to relatively relaxed legal regulations over medical practices and specific cultural notions of privacy that give family members a great deal of latitude in knowing and handling each other's personal matters.[4] Even though proxy is not a desirable arrangement in seeking medical help and comes with many potential problems and limitations, it also makes it possible for families to get expert feedback and medications if needed. In fact, for many frail seniors who suffer from dementia and other mental distresses, sometimes this is the only way to get help unless one can bring a therapist for a home visit. In this section, I share my firsthand experience involving my late mother to demonstrate the benefit and downside of proxy treatment.

My mother, who was born in the late 1920s, had been suffering from a number of physical and psychological disorders for several decades, but we did not know how to name or talk about her distress in medical terms. At age eight, she lost her mother due to illness and subsequently endured an abusive step-mother who put her and her two sisters through many ordeals. I remember that my mother was always fearful about the possibility of her step-mother coming to harm us even when she was already into her adulthood. Then came the turbulent years of the Cultural Revolution, which brought about tremendous stress to most intellectuals like my parents. The political instability and uncertainty of life they had to experience exacerbated her existing mental condition. During her lifetime through the 1990s, psychological counseling was not available and mental illness was heavily stigmatized. My distraught mother basically somatized all her problems as physical illnesses and did not know how to address her psychological torment. In fact, she had not been formally diagnosed by mental health professionals for most of her life, and we in the family just thought she had a bad temper and was overly frightful due to her long-term, multiple physical illnesses (including cancer at age fifty-one) and the trauma of losing her mother at a young age.

Later as I read more and more psychotherapy and psychiatry books for my research, I began to realize that my mother had displayed all the classic symptoms of anxiety and obsessive compulsive disorder (OCD). After she turned eighty-two, her osteoporosis worsened leading to several painful spine fractures. Eventually, she became bed-ridden, and her mood swings became severe. Most of the time, she was irritable, sad, and angry about everything. She was preoccupied by the thought of death and could not control her anxious feeling. Sometimes, she hallucinated and was confused about where she was. Needless to say I was heartbroken to see my mother in this terrible condition. Based on my limited knowledge, I could tell that she was likely suffering from clinical depression and anxiety as well as early symptoms consistent with dementia. But she refused to see a psychiatrist because she believed that all her illness was physical. "I am not crazy. My worries have real basis," she often said. At her request, we brought her to see both Western and Chinese medical doctors frequently to treat what appeared to be somatic ailments.

As her anguish grew unbearable, and after my gentle but persistent persuasion, she finally agreed to see a psychiatrist. It was a major family effort. First, we had to send a relative to stand in line at five in the morning for two hours to get a hospital registration ticket in order to see a psychiatric specialist that day. Otherwise, all the tickets would be gone by seven o'clock, as there were not enough psychiatrists for patients. My sister and I got my mom a wheelchair and called a cab. After arriving at the hospital around ten o'clock, we waited for an hour with several dozen patients in the hallway. Chinese doctors nowadays are under a lot of pressure to see a large number of patients per day—usually sixty or more, which translates to about five to eight minutes per patient. When it was our turn, we were let into the office by a young female nurse. Dr. Chen (listed as a chief doctor and associate professor) was surrounded by four nurses/assistants who were helping with taking notes, reviewing charts, and writing prescriptions to save his time. It was a bit intimidating, as so many people were staring at us. Privacy did not appear to be a concern here. He asked my mom what was wrong with her. But before she could finish her description, he turned to me:

"Are you her daughter?"

"Yes, I am. I just came back from America. It was very hard for us to get my mom out of the house today due to her weak physical condition." I was trying desperately to get his attention by mentioning my connection to the United States.

"It might be quicker for you to tell me her symptoms. You see I have so many patients waiting here and I do not have time for details. You can talk faster and more clearly than your aging mother."

So I did the best I could within a few minutes. He then started to prescribe medications. When he handed the paper to me, he added: "Next time, if it is too hard for your mom to come, you can just come to tell me her progress and I can adjust the medicines." I nodded, and we were pushed out of the office after about five minutes. I glanced at the prescription, which consisted of four medications: Ambien (sleep aid for insomnia), Prozac (anti-anxiety/depression), Olanzapine (anti-atypical-psychotic), and Xanax (anti-anxiety). I was familiar with three of them as they were commonly used in the United States, but I did not know Olanzapine. So I quickly searched it on the internet using my cell phone and found that it was a very strong anti-psychotic medicine that could cause a number of side effects. I was shocked that the doctor prescribed all these medicines with very little knowledge of my mother's illness history and medical condition. And I know that there was no way my seventy-five-pound mom could tolerate all these medicines at once. After returning home, my family had a meeting to discuss how we should proceed. It was difficult, as we did not have any medical background. I did a lot of internet research and consulted several doctor friends. Eventually we decided to give mom Prozac only and Ambien when really needed. But I felt unsettled and responsible for my mom's situation should something go wrong. This experience was not uncommon in China. Many families have to evaluate their options based on limited information and make tough medical decisions for their loved ones, since the medical system is very flawed.

Miraculously, the Prozac, even at a low dosage of 10 mg per day, helped improve my mom's mood a great deal. She gradually became calmer, and was able to engage in a somewhat normal conversation with us. Her hallucinations still occurred from time to time, but she was clearly less anxious and more manageable. About a year and half later however her condition began to deteriorate with more episodes of the fury and anxiety she had experienced before. It was possible that the so-called "honeymoon period" of Prozac (as with other antidepressants) had passed, so she had a relapse. At this point, my mom was too weak to get out of the house, so I decided to see a psychiatrist on her behalf—someone who also offered psychotherapy.

To avoid standing in the long line, I paid 170 yuan—about ten times the cost of a normal ticket—to get a VIP registration for a psychiatrist recommended by a friend. With the special status, I was able to bypass the crowds and went straight up to the fifteenth floor. I was greeted by a pleasant nurse in a quiet and comfortable waiting room. She brought me a cup of mineral water while I was waiting. It was like an entirely different world than the floors down below packed by thousands of patients. Twenty minutes later I was led into the office of Dr. Sun, who was sitting in a chair smoking. I was a bit surprised, but he did not seem to have noticed my frowning and displeasure. He appeared to be his early forties and was not wearing the typical doctor's white coat. He asked me to sit down and occasionally reached out to the ash tray on the table to deposit the ashes. "What brought you here today? Don't worry. We have time." I explained my mom's situation and why she could not come with me.

"That is not a problem. I can get a pretty good sense from your report." Then he asked me some basic questions about my mom's symptoms and medications. I tried to be as thorough as possible since he did not rush me. He picked up another cigarette slowly and said: "I can give her some medications to control her symptoms and improve her mood." I nodded and brought up the issue of side effects. "At this late stage in her life, the quality of life is more important than longevity. Do you agree? Some seniors I have seen in similar conditions live on for ten more years. They can be tough, not as fragile as we think." After about forty minutes I left with a prescription of two medications—Zoloft and Ambien. Dr. Sun thought a different SSRI (Zoloft) might work more effectively. He also gave me an advice: "Just give your mother whatever she wants to eat and whatever makes her happy. You are a filial daughter, I can tell, but there is only so much you can do for her old age." He said that we could also continue to use Prozac at a higher dosage.

Sadly my mother did not last that long. She passed away a month later on a rainy morning. Although the direct cause of death was pneumonia, she was struggling with multiple medical issues. We did not even have time to switch her antidepressant. But I know we did our best given the circumstances, and I was fully aware that acting as my mom's proxy to get treatment for her was highly problematic. From time to time I wonder whether she could have gotten better care for her distress if China's mental health services were more advanced. I could only take some comfort in knowing that my mom at least had a few months of feeling less dread and anguish before she left us forever.

REFLECTIONS

For a long time, I believed that the kind of therapeutic relationship marked by clients' demand for fast, pragmatic diagnosis and treatment, linear progression, and medical authority to direct their life was distinctly Chinese. I have outlined some of the reasons in this chapter and suggested that therapeutic relationships fundamentally reflect different ways of understanding person-hood and sociality. But as time goes by, and based on my longtime personal experience and observation of therapeutic dynamics in both China and the United States, I have come to realize that these urges and traits are prevalent in non-Chinese settings as well. One indication is the increasing popularity of cognitive behavioral therapy (CBT), which claims to offer quick, measurable results and features a more salient role for the therapist in guiding the patient. Of course, cost is another important factor, as the insurance industry does not want to pay for prolonged talk therapy based on traditional psychoanalysis. Thus, to signal my hesitation to call all the characteristics I have identified here "Chinese," I have added a question mark to the title of this chapter.

Having said that, I still want to maintain that the urges for fast, practical and directive therapy without the space for transference seem to be more strongly felt in the Chinese setting, and they are shaped by a combination of historical, cultural, and structural forces.[5] In particular, it is not unusual for Chinese family members to play a proxy role, especially in the case of seeking help for the elderly and children. Given the limits facing most people in the medical system, doctors or therapists are also willing to take the case and prescribe medications and offer advice even though they have not met the patient in person.

Finally, I would like to reflect upon once again the centrality of the therapeutic relationship itself in healing. As I was writing this chapter, I happened to be reading two wonderful books by Irvin Yalom, a well-known Stanford psychiatrist and writer: *Creatures of a Day: And Other Tales of Psychotherapy* (2015) and *Love's Executioner: And Other Tales of Psychotherapy* (1989). They offer vivid accounts and reflections on his therapeutic encounters with some of his clients throughout the years—like a deep meditation on life, death, loss, aging, and other existential matters. In the afterword of *Creatures of a Day*, Yalom concludes: "The most important thing, I, or any other therapist, can do is offer an authentic healing relationship from which patients can draw whatever they need. We delude ourselves if we think that some specified action, be it an interpretation, suggestion, relabeling, or reassurance, is the healing factor" (2015: 209). For him, the true healing power does not come from the "archeological dig" of the past false trail of life, but rather lies in the therapist's loving present with the client (1989: 230). Based on my own years of counseling experience as a client and my extensive research observations, I find these words illuminating. Indeed, much of the redemptive power is derived from the honest, transparent, and authentic bond developed between the therapist and the client—the platform for any exploration. At the same time, I find myself lamenting precisely the lack of such bonds in most situations I observed during my fieldwork for the various social, cultural, and economic reasons I have analyzed earlier. So is Yalom's vision for an authentic healing relationship an ideal that can rarely be achieved? Or is China simply far behind in developing effective talk therapy, one based on the cultivation of a solid therapeutic alliance? My sense is that authentic therapeutic relationships do take place in China too but not so often. In the next chapter, I will show how some therapists attempt to address this challenging issue in their use of the Satir Model.

CHAPTER 4

Branding the Satir Model

In April 2010, I received an urgent email from Mr. Liu Kun, a therapist and friend whom I had been working with for ten years since I began fieldwork in Kunming. He asked me to translate a three-page document into English as soon as possible. I opened the attachment and started to read it immediately. It was an application for establishing the Southwest China Satir Practice and Development Center to be submitted to Dr. John Banmen, the head of the Satir Institute of the Pacific at that time. Liu Kun was the founder and director of a small organization created in 2005 called Soulspa Health Service Institute, and I have been working with his team until today. Because of our close friendship, I felt obligated to help him as much as I could. Essentially, the application was to request formal permission to establish a franchise-like business to teach and spread the Satir Model in Southwest China—involving a combination of for-profit and nonprofit activities. Franchising psychotherapy practice like McDonald's and Starbucks?[1] I was puzzled by how things were developing with regard to the growth of therapeutic practices in China. So, I called Liu to find out more information.

Liu was in his mid-forties when I met him. He made a point to speak Mandarin (rather than Kunming dialect) with me, his clients, and during his workshops to emphasize his professionalism. He told me in the message that he wanted to be the first one to obtain the right to teach the Satir Model and train therapists in Yunnan Province. "This would give me a great deal of credibility and market advantage in the competitive psy world. I would be the one who could supervise other subgroups in the future." He was very enthusiastic about this project and felt that he had an excellent chance to get the authorization.

Indeed, his team, consisting of eight part-time state-certified therapists, was already reputable in the city and had provided psychological services to enterprises, organizations, and individuals for five years. While they initially used many different therapeutic approaches, since 2008, they began to focus on the Satir Model as one of the core components of their teaching and training curriculum. The application detailed their recent training and encounters with various pioneering Satir programs in China, including a four-day workshop led by one of the foremost proponent of Satir family therapy, Dr. Maria Gomori. The document conveyed their understanding of and faith in Satir's basic premises that all human beings possess the inner resources for personal growth and creativity. It also presented their ambitious plan to broadly apply the model to enterprises and schools through a series of workshops. A month later, I got the confirmation that the application was approved and that Soulspa was now the legitimate organization to disseminate the Satir Model in Southwest China. Liu thanked me profusely for my translating work and was excited to delve into the project. They were already making plans for Dr. Banmen and Dr. Gomori to visit and lecture in Kunming.

In chapter 2, I introduced the Satir Model briefly and examined why it is attractive to many Chinese therapists and clients. I suggest that its main appeal is the focus on understanding and changing family dynamics and interpersonal relationships, which resonates well with Chinese people's emphasis on family harmony and the socially embedded notion of personhood. In this chapter, I want to take a step further and explore how a therapeutic model that is little known or has lost its appeal in North America today has been gaining enormous popularity in China and other parts of Asia. I trace the on-the-ground work of marketing and branding this model in the Chinese context in order to transform an "out-of-date" therapeutic approach into something novel, cutting-edge, and suitable for contemporary Chinese society. I also seek to understand how psy experts like Liu negotiate the tensions between doing "public good" (gonyi 公益) and pursuing "profits" (liyi 利益) in this process. I ask: What is the motivation? Why does he want to devote his lifetime to the teaching of the Satir therapy? What is behind his sense of calling?

THE PACIFIC SPREAD

Satir's teaching was once popular in the 1960s through the 1980s in North America but gradually lost its appeal. Today if you ask most psychotherapists in the United States whether they have heard about the Satir Model of therapy, they are likely to say that they know about it or read about it briefly but are not familiar with it. Very few would claim that they are experts on it or actually apply it in their practice. However, this is not the case in Asia where the Satir Model has gained new vitality since it was first introduced there in the 1980s.

According to Liu, the first step of bringing Satir's theory to East Asia was taken by the Chinese Psychological Hygiene Association based in Taiwan, which invited Virginia Satir to teach at a local counseling training workshop in 1983. By that time, Satir was already quite famous in family therapy and spending most of her time providing workshops and trainings in every continent in the world. Later on, several of her colleagues and students such as John Banmen and Maria Gomori went to Hong Kong and Taiwan annually to run workshops dedicated to teaching Satir therapy theory and practice. Hong Kong, Taiwan, and Malaysia thus became the early bases for spreading the Satir Model to Asia. In 1986, Banmen and others from Washington State and British Columbia founded the Northwest Satir Institute. Then in 1998 he established a separate nonprofit entity, called "the Satir Institute of the Pacific" (SIP), based in British Columbia. Originally consisting of twenty-three members, it has now grown to over one hundred thirty members throughout the world. It also supports the publication of *Satir International Journal*, whose goals "encompass therapeutic communication, equality, spirituality, ethical decision-making and global diversity." Its mantra is "healing the family, we heal the world," a deep conviction that Satir held.

With the rapid development of counseling services in Mainland China, Banmen and his colleagues began to turn their attention to Chinese cities. In 1996, a psychiatric hospital in Guangzhou invited him for the first time to give talks at a counseling workshop. In 2003, a series of workshops on the Satir Model were created in Guangzhou, Shanghai, Beijing, and other major cities, featuring well-known trainers such as Monita Choi, John Banmen, Maria Gomori, Cai Minli, Sandy Novak, Marie Lan, and Sok Fun Lam (see Yang and Lou 2013). Since then, because of the perceived market potential, more and more overseas therapists and psychologists who claim to be Satir's true followers have flocked to China to give lectures and run training workshops. The trainees include a broad range of people, such as school counselors, teachers, doctors, social workers, and ordinary parents.

Some researchers have argued that the Satir Model is so popular in China largely because of its compatibility with Chinese traditional values. Yang and

Lou, for example, tease out three fundamental views shared by both and compare them side by side (2013):

> The first is regarding the nature of human beings:
>
>> "People are basically good, but sometimes need help to experience and manifest this aspect of themselves" (Banmen 2008).
>> "People at their birth, are naturally good. Their natures are much the same; although their habits are widely different" (Sanzi Jing 三字经 *The Three Character Classic*).[2]
>
> The second is about the innate ability to grow:
>
>> "We have the internal resources to move beyond the basic coping level as well as the ability to harness our external resources in order to grow" (Banmen 2008).
>> "As Heaven's movement is ever vigorous, so could people ceaselessly strive and grow" (*I Ching* 易经 *The Book of Change*).
>
> The third is about the role of the family:
>
>> "The family system is the basic learning and living unit and, as such, needs to be included directly or indirectly in all therapy" (Banmen 2008).
>> "Harmony in the family is the basis for success in any undertaking" (家和万事兴 An old famous Chinese proverb).

The authors conclude that the congruence between the Satir therapeutic beliefs and traditional Chinese conceptions of personhood and family makes it much easier to adapt this Western therapy to Chinese society. The emphasis on seeking familial and social harmony echoed the Chinese government's project to build a "harmonious socialist society."

I cannot help but notice that the Chinese word frequently used by the followers and practitioners to describe the expansion of Satir's therapy is *chuanbo* 传播, which means "spreading." Although this word can refer to spreading any ideas, information, or schools of thought, it often carries a strong connotation of spreading religion such as Christianity or Buddhism, or ideology such as Marxism. It suggests a certain degree of devotion, passion, and loyalty, and the desire to cultivate a large number of followers. Thus, *chuanbo* signifies a sense of mission. Further, it is also peculiar that another word, *moshi* 模式 ("model"), is used specifically in relation to Satir practices. In China, *moshi* usually refers to something grand or bigger like a paradigm or an economic model that can be replicated and has pragmatic implications for shaping behaviors and life. Thus, it is much more than a theory or school of thought. Both terms, *chuanbo* and *moshi*, are rarely used in talking about other branches of counseling approaches. For example, people would rarely say they seek to spread "the Freud Model" or the "Jung Model." But what interests me more is the business model by which the Satir Model has been adopted, branded, and managed in China.

FRANCHISING AND BRANDING

Indeed, the Satir Model is treated almost like a commercial brand, and its application must be authorized, standardized, and franchised. In other words, in order to be recognized as an authentic Satir center, one needs the official certification from the Satir Institute of the Pacific to operate. To further regulate the application process and oversee the quality of newly created centers, the Banmen Satir China Management Center (BSCMC) was established in 2009. According to its official website, the purpose of the center is "to promote the application of the Satir Model in China" and it will "set standards for certification of therapists, counselors and professional helpers using the Satir Model based on international standards of qualification and set standards for trainers and approve trainers who are running programs using the Satir Model." It seems to be preoccupied with the aims of standardization and centralization of control of the practice.

Because of his intellectual affinity with Satir and his long-term engagement with this therapeutic tradition, Banmen clearly sees himself as the genuine and rightful decipherer of Satir's theory and practice. He felt a sense of responsibility to carry on Satir's work and mission to benefit the entire world. And the excitement he received in China—the sheer number of people eager to follow him with great enthusiasm—was like nothing he had encountered before. It appears that there exists a potential to grow the Satir Model into a mega business that can both help people and generate profits.

In September of 2011, BSCMC held its first nationwide meeting in Beijing. Each regional center sent its representatives to make a detailed report on their programs, activities, services, contact information, webpage, aims, and so on. Then they discussed several key management issues: Level 1 and Level 2 facilitators training and registration fees, a formal contract for new centers to sign, the application process, and marketing strategies. Two representatives from the Wuhan Satir Center made a PowerPoint presentation on their "Distribution Plan," which assessed the market potential, value chain, pricing, and promotion strategies for how to further expand the Satir Model in China.[3] They maintained that since China has the largest population in the world accompanied by fast-growing needs for psychological service, its market potential is enormous. Further, Satir therapy is already a "leading foreign brand in family therapy," thus they predicted that it could be expanded quickly with some marketing efforts and eventually dominate the Chinese counseling field. A map was shown to illustrate the geographic distribution of the existing eleven centers, most of which were in major cities on the East Coast, North and Central China. Then the presenters devoted most of the time to what they called "value chain analysis" with a closer look at several groups of actors: clients, organizers, professionals who want to get the training, and other self-managed individual teachers and trainers. They pointed out that these groups do not coordinate with one another, so things just happened haphazardly. It is "hard to make money through the Satir Model" due to the "lack of a mature business model and consistent development plan, and the lack of united marketing support from headquarters." They also suggested to set up the "one area one center rule to avoid unnecessary competition and improve the cooperation among centers." Clearly, making money was a concern here, and in their opinion a well-coordinated national marketing plan was the key to achieve this goal. It is striking to me that the language used was overtly business-flavored—market potential, pricing, competition, brand, value, marketing, and so on. If one replaces the phrase "Satir Model" with another commercial product or service, one would think this was a business meeting for merchandise marketing.[4]

By 2018, over twenty centers nationwide had been approved by BSCMC and more were in the pipeline to be authorized. In Kunming, there are about four self-proclaimed Satir training centers plus a dozen smaller counseling offices, but only two are certified by BSCMC. Liu told me: "The competition in Kunming is increasing rapidly because some people see that the Satir Model can be applied broadly in other life domains. But my center is the real one and has been in practice the longest." After getting the authorization of BSCMC, Mr. Liu also registered with the Kunming Municipal Industry and Commerce Bureau and the Yunnan Provincial Civil Affairs Department. Once all the paperwork was done, his center began to operate and paid an annual regulation fee to Banmen's management center. Liu was all for strengthening the regulation of certification so that the "sham ones" could not easily make claims and compete with "real centers" like his. "It is not just about market competition but also about credibility. The fake ones not only ruin help-seekers' life but also ruin the reputation of the Satir Model and our true followers," he added.

Next, let us take a closer look into how his center actually engaged in the work of branding and spreading the Satir Model in recent years. I am particularly interested in how therapists like Liu Kun understand their mission and explain the forces that propel them to promote a particular therapeutic approach.

Naming and Visibility

Branding one's center as an authentic Satir institute involves a number of strategies. In addition to obtaining formal authorization, one must show one's close ties with Banmen himself, advanced professional training in this field, smart naming and advertising, a series of free public events and fee-based workshops that apply the Satir Model widely to many social domains (such as family, school, and workplace relations). For Liu's group, as soon as they received the endorsement from Banmen, they immediately changed his center's name from Soulspa to Satir Southwest China Center and redesigned their website to reflect this new status and orientation.

In order to familiarize more people with the Satir Model, Liu began to offer a series of public events free of charge in Kunming. For example, his team held a monthly lecture series at the provincial library located at the center of the city. These events were widely advertised in major local newspapers and on websites. They teamed up with several prominent organizations such as a reading club, Sina Happy Living, and Peking University Resources Group to increase its publicity. Topics ranged widely but a consistent and hot topic was "How the Family Shapes a Person," which examines techniques of improving strained marriage and parent-child relationships using Satir systematic family therapy. The audience included ordinary citizens of diverse backgrounds— some were health professionals interested in psychology; some were teachers, parents, and retirees.

These lectures were very well received because Liu and his colleagues always engaged in dynamic interaction with the audience using a workshop format. They frequently invited people in the audience to come out to experience a simulated counseling situation and talk about their feelings freely and openly. In fact, Liu rarely used a podium or stage; rather, he liked to sit with the audience in a circle to minimize the sense of hierarchy and distance. There were also many opportunities for group interaction and bodily movement to incite affective responses. I participated in some of these events and could tell that the audience found such interaction refreshing and enjoyable. Such events greatly boosted his center's reputation and visibility in the city, even though they did not gain anything financially. Through these public outreach efforts, he was accumulating important social and symbolic capital necessary for branding his center.

Workshopping

Another important component of branding is through fee-based workshops held regularly throughout the year. Each typically lasts for two to three days and costs about 2,000 yuan. I attended eight of these workshops as Liu's guest between 2010 and 2016.[5] They are usually divided into four kinds for different clients: enterprise employees, teachers, parents, and mixed groups. The first kind, for enterprise employees, is generally invited and paid by a particular firm. Liu's most reliable client groups are several highly profitable local tobacco companies. The issues they tackled include stress-management and team-spirit building, reshaping enterprise culture, making harmonious relationships, and more. The approach is based on the Satir Model through self-exploration and reflection in the context of one's social nexus. The workshops for teachers, parents, and mixed groups tend to focus on nonviolent forms of communication, personal growth, and family dynamics—something derived from Satir teaching. Liu explained to me: "As you know, Chinese people put a great deal of emphasis on cultivating of harmonious family and social relationships. But nowadays it seems to become more and more difficult to do so given increased competition, faster pace of life, and multiple demands. People are often stressed out, anxious, and uncertain about their future and how to balance between individual desires and social expectations. Satir is the answer, or at least offers people a means to examine and change their state of being in a hopeful way."

One of the core Satir theories taught at these workshops is through a famous metaphor called the "Personal Iceberg" (figure 5). According to Satir, the visible part of the iceberg above the water surface usually consists of our behaviors and coping acts. What lies beneath the surface are the feelings, perceptions, expectations, and yearnings that together shape our behaviors. Beneath all these layers is the core: self-wholeness, which Satir called "I AM." Thus, changes in behaviors and feelings depend on transformations at the deeper levels. Any transformations on one level can cause disturbances on other levels, but they can also lead to eventual self-integration. Liu's teaching usually does not go into the theory itself deeply; instead, he focuses on how

The personal iceberg metaphor of the Satir Model

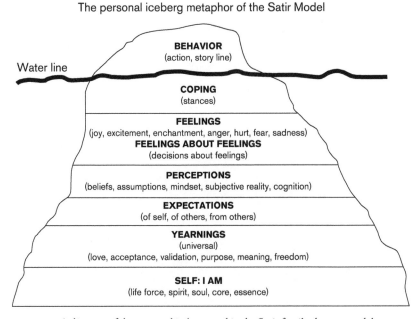

FIGURE 5. A diagram of the personal iceberg used in the Satir family therapy model.

to identify patterns of perception, longing, and expectation behind one's own emotions and behaviors through interactive practice. He told me, "I want my clients to learn to explore what is beneath the water—the iceberg behind a series of events and behaviors. Passing beneath the surface, we begin to see that behind anger is helplessness and longing for acceptance, behind the act of pleasing others is the attempt to control and the need to be loved and respected, behind conceited lecturing is fear and panic. We also begin to understand the unfulfilled expectations within the family and the yearning for intimate connections to one's self and family members."

The second core concept Liu taught is Satir's innovative idea of "family sculpting" (*jiating diaosu* 家庭雕塑). Satir recognized that people could express their inner feelings and raise awareness through verbal and nonverbal ways. Sometimes the affective expressions were far more powerful than words. Sculpting—"an in-motion interaction that used bodies in space to make overt the family's (or other system's) pattern of interrelating"—is an alternative to being mired in words. As Banmen and others put it, it is "a (usually) nonverbal use of oneself in space (figure 6). It offers another set of awareness that gets

FIGURE 6. Experiential practice through bodily "sculpting" at a Satir workshop for a local firm. Photo by Liu Chengzhe.

beneath the defenses of denying, ignoring, and distorting. Instead, it taps into our kinesthetic responses, which can be very powerful" (Satir et al. 1991).

In all the workshops I attended, Liu always inserted such sculpting exercises. He asked the trainees to take up a family member role (father, mother, son, daughter, husband, wife) in a dysfunctional family situation. Then they used body sculpting to cast their attitudes and behaviors as if they were frozen in space. For example, a critical husband standing high with one hand on his hip and the other pointing down as if scolding; his wife kneeling as if in distress (figure 7). By sculpting this situation, they experience it with their body and heart, and then they talk about how they feel (*tiyan* 体验) about their own and the other's situation, rather than using a set of preconceived words. "Seeing myself pointing a finger at my 'wife' like this makes me realize how hurtful it must be to her. I normally just do it to a family member without realizing the impact of my gesture. I was too busy expressing my anger and dissatisfaction without paying any attention to how others around me might feel," said a male trainee. Another trainee commented: "In daily life we usually act automatically and reactively, but rarely pause to examine our

FIGURE 7. Sculpting a mock family situation in a Satir-based
personal growth workshop. Photo by Liu Chengzhe.

own behavior and impact on others objectively. Sculpting gives us an opportunity to do just that."

In sum, such "kinesthetic responses" or "affective acts" help externalize our
inner processes and the way family members communicate, allowing clients
to transcend their habitual perceptions and defensive words to reach a deeper
understanding of the interaction between themselves and others.[6] Awareness
is the first step toward therapeutic progress and meaningful change.

The third concept and intervention closely related to sculpting is "family
reconstruction" (*jiating chongsu* 家庭重塑) with the aim of reintegrating the
client into the historical and psychological family matrix. Satir believed that
one's own natal family (*yuansheng jiating* 原生家庭) has profound influences
on one's life. In order to better understand the present and the future, one

must grasp this matrix and its history. Family reconstruction, however, is a time-consuming and complex process that often takes two to three days. It begins with identifying the "Star" as the person whose family is to be enacted, and the "Guide" as the facilitator. Together they work on the family map, the family life history of three generations, and a "Wheel of Influence" charting all the people who had influence on the Star. The next step is for the Guide to tell the Star's family story while the Star just sits and listens. A large group of people as players must be made available. This entry eventually leads to the sculpting of the Star's family origin and key events such as parents' dating and wedding and the birth of the Star and siblings if any. The Star is often asked to recall and sculpt traumatic events with other players. The final part of this process is for the Star to verbalize and express openly any personal expecta-tions and yearnings that have gone unfulfilled, to accept his or her own as well as the parents' personhood, and to acknowledge that the parents did the best they knew how. Much of the effort is on reworking the relationship between the Star and the Star's parents with a new level of acceptance and self-esteem (see Satir et al. 1991).

Since a full family reconstruction requires a good deal of time and many participants, it is often not a practical procedure to carry out. Liu only used a much-simplified version at some workshops, involving just a few players (often limited to two generations) and a brief family map and history. Never-theless, this novel method still made a strong impression on his trainees, who were eager to participate. He reminded the trainees: "Our goal is not to focus on family pathology, but to learn how to cultivate positive ways of expressing, relating, and growing up when we have a fuller understanding of where we come from." A young mother of a two-year-old son was a single child in her natal family and volunteered to be the Star at a workshop. She told me: "Satir's family reconstruction makes a lot of sense to me. We Chinese tend to have a tight family system, so its influence on our development must be strong and long-lasting. Being able to reenact some of the relationships and milestone events really gives me a rare chance to feel things viscerally and reflect upon my experience." Dissatisfied with her own problematic dynamic with her parents, she wanted to learn from experts how to communicate with her husband and raise a wholesome child.

In my view, the power of these workshops was derived from not merely the learning of certain self-techniques and family dynamic theories but more importantly the very human connections made in a trusted space that was not often available in everyday life. This new form of sociality is similar to what Tomas Matza (2018) has called "psychosociality" found in contemporary Russian psychological practices. People who faced similar problems and shared the intention for self-exploration came together to create a safe space under the guidance of a charismatic therapist. I was often amazed by the high degree of candidness and trust, albeit temporary, that was developed in these workshops. At the end-of-the session reflection time, many trainees remarked that they had shared some of their most intimate feelings and personal circumstances that they would not share with friends of many years. One woman in her thirties put it this way: "Perhaps, we are all like-minded people. Otherwise, we would not show up here voluntarily. At the same time, we are also strangers to each other and do not compete for any utilitarian gains. Thus, it is easier to open up in this intimate yet unfamiliar group and share our problems and feelings. Look, there is nothing to lose—not even losing face (*mianzi* 面子)." In this shielded experimental space, engaging in self-work through affective exercises made it even more appealing to the participants. They not only *learned* something with their brain but also *felt* 感受 something with their heart.

The Master Effect

In China, there is a catchphrase, *dashi xiaoying* 大师效应 ("the master effect"), frequently invoked in marketing and branding. It means that by casting and using someone as a master/guru of a school of thought or practice surrounded by some mystique and aura, one can potentially generate a large number of devoted followers and capitalize on its far-reaching effects.[7] This is a common strategy adopted by the popular cultural industry to increase one's market share and prominence. Certain techniques are usually involved: exaggeration, showing global recognitions, using seemingly impressive titles, claiming lofty goals, citing big numbers, wide media exposure, and creating a good story.

In branding the Satir Model in China, two figures are central to the production of the master effect—Virginia Satir and John Banmen. For example, in all the workshops run by Liu's team, they produce and hand out a booklet, which normally begins with a brief introduction of what the Satir Model is. It opens with a paragraph casting Satir as "America's first generation of family therapy master," and "a pioneer of family therapy much like the contribution made by Columbus." It claims that Satir was recognized by the American Psychiatric Association as one of the twenty-one most influential therapists in history. Since most Chinese people do not read English materials and have little knowledge of the global therapy field, they take such writings at face value and nobody cares to check the inaccuracy. The goal here is to incite respect, amazement, and admiration. More important, what is conveyed is that Satir was not just a therapist treating personal and family problems, but also a tireless proponent of a positive, humanistic personal growth model and ultimately of humanity's well-being and world peace. She is portrayed as an altruistic person who dedicated her entire life to research, therapy, and teaching for the benefit of humankind.[8] She is portrayed as motherly, sagacious, compassionate, and efficacious all at once. Further, the qualities that set her apart from other therapists are her broader vision, caring spirit, and transformative power as a *dashi*.[9] Thus, while virtually unknown to the general public in North America today, Satir is entering ordinary Chinese middle-class households as a charismatic self-help master.

Another key figure is Dr. John Banmen, now a big star and popular guru in China (and Asia more broadly) with tens of thousands of followers. He received his PhD in Social Psychology from Northwestern University and taught many years at the University of Nebraska–Lincoln before being appointed to the faculty of the University of British Columbia for twenty-one years. Although Banmen has held many prominent professional titles and leadership positions in psychotherapy, he is not widely known outside the family therapy world, certainly not a household name. But in China, his influence has far exceeded what he could have imagined. As one reporter describes, "compared to Canada and the U.S., where a psychologist might teach a few dozen graduate students a year, the president of one university in Shanghai recently asked Banmen to establish a program to train 10,000 Chinese therapists" (Todd 2010). Banmen, a retired professor with a modest demeanor, has been frequently invited to lecture and lead workshops throughout Chinese cities. Each time his audience often surpasses several hundreds or thousands. His experience, age, modesty, and close connection with the late mentor Satir, as well as his being a white male, all became an asset in marketing.

Let us have a close reading of a recent advertisement for a five-day Banmen Workshop held at a luxury hotel in Kunming (November 23–27, 2018) organized by Liu. The cost is quite high—8,800 yuan (roughly US$1,300) per person. Titled "Healing and Growth: A Workshop on Harmonious Relationships," it is listed under the heading of "2018 Master's Workshops," followed by these words in bold font: "The top international master on Satir family therapy, Dr. Banmen, will be coaching in person!" Note the usage of these words: *master* (twice), *doctor*, *top*, and *international*, all with the intention of solidifying his high status and reputation. Then there is an uplifting narrative to cast Banmen as a selfless person whose calling is to come and help Chinese people reach health, happiness, and success. He was even compared to the famous Canadian physician, Norman Bethune, who came to China during the 1930s for the revolutionary causes:

> Despite living far away across ten thousand miles, a Canadian man travels to China again and again! Driven by his dream and mission in his heart, he seeks to spread Satir's faith—"peace within, peace among, and peace between." As he says, "It is not you who come to see me; it is I who come to see you because you all make my life more meaningful and worthwhile."
>
> His goal: Making sixty-five million Chinese people healthier, happier, and more successful! He is an experienced, wise man with a compassionate and pure heart. Perceptive yet humorous. He understands you before you even open your mouth. . . .
>
> Every year Dr. Banmen comes to China in order to lead various kinds of workshops. Regardless who the audience are—individuals, married couples, families, and youth, their lives have all been touched and transformed by this eighty-year-old man The participants often weep in joy because they, for the first time, are discovering their innate longings and vital energy.

This style of writing—using flowery but empty language and invoking legendary historical figures, is commonly found in Chinese popular advertisement. I find it hard to translate into English since it does not make much sense or flow in thought. It jumps from one grand statement to another. Its intention is to impress and excite readers, rather than convey information accurately or logically. The first sentence here is a smart replay of the first sentence in Chairman Mao's famous eulogy for Dr. Bethune. During China's Civil War, Bethune left his home country—Canada, joined the Chinese Communist Party in Yan'an, treated countless wounded soldiers and villagers, but eventually died of blood poisoning after he accidently cut his finger while operating on a soldier. The eulogy, in which Mao lavishly praised Bethune's selfless commitment to the Chinese revolutionary cause, was read by virtually every one of my generation or older in elementary school. Here, Liu compares Banmen's commitment to helping Chinese people obtain well-being to that of Bethune. In my view, it is quite a stretch, but the intent to brand Banmen as a self-help sage and an emissary of peace is abundantly clear.

Like Satir, Banmen's teaching focuses on self-growth in the context of family and social relations. On May 15, 2018—the International Day of

Families, his organization issued a press release announcing that he would begin with a grand lecture tour in China on the theme of "Creating Happy Families in the New Era." The goal is to make more Chinese people happier and healthier. He was cast as a psychological *taidou* 泰斗 (grand master). In an interview, he said what motivated him was not money but a calling to finish what Satir did not finish: "Part of what I'm doing is a spiritual journey, because I'm helping carry on her goal of helping people connect with themselves at a deeper level."[10] Even in his eighties, Banmen is enthusiastically striding out as a grand master on this newly discovered grand stage of China and Asia.

BETWEEN *LIYI* AND *GONGYI*

One of the most interesting aspects regarding the spread of the Satir Model in China is its incredibly broad application beyond the clinical setting. In fact, it is becoming almost a panacea adopted by more and more firms, government organizations, and schools for diverse purposes. Outside the family, the model is used as the basis for positive emotions and stress management, increasing leadership capacity, conflict management, improving communication skills for managers and teachers, creating a positive workplace environment, and many other applications. For those who want to promote the Satir Model, such a broad compendium of uses can achieve at least two different yet related goals: It helps develop a bigger market for generating income and, at the same time, it enhances its popular influence and reputation through serving the general public. These two concerns—economic interests (*liyi* 利益) and public good (*gongyi* 公益)—are not necessarily in conflict with one another; instead, they are complementary if handled properly. How to balance the two is an art: "I must prioritize generating enough income. I have a family and a team to support and certain lifestyle to maintain. But as you can see, I also engage in a great deal of gongyi activities. There is a sense of calling once you are deep in the Satir world," Liu said with sincerity.

Recall Liu had quit his permanent job at a local university many years ago, thus therapeutic training is now his primary source of income, although he continues to see some individual clients. His fee for private counseling is about 500 yuan per hour, but a weekend group workshop can generate 30,000 yuan (about US$4,400) after other expenses (such as paying for assistants). A larger training workshop paid by a state firm for their employees can bring in 50,000 yuan (US$7,350) or more. As far as I can tell, Liu lives a comfortable life with his wife, who is a college teacher, but he is not interested in showing off. They own a nice but modest apartment and a decent domestic car. Their daughter attended a university in Hong Kong for four years, and he paid for all the tuition and living expenses with cash. He and his family like to travel within China and abroad yearly. To support this lifestyle, he needs to run monthly training workshops at his center and other larger ones for several big clients (corporations, police stations, schools, and other government organizations).

In China, in order to gain competitive advantage and expand market share, one must also obtain official recognition and team up with government or public agencies. This is precisely what Liu's team does. One day he showed me a document with great excitement. Mimicking a typical Chinese official notification with a red seal on, it read "Regarding How to Promote the Training of Psychology Teachers in Higher Education and Vocational Schools Using Satir Model's Systematic Therapy." The issuing authorities were the Counseling Committee for College Students under the Chinese Association for Mental Health, and the Working Committee on College and Vocational Students' Psychological Health Education. They both sounded very impressive, suggesting a national-level recognition, and could be easily mistaken by someone as an official call from the Ministry of Education. After citing a number of official documents stating the importance of teachers' training in students' psychological health, the Notification turned to what was essentially an advertisement for an eight-day training workshop run by Liu and supported by the Banmen Satir China Management Center.

Note the change of the operational scale: this time the target group expanded from those from Kunming to nationwide. The cost (not including meals, lodging) was 2,800 yuan per person, and each session was capped at forty-five. As usual, a certificate was promised at the end. The purpose of having the backing of the two important-sounding entities was to suggest that this training and certificate would be an asset and possibly a necessity for all teachers in the near future. If the latter became true, one could imagine the magnitude of this program and the money generated. Liu admitted with a dreamy smile: "We would have an endless source of trainees if this program works out. At the same time, we would also do some good for society because we believe that all teachers could benefit greatly from such training and applying the skills to their work. It is a win-win situation!" This was another way he tried to rationalize and bridge the two ends—increasing earnings and taking care of public welfare.

REFLECTION

Over the years of working with Liu's team and watching their effort to brand the Satir Model as a vital therapeutic practice, I am stunned by how quickly a previously little-known counseling theory and practice took firm hold in China and was adapted to address present problems concerning Chinese people. The branding of the Satir Model started with a clear focus on intimate relationships (*qinmi guanxi* 亲密关系) and parent/child relationships (*qinzi guanxi* 亲子关系), and then expanded to other social nexuses including but not limited to workplace, peer, and teacher/student relationships. Recast essentially as a panacea for multiple problems facing Chinese society, the Satir Model has attained a special status in China with the ascribed potential to transform lives as nothing has done before.

Several of Satir's basic principles are particularly inspirational to the Chinese audience and can be applied to real-life situations: (1) Change is possible and must involve a deep reconfiguration of the self. (2) Therapy must be experiential and affective. (3) Effective treatment must be systematic and oriented toward positive potentials. (4) Problems themselves are not the problem; how to respond wisely is the key. These ideas—self-care, positivity, change, responding—may seem banal and simple to the Western audience, but they are powerful and refreshing to many Chinese, as they run against the conventional ways of thinking.

I am further intrigued by how Chinese practitioners like Liu manage to justify and intermingle a number of seemingly opposite goals in their branding practices: embracing a franchising-based commercial model of operation to maximize market share while still holding to a sense of mission and higher calling; making money while doing good for society; appearing humble and genuine while desiring bigger crowds and followers. The trainees and followers I spoke to do not see these efforts as contradictory but tend to buy into this mixed operational model. A young woman who attended one of the workshops once said to me: "If you want to get the remedy for your problems, live a good life, and create inner peace, you have to pay for it just like you pay for everything else. We live in a highly commercialized world. There is nothing wrong with franchising psychotherapy."

So far in this book, I have focused on what particular forms psychotherapy takes in China today, including the unique mode of therapeutic relationships emerging in this process. I seek to answer the questions of why and how through detailed ethnographic accounts. Yet, bentuhua is not the endgame, but only the starting point of unraveling a myriad of social and psychological problems (or what Chinese people call the "knot of the heart" 心结). In the next three chapters, I will explore how this popular engagement with a new therapeutic culture profoundly impacts the remaking of selfhood and sociality, well-being, and governing practices for individuals, families, and organizations.

CHAPTER 5

Crafting a Therapeutic Self

On a warm summer afternoon in 2009, amid light rain, I met Ms. Zhu Ling, a part-time therapist in her early forties, at a tea house near Green Lake in Kunming. After a mutual friend introduced us via phone, I set up the meeting immediately. Zhu was a tall and slender woman with long dark hair and a pair of big inquisitive eyes. She arrived before me and had already ordered a pot of green tea for us. As we sat down in the comfortable bamboo chairs sipping the refreshing tea from small ceramic cups, Zhu began to tell me about her initial encounter with psychological counseling and subsequent personal transformations:

> About seven years ago, one day as I was reading a newspaper, I saw an advertise-
> ment on psychotherapist training classes offered by the provincial health bureau.
> I had no idea that there existed such a field and occupation. I had always liked to
> listen to my friends' problems, but did not know how to help them. So I thought
> I would enroll in the program and learn something to help my friends. The classes
> lasted for three months, mostly on the weekends and in the evenings. I passed the
> certificate exam easily. But in this process, I began to realize that I was deeply
> troubled by many unresolved issues and I myself needed help.

The psychology program she enrolled in was a typical one for China, as it packed many psychology topics into a short period of time. Zhu had obtained a college degree in literature from a reputable university and held a well-respected and well-paid civil servant position in a provincial government agency. With this career, she enjoyed job security and would retire with a lifelong pension. Friends envied her secure situation, a so called unbreakable "iron rice bowl" (*tie fan wan*) of state-guaranteed earnings that had become harder and harder to acquire since the economic reform period. For her, entering the psy field was accidental, yet it became a long journey of self-discovery and self-healing that had profoundly altered her life and mindset.

This chapter examines how psychological training and therapeutic interventions play a vital part in the Chinese urban middle-class project of self-making.[1] I explore how the Chinese notion of the self (*ziwo* 自我) is turned into an object of intense inquiry and how various therapeutic projects are used to achieve self-development and personal fulfillment in the current context.[2] By *therapeutic self*, I specifically mean a different sense of self emerged in the process of one's therapeutic encounters. This new form of self in turn produces healing effects on the subject and that person's close contacts. Further, a therapeutic self is at the same time a social self (embedded on the social nexus) and a reflexive self (requiring inward personal reflections). This reflexive quality and social nature in psychological exploration is a distinct feature of contemporary self-development in urban China. More importantly, I maintain that newly crafted forms of the self (including self-healing and healing by others) through using psychotherapeutic techniques, continue to intersect with and complicate the existing social nexus, cultural sensibilities, and local notions of personhood. My analysis will focus therefore on two integral processes of self-work among Chinese middle-classes: Disentangling, and Re-embedding. I argue that such therapeutic work contributes to intricate forms of subject-making that challenge conventional conceptual binaries such as the private versus social self, the inner versus outer life, and psychological versus social problems. It is important to note that the new middle-class in China is not a monolithic entity, but an emergent, fragmented, and amorphous collection of social groups. Although it can largely be defined through external indicators such as home ownership and consumption practices, the "middle-class" is a relational and fluid category without any fixed boundaries. This fragmentation further complicates how the refashioning of the self is carried out, since there is not a single trajectory individuals can identify easily.

Earlier in this book, I raised these questions: Why do so many people flock to counseling training yet so few become full-time therapists or use it in treating mental illness? And what do they hope to gain from such seemingly "impractical" training? I suggest that the answers partly lie in the growing desire among middle-class Chinese to reconfigure the self and its relationship with the social nexus in order to achieve self-actualization and the "good life" dream. With the influx of psychological knowledge and practices from over-seas, attending to one's own psyche and emotional well-being becomes a new tool for self-management, among not only urban professionals but also mar-ginal groups (see Zhang 2014; Yang 2013a, 2013b). A quick look at the titles of some of the mushrooming advertisements by psy experts for workshops clearly indicates the intense popular interest in therapeutic work on the self: "Self-Loving, Self-Care: A Balanced Development," "Unpacking Self-Growth," "Encountering the Unknown Self," and so on. As one workshop declares, the aim is to "help you unearth the inner-self strength, pursue the happiness brought by the growth of the soul, and greatly improve your personality so that you can live a life with a brand-new, authentic self."

Moreover, while the teaching of "self-growth" and "self-development" is becoming a popular profitable industry catering to China's urban middle-class professionals and youth, it tends to carry a flavor of religious zeal in the pur-suit of self-salvation. American writer Barbara Ehrenreich once depicted the "new psychology" that gained wide popularity in the 1970s America as "both an industry and a kind of secular religion, enlisting hundreds of thousands of middle-class Americans in the project of self-improvement through psycho-logical growth" (1983: 91). This observation echoes what I find in China today, that the psy industry is capable of combining therapeutics, secular religious spirit, and profit motives, which greatly enhances its rapid expansion.

In the final section of this chapter, I show that while this new regime of self-work is becoming a profitable industry and has certain key neoliberal traits (such as promoting self-governing and self-reliance), it also dovetails with the post-reform state's project of building a "harmonious society" that emphasizes social harmony and conflict reduction.[3] So what is emerging here is not the usual "neoliberalism" story of self-advancement but a more complicated picture of assemblages. In this context, therapeutic self-practices, while very much influenced by global psychotherapeutics, are not only rooted in Chinese history and culture but also have important political implications for Chinese society in the face of soaring inequality and growing social insecurity.

DOING SELF-WORK

Zhu Ling, the woman I met at the tea house, was facing a set of misfortunes and challenges in her life when she first encountered counseling in the early 2000s. Her fifty-eight-year-old father had fallen ill two years prior and become bed-ridden at home. As a good and filial daughter, she moved him into her own house and took care of him. Her own child was born with Down syndrome, a disorder that at that time in China was rarely known. Zhu was scared and felt ashamed, as if her child's condition was her fault. Meanwhile, her husband's small private business went into bankruptcy, putting great strain on their marriage. They argued a lot and felt frustrated by everything. She was physically and emotionally exhausted, as if "the sky were going to collapse suddenly," to use her own words. Zhu felt lonely and hurt yet tried to bottle up the distress and avoid feeling the pain by keeping herself busy. But bewilderment and despair were engulfing her. "I was in a very dark place. You would not recognize me if you had met me then," said Zhu with a hint of sorrow in her voice.

In studying psychotherapy, Zhu found some comfort and hope, and came to realize that she must first "do her own homework" allowing herself to explore who she was and what she wanted in life. She described her state of mind then as if "my head were full of clouds and cottons." She was convinced that she must cleanse (qingli) her own mind before she could take care of others. After careful consideration, she made a bold and unusual decision. She hired a live-in domestic worker to take care of her daughter and father, and took an unpaid leave from work. Then she left home with a backpack and embarked on a two-year journey to Tibet. Her family, friends, and neighbors thought she was out of her mind. I asked her whether it was very difficult and whether she worried about her daughter, she replied, "Of course! I was crying every day before and after I left, but I knew I had to do this for myself. Otherwise, I was going to implode or die, as I saw no way out of the situation. I was on the brink of a total breakdown."

The choice of her destination was not accidental. Tibet, in her and many Chinese and Western people's imaginations, stood for a place of unworldliness and purity. She described this journey as a physical, spiritual, and psychological expedition.[4] She arrived in Tibet by bus after several days of traveling on winding and bumpy roads. Then, she walked and hitch-hiked from place to place every day with her heavy backpack and little money. No cell phones, no credit cards in those days. Zhu described her experience:

> The Tibetans I met were extraordinarily kind and generous. Wherever I went, I was offered food and a place to sleep in their home for free even though I was a total stranger to them. I saw gorgeous sunrises and sunsets. I was sometimes drenched in rain storms and shivering in icy cold wind. But I felt happy and calm.

Even though I did not speak Tibetan and many of them could not understand Mandarin, I felt more connected with them than at home. And I had a lot of alone time to reflect and get in touch with my own feelings.

Traveling alone as a young woman on foot in remote areas was not easy, but Zhu was determined to go on. She felt that physical hardship was good for training her mind and fostering endurance. Along the way, she participated in many daily activities and rituals at the invitation of some Tibetan families. What impressed her most was their funeral rites and attitude toward death: "For them, death is not a horrible thing; rather it is the time for the soul to ascend to heaven. There is calm and joy in praying and singing for the loved one to go serenely. What a contrast it is with our Han ceremony, which is usually full of tears, fear, and misery," she recalled. Toward the end of this journey, Zhu was converted to Buddhism and became passionate about combining her newfound spirituality and psychotherapy in the years to come.

The initial goal Zhu set for herself was to disentangle temporarily from the web of family obligations and other social relations in order to reclaim a more composed and resilient self, capable of accepting life as it is. It was not an act of total retreat to the self, but one of reshaping "its relations with others so that it will best fulfill its own destiny," using Nikolas Rose's words (1996: 159). The temporary withdrawal from the social world eventually prepared her for a better reentry into her family and work. It was also like a rite of passage for her to be reborn and evolve into a good therapist. She once explained to me the importance of prioritizing self-care and maintaining mental clarity this way: "No therapist can heal others if she cannot heal herself first. Her mind must be like a body of lucid and tranquil water in order to reflect upon others' life and help them untie the knots of the soul." The language she used throughout the interview was imbued with the ethos and images of Zen Buddhism that stress mindfulness, clarity, and tranquility.[5] Her narrative also echoed a popular method of self-inquiry, known as "The Work," which was created by a contemporary American self-help writer, Byron Katie (Katie with Mitchell 2002) and was spreading in East Asia. For Zhu, the Tibetan trip was the best way of doing her own homework, through which she was reborn as a new person.

Zhu Ling's story is a narrative of self-inquiry and self-development widely shared by other Chinese drawn to the psy field. During my fieldwork, many informants recounted the moments of self-enlightenment and self-salvation brought on by their therapeutic work. They eagerly explained to me how they finally found clarity in their mind, how their depression was gradually lifted, how their anxiety steadily decreased, and how their troubled hearts began to find new hope and serenity during their encounter with psychological counseling. In sum, their enthusiasm was palpable. they saw such efforts as a pivotal project that could generate healing, personal growth, and happiness.

It is important to point out another distinct feature of self-work among Chinese: Such work often involves not only psychotherapeutic efforts but also regimented physical activities. The belief that physical well-being and mental well-being cannot be separated reflects a common view among therapists and ordinary people in China. Several decades ago, the anthropologist Arthur Kleinman famously claimed that Chinese people tended to somatize mental and psychological illness—that is, they expressed their emotional distresses through somatic terms (1980, 1986). His study suggested a close connection of mind/mental and body/physical, but the latter tended to dominate the former. Several decades later, during my fieldwork, I find that the tendency of somatization is still present, but more and more urban Chinese increasingly emphasize the mutually constitutive processes of the physical and the mental, the body and the mind.[6] Thus, while they seek psychological treatment, they also include physical exercise as part of the healing program.

For example, in 2013, I met Mr. Xiao, a self-fashioned counselor in his mid-forties. In other people's eyes, he was a very successful educator and entrepreneur—the owner of a profitable vocational school in Kunming. His office, located on the twentieth floor of a luxury high-rise, was sunny and spacious. We sat down on a comfortable black couch to talk. Xiao had suffered from bouts of deep depression for several years but was ashamed of admitting his emotional problems to anyone for a long time. When he began to study counseling, he realized that depression was an illness that afflicted millions of others and that it was not his fault or personal weakness. Further, he learned that depression could be treated with proper care. Xiao told me that his project of self-discovery and struggle with depression consisted of two essential and intertwined parts—participation in psychotherapy plus daily long-distance walking. He sought psychological counseling from a therapist and also used the techniques he learned from cognitive behavioral therapy to help himself. Meanwhile, he firmly committed to one physical activity—walking. He was animated when he described his "secret" to me: "I have been walking some twenty kilometers every day between my home and work for several years. By now if you calculate the total distance of my walking, I could have walked from Kunming to Beijing. This journey along with my therapeutic experience has not only strengthened my physical body but, more importantly, transformed my psyche. I am a much happier and composed person now in comparison with the disturbed and confused me eight years ago."

Xiao strongly believed that one's physical condition and psychological state of being were closely related. He was very taken by modern neuroscience theory that exercise could increase the level of dopamine in the brain and thus regulate emotional responses better. "One cannot rely on talking or taking pills only. You must do everything you can to get the maximum benefit," said Xiao. By the time I interviewed him, he seemed to be energized and fully functioning at work. Xiao was not alone; many people I met during my research liked to take an integrated approach by seeking both psychological and physical care.

Although the "psy fever" foregrounds self-queries and self-improvement, the ultimate aim of self-work is to create an enhanced person able to handle family and social relationships better. Recall that after the long journey, Zhu Ling eventually returned home and found herself in a stronger position to take care of her family and work responsibilities. Having gained more inner strength to handle stressors and with a new perspective on life, Zhu felt less frustrated and burnt out. She told me that going away for two years and learning psychology were the best things she did for her own healing and rejuvenation. In other words, the newly emerged self should not be read as a turn to individualism, but a move toward better management of one's own emotions and social nexus. I call these two simultaneous processes "disentangling" and "re-embedding," which I will next examine in depth.

DISENTANGLING AND RE-EMBEDDING

It was a breezy July morning in 2010. I was sitting in a small conference room to attend a three-day intense workshop on sandplay therapy offered by a local training center I call Xinshi ("a chamber of the heart"). This center was created by a private vocational school that specialized in training young people for obtaining various kinds of certificates. It also provides post-exam, advanced training for those who have obtained their certificates. The room was cozy with several chairs and sofas, a tea table, a white board for writing, and a sandbox. On the walls there were several ink paintings done by previous art therapy clients. That day there were eight other trainees there—three men and five women, all in their late twenties or thirties. These young men and women had recently passed the counseling certificate examination after taking intensive prep classes there for two months. The cost for this workshop was 2,000 yuan per person, and they all had paid it out of their own pockets. During the self-introductions, I learned that all of them held regular jobs— three school teachers, one policeman, two state agency employees, and two private firm employees. The instructor was an experienced therapist and teacher I had been following for several years. He was very kind to let me participate in most of his advanced training workshops and to talk to his students. I eventually received a certification myself on sandplay therapy from this workshop.

During an extended tea break, we engaged in an animated conversation. I asked: "Do any of you here plan to become a psychological counselor?" Several of them started to giggle. One shy woman said: "Someday maybe, but certainly not now. Even though we have the certificate, it is just a piece of paper. We do not know what we are doing. But the training is extremely helpful for me personally." I then asked why they were there and what they hoped to achieve through the therapy program. I quickly learned that most of them sought psy training as a form of self-development and self-help to improve their lives and interpersonal relationships. They all believed that a better understanding of one's own emotions and enhancing communication skills would not only generate more happiness but also increase social and professional success. There was a great deal of what Tomas Matza calls "the success complex" (2018) shared among these young interns: It seemed that everyone was afraid of being left behind and craved to move ahead in the race for success—whatever it might mean.

Xiao Wang, a young female middle school teacher, spoke first with a confident smile: "For me studying psychology and counseling is a way of understanding myself and my own issues so that I can understand the social world around me better. I discovered this field by accident but soon fell in love with it because it helps me see myself with clarity. Prior to this encounter I was in a state of *huntun*." *Huntun* 混沌, which means "chaotic and blurred," is a Chinese phrase used by many to describe their state of mind before they encountered psychology and counseling. For them, psychological knowledge and explorations functioned like an act of enlightenment that brought inner clarity and harmony. There was a sense of mystery and magic experienced by these young participants, which pulled them even deeper into this field. Xiao Wang admitted that psychology was not a panacea and her problems did not simply disappear, but she now felt that she had a tool to work with, so she was not too vulnerable. This sense of self-reliance was important to people like her.

Another key factor that motivated these young men and women to be trained was a financial consideration. Even though the fees for enrolling in the prep classes and the national certification exam are not small, costing about 2,000–4,000 yuan per person, which is about two months' salary of an average wage earner in Kunming, my interlocutors reasoned that mastering the skills themselves was cheaper than paying for professional counseling at the rate of 300–400 yuan per hour in the long run. In other words, acquiring self-help techniques through systematic learning—solving one's own problems and gaining a deeper understanding of oneself and family dynamics—was seen as a more reliable and cost-effective approach. This way of thinking was widely echoed among others beyond this workshop.

Then our conversation turned to the question of *ziwo* 自我. The Chinese word *ziwo* can be roughly translated as "self," "selfhood," or "one's self." It is often associated with several other notions: self-consciousness (*ziwo yishi*), self-worth (*ziwo jiazhi*), self-development (*ziwo fazhan*). The first one—the ability to be aware of one's own existence—entails a long-imported Western tradition of philosophical discussions. In the Chinese cultural context, *ziwo* implies at least two layers of meaning—*dawo* ("the big self") and *xiao wo* ("the small self"). The small self, consisting of one's own needs, desires, and body/mind, is always embedded in the big self, consisting of one's obligation to the family, community, and nation (see Yang, Huang, and Yang 2008). In other words, there is no strictly private self without any broader social embeddedness. Confucianism also refers to these two layers of self as *xiaoti* 小体 (small body) and *dati* 大体 (big body), signifying an inherent connection between the body and the mind in thinking about one's self. This embodied view of the self continues to be prevalent today.

The workshop participants were aware of such traditional Chinese interpretations of self or what some called "embedded individualism" (Sampson 1988), but interestingly the language they used in the discussion was more in line with the humanistic psychology developed by Abraham Maslow (1954) and with the client-centered therapy of Carl Rogers (1951). In particular, the notions of "self-actualization" (*ziwo shixian*) and "self-growth" (*ziwo chengzhang*) were frequently invoked as they talked about what constituted the fundamentals of self-work. Like Rogers, they regarded self-actualization as an ongoing process of constant reflection of experience, enhancement, and change, and defined one's interactions with significant others as a key component of self-actualization. They believed that this was a continuous process, which ran through different stages of the life cycle, therefore individuals always needed to engage in self-work in order to truly thrive and adjust. Free appropriation of both Chinese and foreign ideas and languages to talk about self-work occurred in all the workshops I had attended. It was this kind of eclectic bricolage that had caught my attention from the very beginning of my fieldwork. I then asked each of the workshop participants to explain what *ziwo* meant to them and whether and how their understandings had changed over time. The first person who responded was a woman in her mid-thirties wearing a dark floral casual dress and a pair of leather sandals. Her name was Wan Qing, a divorced mother with an eight-year-old daughter. She appeared a bit older and more urbane than the rest of the trainees there. Her hair was short but fashionably styled. Holding a mug of strong green jasmine tea, she did not hesitate to articulate her understanding of ziwo to the group: "Ziwo is like a circle demarcating the boundary between one's own self and others. Within the line, one must love and accept oneself. Outside the line, one must respect, understand, and appreciate others. I try to teach my eight-year-old daughter how to draw this line and respect the boundary. For example, she likes to go through my purse for fun. So I tell her that the purse is my private belonging and she must get my approval before handling it. She must know the boundary between ziwo and others. This is the first step toward personal growth."

I later learned that Wan Qing had worked for some years at a real estate firm selling newly built housing units. Although the income was very good, the work was highly demanding and left little time for family. Four years ago, Wan's marriage fell apart as she discovered that her husband was having an affair with a younger woman from work. After the divorce, she decided to quit the real estate job so as to spend more time with her daughter, whom she had custody of. Wan implied to me that she had got a good settlement from the divorce and saved enough money to live on for a while: "I needed some time to think about what I did wrong before and what I wanted to do with my life. I just cannot run around selling houses and wasting my life anymore. My daughter is growing up fast, and I want to make sure that she has good parental guidance and lives a good life." Two years ago, Wan started an afterschool care program helping some elementary school children with their homework and providing lunch. This is a popular practice in urban China today because busy working parents simply do not have time to bring their kids back home for lunch or supervise them until six p.m. The home care program brought in good income while still allowing Wan to spend enough time with her daughter, who could at the same time socialize with other children in the program.

The reason why Wan Qing decided to study counseling was to be better informed by psychological science so as to, in her words, "help myself and guide my child to grow up better." For her, mastering psychological counseling was a form of empowerment so that she would not need to rely on another person (a therapist for example). It was an effective way of developing self-understanding and improving social relationships with others. Wan Qing's view of the self as a demarcated entity was intriguing to me since most people I met with did not speak in such strict terms. Rather, they tended to relate the notion of the self to discussions of broader interpersonal relationships—especially family dynamics. So I asked Wan why she placed such great importance on the self/other boundary. She said that based on her personal experience she felt that Chinese social relationships were too entangled, which could give rise to a host of problems. "I often feel trapped in such tightly knit social bonds and find the situation suffocating because one needs some space to grow. Lately I have come to realize that Western psychological theories that underscore greater individuality and personal space make more sense, at least to me. This does not mean that I do not care about my family and friends around me, but I have a new perspective now that enables me to enjoy more personal autonomy without feeling guilty."

Wan's emphasis on a demarcated private self is in sharp contrast with the view of another trainee, Lu Minxin, a twenty-five-year-old temporary junior high school teacher and former enlisted army soldier. At the workshop, Lu was most concerned about social acceptance and public opinions. He passionately declared: "Anyone who enters the world must be recognized and accepted by society. Only when the society acknowledges me can there exist the self. If you are not connected with the society and people around you, how can you have a true ziwo?" He acknowledged that he had recently become more drawn to psychological exploration of his inner experiences even though focusing on one's own feelings and reflecting on one's life, as usually required as part of the learning, was often unsettling to him. After a bit of hesitation, he decided he should share his personal background with us, which might help us comprehend his situation:

I came from a mountain village in Guizhou Province. My family was poor and I did not have much education. In the military, I always felt inferior to others, as if my brain were empty. So I tried to follow the orders and win the recognition and approval of the people around me. I tried not to think about myself or how I felt. When I first began studying psychological counseling, my goal was to obtain the skills to help my students and improve my teaching. But soon I realized that I wanted to understand my feelings and myself even though the concept of ziwo is quite new to me.

In the Chinese spatial hierarchy, Guizhou Province is one of the least developed areas and is generally considered to be lagging behind the national race toward modernity. Lu who came from a poor farming family was keenly aware of his doubly disadvantaged origin and felt a strong sense of inferiority in the city. In addition, the military was a setting in which toughness (rather than sentimentality) and masculinity were valued. He was clearly trained to conform to such conventional expectations.

It was not difficult to notice that Lu had trouble talking about his personal feelings at the workshop. He was a bit flustered and timid when it was his turn to speak about his inner conflicts or emotions. He constantly referred to how he might be viewed and judged by his fellow soldiers and coworkers and was disturbed by his uncertainty of whether his behaviors would be accepted by others. Deep inside was the anxiety of losing face and the fear of social abandonment if he failed to fit in.[7] In the early phase of the three-day workshop, he felt exposed and was particularly wary about how we might judge him as a person or his words and ideas. He reminded me of my parents' generation, who grew up under socialism and largely sought social conformity, fearing exclusion—it was safer not to stand out from others and not deviate from sociopolitical norms.

Lu was rather conflicted and unsure. Yet part of him wanted to explore a dormant realm in his heart. He hoped that cultivating some self-awareness and self-efficacy would enable him to craft a new kind of person capable of engaging with the social world and becoming more confident. The lead trainer and fellow trainees who sensed Lu's inner struggle were very supportive. They encouraged him to stay with this experience and explore further even if it was uncomfortable for him. They listened to him carefully and applauded after he spoke every time. On the third day, Lu became more relaxed and was less awkward at sharing his thoughts and feelings. He told me that he felt assured in this setting and was grateful for this rare opportunity that was simultaneously personal and social, therapeutic and exciting. At the closing session, Lu said, "Even though we did not know each other in the beginning and we may not see each other again, I feel like I have known you all for a long time. I have shared more about myself with you in the past three days than with anyone else. I know I will be back to more training." People started to applaud and I saw tears in his eyes.

The third person I want to introduce is Feng Gang, a thirty-three-year-old city police officer. We first met at the sandplay workshop, and I must admit that I was a bit surprised to see a policeman there. He was quiet and modest, with a touch of melancholia. He had short hair and wore a casual light blue checkered shirt. We eventually became good friends because we happened to share a special moment when I was assigned as his therapist in one simulated sandplay therapy session.

We began by greeting each other at the sandbox and, following the methodology, I gave Feng as much time as he needed to choose some objects from the shelves in the room. There were well over several hundred pieces of sandplay items (shaju) of diverse kinds—miniature trees, plants, animals, shells, rocks, human figures, small pagodas, bells, boats, houses, and so on. Feng looked at them carefully for a while and finally brought over a few objects. The arrangement he created was very telling (see figure 8). It was a desert scene, with a red snake that appeared to be stranded in the sand. Nearby there was a cluster of green cactus and a jade horn. It took him twenty minutes to put them together, and then he was silent for five minutes with his eyes looking down at the box. Finally, without looking up Feng murmured: "I feel that the snake is very lonely and stuck there. It is trying to move toward the green plants—perhaps an oasis in the dessert. But it is very tired and will probably never get there." At that time, even though I did not know much about Feng's personal circumstance, I could sense a great deal of tension inside him. I asked carefully: "Does this scene speak to your current situation?" He nodded, and tears came rolling down. He took a piece of tissue on a nearby table to wipe his eyes and then said slowly: "This snake is just like me. I never had a chance to look at myself like this before." He continued to weep while staring at the snake.

I was somewhat shaken at first because I did not expect to encounter such an emotionally charged situation. I also did not know that Feng was experiencing a great deal of confusion and anxiety caused by growing tensions with his boss and his family. I looked at him with sympathy and said gently: "It is

FIGURE 8. A sandplay arrangement made by Feng Gang. Photo by author.

OK. I can feel your loneliness." I then stayed silent for a while until he calmed down a bit and was ready to talk.

I learned that Feng Gang was a plain-clothes policeman responsible for apprehending pickpockets on city buses. His work was highly demanding and sometimes dangerous, yet his supervisor did not trust him and accused him of slacking off. He felt stressed and resentful. When Feng began to take counseling classes in his spare time, he had to hide it from his supervisor and coworkers. At home it was also difficult for him. His wife's parents, who lived with his family, questioned why he was studying psychology, and they complained frequently. Luckily his wife, a full-time white-collar worker, was supportive, but she needed his help in taking care of their newborn baby. "I come home after work feeling exhausted, but I am expected to help wash baby diapers and do housework." Feng continued, "My in-laws think I am just lazy if I need some rest. They also believe that studying psychological counseling is impractical, a waste of time. I am under so much pressure at work and at home. And I do not have a moment for myself. I am stuck and feeling very lonely." I was touched by Feng's honesty and trust, and I got a bit teary-eyed. He saw it and I knew that he appreciated my empathy.

From our first meeting, Feng looked depressed, but he never went to see a psychiatrist or got a formal diagnosis, partly because mental illness was stigmatizing and partly because he thought he could just toughen up. Yet, he was slipping into deeper isolation and sadness. Feng's personal experience of depression and bewilderment was a main factor pulling him toward psychological training. He cherished the moments he crafted for himself to look deeper into his own psyche and affects, and largely attributed such opportunities to the encounter with psychology and counseling. Attending to his anguish and opening up his feelings to others in the therapeutic setting was a first step toward healing, even though this experience was painful.

As a man and a police officer, Feng was expected to be tough and not to express his anguish, but the therapy training provided him with a safe space to explore his inner fears and desires against gender stereotyping. He was able to engage in a deep introspection while reaching out for help from the mentor and fellow trainees. Thus, Feng felt he was not alone but at the same time still had his own space to feel and reflect. And the most valuable part, he noted, was to be able to get in touch with his own affects—the feelings that were embedded in the bodily experience but might not yet be articulated by language (see Massumi 2002; Clough and Halley 2007). At the end of our session, Feng mentioned that the green plants and jade horn he had placed in the sandbox represented hope, faith, and good luck. "I am not sure where it is yet, but I have a feeling that I have begun to see sparks of hope in this rather desolate situation. And that is why I keep crawling like that snake," said Feng with a faint smile. After the session, Feng thanked me for listening to him and for being there for him. He genuinely appreciated the workshop that gave him an opportunity that he called "cathartic." When he was feeling more composed, he offered this reflection to me: "Ziwo has two layers of meanings. One is *dangxia de wo* 当下的我 (the self that is living here and now), which is deeply embedded in the family, kin, and society. The other is the *yuanshi de wo* 原始的我 (the primeval self) detached from the reality, which can only emerge from time to time when I am alone in meditation. I am longing for the disentangled self, but at the same time I cannot abandon the socially embedded self because both together make me human."

This is a powerful statement that highlights the complexity of the self as relational and dynamic, constantly being constituted and reconstituted through different layers of sociality and personal desires. One of the precious experiences Feng gained through psychotherapy training was introspection—what Haag defines as "the capacity to experience and observe oneself simultaneously" (2018: 26). By splitting the self temporarily, the person becomes the subject and the object of observation at once. Two years later, we met again at a small restaurant for lunch. I found Feng's mood and personal situation had improved greatly. He continued to study counseling in his spare time and practice self-cultivation. At the same time, he was actively engaged in his family's and other social activities. He summarized his progress like this: "I have learned to adjust my mindset constantly, which helps enhance my family life and work relations. Even though I cannot change the reality, I am much better at seeing different options and deciding how to respond." Responding, rather than reacting, was central to Feng's personal transformation. When he felt more confident interacting with others, he felt more at ease and was more willing to be an active player in the social world. To his surprise, his in-laws' attitude toward him had also altered gradually, as they sensed the change in him and felt it easier to communicate with him. Feng also began to volunteer at a small, private counseling center offering free psychological service to elementary and high school students with emotional troubles. He found this act of giving by helping others in need highly gratifying because it offered new social connection, more training experience, and public recognition. Feng's dream was to open a service facility like this of his own someday and help those in distress.

The above three cases illustrate heterogeneous ways of conceiving a therapeutic self that have emerged in contemporary urban China. For them, therapeutic knowledge and practice served as a primary conduit through which new self-awareness and self-practice are made possible. Yet what they took away from this process was not the same. Wan Qing stressed the importance of a private self and maintaining a boundary between public and private, yet she was also aware that the formation of this private self could not be isolated from the social world. Lu Minxin advocated a mode of selfhood deeply rooted in and shaped by social norms and expectations, based on his past interpersonal dynamics. Disentangling one's self from others, even for a moment, was unsettling for him. However, we can see some gradual changes in him—the propensity to open up for new self-experiments. Feng Gang's notion of self-work was more sophisticated and dialectic. It first required the undertaking of disentanglement so that the inner self could find a safe space of healing and regain clarity and strength. Yet the work did not stop here; the new self cultivated by psychotherapeutic practices needed to be re-embedded in the social world.

The dialectic relationship between disentangling and re-embedding was also reflected in the story of Zhu Ling, whom we met earlier in this chapter. Although she left for Tibet in search of peace and self, she eventually came back to her former social world after the extended journey. She told me that she felt like a new person afterward, but her self-work continued into the years that followed. I visited Zhu at work three years later and found the combination of the books on the shelves in her office fascinating: psychology, counseling, Buddhism, and government documents. She continued to take many advanced counseling training workshops to refine her skills, and she joined a small team of therapists offering individual counseling and collective training for work units. She felt happier and more effective at home and work: "Once in a while, I also disentangle myself from the busy world around me, but not necessarily to be away physically. Now I can do it mentally or through meditation." Her daughter's condition continued to be a challenge, but instead of feeling shamed and guilty, Zhu accepted the situation and tried to enjoy whatever sweet moments she could have with her daughter. "Buddhism taught me that my suffering comes from my inability to accept what is. When I stop fighting against what life presents to me, serenity arrives. Of course, it is easier said than done. The art is how to strike a balance between attending to my feelings and taking care of others around me." By combining insights from both worlds—spirituality and psychology, Zhu became more poised in facing difficulties.

Despite the differences, the one thing that my interlocutors had in common was their faith in psychological work, seeing it as an effective tool of enhancing themselves. For them, self-efficacy and social efficacy become one and the same project, with promises of happiness, success, and fulfillment. Many informants I spoke with echoed this view, especially as they witnessed the positive effects of therapeutic self-work on their family relations and social lives. The dual process of disentangling and re-embedding, the self and the social, the inner (nei) and the outer (wai) constitutes a dialogic relationship that strengthens rather than opposes one another.[8] Here I borrow Bakhtin's notion of "dialogic" to describe this form of dynamic in which the two seemingly contradicting dimensions actually interact and transform one another to generate new meanings (1981).

REFLECTION

For many urban Chinese professionals, ziwo is becoming an object that one can work on, adjust, and improve with psychotherapeutic techniques. In this vein, two things—selfhood and therapeutics—are increasingly interlocked and configure each other. Many people who are drawn to psychotherapy are not interested in treating mental illness per se, but rather want to enhance their well-being and cultivate a better self in order to live the "good life" in the boisterous era of fast economic growth and social aspiration.[9]

Managing the evolving relationship between the self and the layered social nexus remains a key challenge for my interlocutors, who hope to live a better and balanced life. I have identified a distinct dual process of "disentangling" and "re-embedding" as central to the formation of this new therapeutic self. Yet, as we can see, much of the focus on the social here is on the intersubjective level, namely one's relationship with family members, friends, coworkers, and others in social networks. Less emphasis is on changing broader social processes, which many people feel to be beyond their control. As Jie Yang (2015: 84) points out, this innovative therapeutic approach can end up bypassing current social and economic problems that may be the main sources of many people's distresses. Thus, the social, in relation to the question of the self addressed by modern psychology, is a specific form with its own limits.

Three important features about this emerging therapeutic culture of the self are worth noting. First, multiple notions of selfhood—traditional, socialist, and neoliberal—coexist and are entangled with one another. Individuals must navigate this plurality in their life and try to make sense of the different forms of the self that are often in friction with one another. Therapeutic engagement with self-work is becoming an important tool for not only enhancing *ziwo jiazhi* (self-worth) and *zizun* (self-esteem) but also easing the tension created by different self-modalities. While in the earlier reform years (1980s–1990s) material wealth was the prominent marker of well-being, today health and an enhanced self are vital registers of living a better life (see Borovoy and Zhang 2016; Farquhar and Zhang 2012).[10] A recent article in a popular Sina blog site, widely circulated among some middle-class professionals, states boldly: "Willing to receive psychological counseling is a sign or indicator of self-confidence and affluence." This article claims that almost every middle-class American has a therapist and this is one of the secrets of their success and happiness.[11]

Second, sharing personal life stories and narratives of feelings is essential in the cultivation of a new therapeutic self and for personal growth. Bradley Lewis highlights the centrality of self-stories this way: "These culturally located 'self' stories and the priorities within those stories combine with other cultural stories to scaffold our narrative identity and provide us with a compass for living" (2013: 398). From this perspective, such narratives are not merely a reflection but a form of practice that *does* something important for us— scaffolding and guiding a new self. A common theme that emerged in the narratives I collected during my fieldwork is that individuals often started to engage in psychotherapeutic work out of curiosity or the desire to help others and then discovered that they needed to do self-work for themselves. And this self-work started them on a life-changing process toward illumination. More importantly, talk therapy training, as conducted in China (mostly in small groups), offers a unique opportunity for participants to share their own stories and self-experiments in an intimate setting with others. This emerging form of sociality is critical for maximizing therapeutic power in remaking a person. In his study of the new psy regime in postsocialist Russia, Tomas Matza has observed a similar phenomenon, which he calls "psychosociality"—"a form of 'social proxy,' where imagined intimate stranger relations in public are mimicked in therapeutically attuned settings" (2018: 28). He shows that through this form of public intimacy, people can feel free to share their inner struggles, personal problems, and even political traumas, which otherwise would remain hidden and un-articulated. Likewise, many of my interlocutors find this new therapeutic sociality powerful and refreshing. They demonstrate that self-cultivation is not the antithesis of the social but in some ways depends on a new kind of social.

Third, this regime of self-work is very much shaped by class and gender. The primary consumers of this new industry are members of the urban middle classes. The working-class, the poor, those on the margins of the society, are largely excluded, lacking the time and money (and perhaps interest) to embrace these therapeutic experiments of self-actualization.[12] Women make up nearly 80 percent of the participants at the self-growth workshops and psy training classes I attended. This may be due to ideas that women are primarily responsible for taking care of familial relationships and engaging in emotional labor. But urban Chinese women now have the possibility of acquiring a professional toolbox to take charge of their affective relationships. For many of them, this change is simultaneously powerful and demanding, hopeful and stressful. At the same time, this gender imbalance does not mean that men have fewer psychological conflicts or need less help. Many therapists feel that it is imperative to break down cultural barriers and gender bias to include more men in this new therapeutic realm.

While the new therapeutic culture provides a unique and safe space for self-exploration and self-healing, its impact goes far beyond the personal realm. Self-work is not merely personal but also political. As Barbara Cruikshank (1996) has shown in the case of the self-esteem movement, which started in the 1980s in the United States, this project forged a new mode of governing the self through therapy and presented self-work as the core problem of neoliberal governance.

Nikolas Rose (1996) has also reminded us that the regime of an enterprising self is itself a central feature of contemporary governmentality and an indispensable component of neoliberal political programs in advanced capitalist societies. While my research shows that this culture of self-engagement is emerging outside of Euro-American societies, it takes a distinct form in these contexts that have their own deep cultural and historical understandings about what it means to cultivate oneself. Here what we see is a blend of new and old, foreign and local narratives of soul searching and self-discovery, rather than a simple storyline of a neoliberal takeover of self-care from tradition.

This new self-work joins with the postsocialist politics of reshaping persons and society. A core element in the official project of building "a harmonious socialist society" is a higher degree of stability and contentment among citizens. In this context, the Chinese state and social scientists have come to embrace "positive psychology," a distinct branch of psychology developed by Martin Seligman (1991, 2002) and others. Despite critiques of positive psychology by scholars like Louise Sundararajan (2005) for its lack of a moral map and reluctance to tackle structural problems, self-work is regarded by some Chinese experts to have the potential to engender broader social interventions through improving citizens' emotional outlook and fostering a sense of satisfaction (see Zhang 2015). With the help of psy experts, Chinese people are told, it is possible to turn social problems and suffering into a technical matter of sound personal choice and self-management.[13] At this stage, it is unclear whether psychotherapeutic work will generate a stronger sense of individual autonomy and well-being among some people, or help accommodate the existing sociopolitical system by sidestepping concerns of social conflict and inequality.[14]

CHAPTER 6

Cultivating Happiness

For those who suffer from alienation, cure does not consist in the absence of illness, but in the presence of well-being.

—Erich Fromm, "Psychoanalysis and Zen Buddhism" (1960)

In the midst of rapid and often disorienting socioeconomic transformations, a new form of urban aspiration is emerging among China's middle-class professionals: namely, an intense interest in and a fervent pursuit of personal happiness under the twin banners of science and well-being. This "happiness fever" (*xingfu re*), which often calls for psychological intervention, is taking place against the backdrop of a society that is becoming increasingly competitive and distressed as unprecedented surges in the desire for material wealth are coupled with mounting social inequality and moral crisis. These changes are magnified in the cities, where competition for resources is fierce and palpable. Novel notions, mostly imported from the West, such as "the science of happiness" and "the happiness index," are being introduced to urban Chinese by psychologists and psychotherapists who have recently "discovered" positive psychology and the fusion styles of healing approaches to well-being (much inspired by Buddhism and Daoism) brought from Japan, the United States, and other places. These hybrid therapeutic techniques that attempt to blend science with secularized religious teaching claim to be not only *efficacious* in promoting emotional outlooks and the quality of life, but also *suitable* for the Chinese social and cultural conditions. By reducing anxiety, stress, and other existential sufferings, the ultimate goal here is not to just eliminate illness but to foster a richer sense of well-being or what Martin Seligman calls authentic "human flourishing" (Seligman 2002).

This chapter explores the logic, practice, and impact of this zealous quest for happiness by addressing the following questions: Why is the search for personal happiness quickly gaining such a salient place in contemporary Chinese urban life, especially among educated professionals? What fusion techniques of self-cultivation and well-being do these people embrace and reinvent? How do the therapists and clients make sense of and reconcile such dichotomous concepts as "scientific" and "religious," "modern" and "ancient" in practice? What does this new trend tell us about the possibilities and limits of reinventing the self and cultivating the "good life" in a globalizing China? My account primarily draws from ethnographic data I collected through participant observation and interviews, but also from my research on how the new study of happiness, positive psychology, and Buddhist psychology in North America are making their way into everyday life in urban China.

This emerging pursuit of happiness beyond material wealth, I suggest, is largely propelled by Chinese middle-class urbanites' aspiration to live the "good life" (meihao shenghuo)—a powerful motif or mirage that is alluring to many today (see Zhang 2020; Hsu and Madsen 2019). But it is also driven by the mounting distress they are experiencing in a time of profound societal change—urban restructuring, a shift to a market-driven economy, the loss of job security, increasingly fragile family and kinship ties, higher health care costs, and the pressure to accumulate more things, to name a few. It is in this context that the notion of happiness or well-being becomes particularly appealing to those individuals who are hopeful yet anxious, animated yet fretful.[1]

Further, in exploring the efforts to blend modern psychotherapeutics with Buddhist and Daoist techniques, I suggest that spirituality is not retreating in China today; instead it constantly finds its way into diverse domains of urban social and mental life in secularized forms. These innovative, eclectic approaches to the cultivation of emotional well-being both within and beyond China may further recast urbanity in a way that integrates rather than conceals spiritual practices, and provides a space for meditating on the possibility of a modernity in which science and spirituality do not oppose each other but come together to enhance human experiences. There exists an interesting paradox here though: While many Chinese psychotherapists and their followers are enamored of the modern, scientific aura/claim of new hybrid healing methods, in practice they do not seem to be genuinely concerned about the actual efficacy of what they offer. Instead, it is the *promise* of healing and living a good life beyond material success that sustains their search for a path to happiness. At times, however, I detected disappointment and dissatisfaction when the promise became frail.

XINGFU RE

The pursuit of happiness or well-being has long been an enduring universal theme of human experience.[2] Yet, how happiness is conceived and the ways in which people strive to attain happiness vary across different times, places, and cultures. Throughout the past century, Chinese people pursued various forms of happiness (*fu* 福, later *xingfu* 幸福) in everyday life, but never before have we seen such an explosion of discussion about happiness and the possibility of technical intervention as appears today.[3] In the past, the idea of happiness was largely produced in relation to the family, collective institutions, or the nation-state.[4] But today happiness is primarily treated as an individual project (although often relational and embedded in social contexts) that can be analyzed, measured, discussed, and improved through psycho-technical means.[5] This turn represents two significant departures: a shift away from the single-minded national focus on economic growth and material comfort we have witnessed over the past three decades, and a move toward a psychotherapeutic regime of well-being that directs the questions of the self and the meaning of life to individuals' psychic and emotional experiences.

The scale of this new "happiness craze" (*xingfu re*) is massive. Books, magazines, websites, talk shows, conferences, and workshops devoted to the pursuit of happiness and the "good life" have been mushrooming. Recently, the word *xingfu* (happiness or well-being), even appeared in a major speech delivered by China's president, Xi, on the Twelfth National People's Congress in 2013, as he elaborated on his ambitious vision for the "Chinese Dream"— "realizing a prosperous and strong country, the rejuvenation of the nation and the well-being of the people" (Sebag-Montefiore 2013).[6] To give readers a sense of the magnitude of this fervent turn to happiness, let us look at a *Time* article, titled "Chinese Flock to Free Lectures on Happiness, Justice" (Jiang 2011), which reports an interesting phenomenon: A popular Chinese internet portal, NetEase, began to offer Open University–style lectures in English on a variety of topics in 2010. It was expected that most Chinese netizens would rush to pragmatic seminars on marketing, robotics, trade, communication technologies, and so on. But to many people's surprise, the two top hits are a course on happiness delivered by a Harvard psychologist (Tal Ben-Shahar) and a course on justice by a Harvard philosopher (Michael Sandel). It was estimated that by now some three million Chinese people have watched them according to the *Time* report.

Ben-Shahar's lecture series on *Positive Psychology: The Science of Happiness* is popular because it strikes a chord with young and middle-aged Chinese professionals who are eager to find both success and happiness. Last summer when I was in Kunming, I noticed that a pirate version of this course with Chinese subtitles was already available in many DVD stores. Ben-Shahar's best seller, *Happier: Finding Pleasure, Meaning and Life's Ultimate Currency*, was translated into Chinese in 2007 and featured prominently in local bookstores. The Chinese translation of the title is somewhat different from its original English one. It roughly means *The Methods of Happiness*. The term *fangfa* ("methods," "means," or "ways") implies a systematic, scientific approach that can be learned and mastered through study, coaching, and practice. Therefore, the intended message to Chinese readers is that reaching the realm of happiness is not surreptitious or haphazard; instead, one must rely on scientific methods. To differentiate its superior status from other numerous books on this topic, its preface is simply titled "Happiness Is a Science."

There are more indicators of this rising interest in the quest of happiness. A nationally popular magazine, *Xinli* (Psychologies) that caters to urban middle-class professionals (especially women), has published several featured articles on inner well-being. The most intriguing one (see the 2010 June issue) is an extensive discussion on the "2009 Chinese Happiness Index Report," jointly conducted by the Jiangsu Satellite Television Station and the Horizon Research and Consultation Group.[7] Based on a survey of 15,801 urban and rural individuals who returned their questionnaires, this report is the first of its kind and thus attracted a great deal of media and public attention. Two significant findings are that the overall sense of emotional well-being among Chinese citizens today is considered very low and that higher income (more than 15,000 yuan per month) does not lead to a greater sense of happiness. Thus, the heated debate concludes that it is imperative to shift our focus from gross domestic product (GDP) to gross national happiness (GNH). Further, it is said that since material wealth does not necessarily foster a subjective experience of feeling happy, it is necessary to unlock the secret of well-being by studying how a less "developed" place like Bhutan can emerge as the happiest place on the earth.

In 2012, Central Chinese Television (CCTV) launched a popular special series titled "The Happiness Lessons" (*xingfu ke*). International and Chinese psychological experts were invited to talk about how to obtain authentic well-being and a positive mindset, cultivate self-fulfillment, and raise optimistic children. In the same year, the Second Chinese International Positive Psychology Conference was held in Beijing and dedicated its theme to "Positive Mindset, Happy China." All of this indicates that by now the happiness talk has gone far beyond the academic sphere and caught the popular urban imagination.

One cannot help but ask: Why is the "happiness craze" emerging in Chinese cities today? What does the notion of happiness mean to Chinese people? How might it redefine Chinese urban life? While I am reluctant to resort to a simplistic causal explanation, it is important to understand the broader socioeconomic context in which this "fever" takes place. Let us first look at the statement of the Second Chinese International Positive Psychology Conference, which attributes the question of happiness to the following structural changes that China is undergoing in recent years: the intensification of multiple contradictions embedded in the new economic system, the slowing down of economic development, mounting social conflicts, escalating competition among different social strata, and the increasing difficulty for the party-state to govern Chinese society. It is suggested that these macro-structural transformations and ruptures are bound to be felt on the micro-personal level and thus profoundly impact the individual psyche. The city is where all these contradictions embedded in the pursuit of postsocialist modernity and urbanity are crystallized, and where yearnings, agonies, and struggles are negotiated constantly. The city is also where new internet technologies, mass media, a reading public, and global influences are readily available. All this helps facilitate the spread of the discourses on happiness and the need for intervention. While the existing literature on the reconfigurations of Chinese urban life has focused on the economic, social, spatial, and political dimensions, little attention has been given to how the *affective* elements—emotions, spirituality, and mentality—are transforming.[8] In other words, we need to know more how city dwellers actually *feel* and attempt to cope with these external changes and distress.

When I spoke to people of different backgrounds in Kunming, I frequently asked them how they would characterize the overall state of being—both for the society and for themselves. The two words that came up most often to describe their affective experiences are: *fuzao* ("impetuous" or "restless") and *jiaolu* ("anxious"). Both terms suggest a strong sense of uncertainty, precariousness, and uneasiness with the reality and the future.

Liu Hui was a high school teacher in her mid-thirties. She and her husband (a civil servant in the provincial government) had a five-month-old boy and bought a modest two-bedroom apartment in a decent residential community in 2014. She felt very lucky to have a place of their own but also was stressed out by the mortgage and other looming demands: "I feel that everyone is running after something or going somewhere, so I have to catch up too—getting a bigger house, buying a nicer car, getting my child into the best school. There is simply no end and no purpose. But I feel like in a sea of people and the waves just keep pushing me to move. I do not have a moment that I can slow down or stop in order to really feel life around me and get in touch with my inner feelings." For her, life was an endless race. This fear of falling behind and the pressure to compete and rush forward can be exhausting emotionally. During my conversations with several middle-class women in Kunming, they shared similar sentiments and social anxieties. As one of them expressed: "We are now worried about how the new property policies are going to impact our life. We are also worried about our children's future, since the competition facing them is so severe. They must fight for the best education, yet there is still no guarantee in the job market." When I met her in 2017, the Chinese government was about to announce a new property ruling that might increase property taxes significantly. Many homeowners were anxious. Children's schooling is another major stressor, since every family wants to send their child to the few top-ranked schools in the city. One's household registration status, cost, test scores, guanxi (personal connections), and commute are all important factors involved, adding complexity and worry to the mix.

Like these women, many middle-class Chinese feel trapped and alienated by the world around them, a world that is supposed to be developing and improving materially—more roads, more high-rises, more cars, more housing, more food, more clothing. Yet, the sense of happiness, security, and contentment they have anticipated does not follow. Instead, they are troubled by confusion, emptiness, and uncertainty, despite living a materially comfortable life (see also Liu 2002; Zhang 2011). One day I ran into Renhua, a young professor of economics at a local university. She put the dilemma of the Chinese middle class this way: "We seem to have everything now, but actually something important is missing. We are living in a society that lacks justice, safety, and fairness. Just look around: the environment is deteriorating, food safety is questionable, health care is unaffordable. . . . How can one be truly happy?" For people like Renhua, happiness is not just feeling good or possessing housing, cars, and expensive food. It is about fulfilling a higher level of necessities and meaning.

In short, it is this anxious and precarious urban environment that gives rise to the popular desire to search for personal happiness and well-being. To gain a sense of better control, some people also resort to fortune telling and the Feng Shui practice of ensuring good luck by getting auspicious numbers (for their phones, car license plates, wedding dates, etc.), identifying lucky house locations, and making sure that their home design will bring blessing and happiness. But these efforts tend to generate only a fleeting sense of luck and implied protection instead of a long-lasting sense of joy and security. Others also seek temporary retreat in the countryside for happiness by leaving the crowded and stressful urban living environment and getting in touch with nature.[9]

"THE SCIENCE OF HAPPINESS"

What is distinct about the current trend of cultivating happiness is its unmistaken claim on science via modern psychology and its simultaneous openness to incorporating the wisdom of spirituality. Examining the phenomenon more closely, it is not difficult to find that much of the language and the logic of the happiness quest is directly imported from certain psychotherapeutic strands based in North America and then modified to fit Chinese society. Under the banner of "psychological science," some experts claim to be able to effectively ease personal and social suffering. Here I would like to trace three important therapeutic threads and the connections among them: positive psychology, Buddhist psychology, and a recent neuro-scientific study on the effect of meditation on the mind and the body. I will examine the role of what I call "cultural and therapeutic brokers," who play a critical role in the global circuits of healing knowledge and practice. It is important to note that while my inquiry below largely focuses on Buddhist elements (and to some degree Daoist elements) among other indigenous cultural influences on psychotherapeutics, I by no means claim that these are the only significant forces in shaping the happiness and well-being craze in contemporary China. Indeed, as other scholars have shown, Daoism, Taiji, Qigong, and Yoga, among other practices have also been quite popular in the quest for personal well-being among the Chinese (see Palmer 2007; Chen 2003).

One of the key figures of spreading "the science of happiness" to China is Professor Kaiping Peng at the University of California–Berkeley and the founder of the Berkeley-Tsinghua Program for Advanced Study in Psychology.

Growing up in China and later trained in the United States, Professor Peng is in an ideal position to "translate" psychological science between the West and the East, and is widely regarded in China as an authority on the science of happiness. He holds joint positions at both institutions and exchanges research ideas and resources frequently. He once stated that he was "the right person in the right place at the right time" to do this bridging work.[10] On March 20, 2014, he delivered a high-profile keynote speech at the United Nations headquarters in New York to commemorate the International Day of Happiness. It was televised by CCTV and viewed by some two hundred million Chinese. This event elevated his status to that of a superstar and drew greater attention to the science of happiness in China.

In a recent interview, Peng declared, "We want to switch the focus in China from the gross domestic product to happiness, from the culture of competition to the common good. We are seeking to correct that imbalance by spreading the science of happiness in China" (Bruce 2010). He is confident that positive psychology can provide much-needed answers to social problems facing Chinese society in transition. Peng also believes that it is much easier for Chinese people to embrace positive psychology because it emphasizes the constructive potential and optimism in humanity and shuns the dark aspects and the heavy sexual overtones in Freudian theory. Further, positive psychology is welcomed by the Chinese government because it articulates well with the official notion of building a harmonious society. As a public intellectual, Professor Peng has been a frequent guest on prominent Chinese television talk shows and interviewed by major Chinese newspapers. He argues that raising popular awareness of psychological well-being and finding reliable methods to achieve positive emotions is a pressing issue since Chinese society has become too materialistic, utilitarian, and spiritually unfit.

So how and why is positive psychology spreading so quickly in the world today? Dissatisfied with the dominant trend in psychology and psychiatry that focuses on pathology and what is wrong in people/patients, as crystalized by the *Diagnostic and Statistical Manual of Mental Disorders* (DSM), proponents of positive psychology declare that the aim of this new approach is to "begin to catalyze a change in the focus of psychology from preoccupation only with repairing the worst things in life to also building positive qualities" (Seligman and Csikszentmihalyi 2000: 5). The critical task is to explore what enables well-being, and how to nurture the strengths and optimism that lead to enduring individuals and communities (see also Seligman 1991). It is argued that positive traits such as courage, wisdom, spirituality, perseverance, self-determination, and optimism can be learned and cultivated through positive psychology.[11]

What fascinates me is a rising passion among some psychologists like Peng for exporting or importing positive psychology into developing countries like China, India, and Vietnam. They see China almost like a huge potential market for exporting ideas. For the reasons I have briefly discussed earlier, this shift from the language of mental illness and suffering to the focus on well-being and flourishing seems particularly alluring to the emerging middle-class Chinese who are grappling with profound societal changes. Positive psychology is often treated as the "scientific" basis for the new "happiness craze," but it is unclear just what exactly constitutes its scientific foundation and how it is practiced beneath the "modern" and "Western" aura.

By now, positive psychology has been widely applied to different social settings across the globe in the hope of raising optimistic children, happier workers, and resilient soldiers.[12] Seligman further declared that positive psychology is not just about happiness or feeling good, it is more about well-being, which encompasses a deeper sense of fulfillment and purposefulness. But the latter is precisely what is lacking in the Chinese psy field. With this new attention to deeper meanings and self-cultivation, a therapeutic approach seems no longer adequate; a spiritual dimension is also called into play.

MINDFULNESS, MEDITATION, AND SPIRITUALITY

Another major current in the pursuit of happiness that influences China is what is called "Buddhist psychology," which seeks to blend the notion of science with the ancient wisdom of Buddhism. A central figure embodying this fusion approach is Jack Kornfield, a renowned meditation teacher and prolific author based at the Spirit Rock Meditation Center in Northern California. He trained as a Buddhist monk in Thailand, Burma, and India and later obtained his PhD in clinical psychology. In *The Wise Heart: A Guide to the Universal Teachings of Buddhist Psychology* (2008), he cites the Dalai Lama: "Buddhist teachings are not a religion, they are a science of mind." Kornfield is very successful at walking a fine line between science and religion. He bypasses the language of religion by secularizing it in order to retain the power of spirituality and craft "a science of mind," one that coalesces modern psychology, neuroscience, and ancient Buddhist teachings. Kornfield aspires to demonstrate that Buddhism is a "living psychology," which "makes no distinction between wordily and spiritual problems" and can offer rich insights to the growing dialogue between Eastern and Western psychology (1993: 3–5). Kornfield's books have been translated into Chinese and embraced warmly by readers interested in the "new" psychology of the heart, not just the mind or brain.[13]

Another prominent figure hoping to integrate psychotherapeutic and spiritual approaches to healthy emotions is Jon Kabat-Zinn, the founding director of the Stress Reduction Clinic and the Center for Mindfulness in Medicine, Health Care, and Society at the University of Massachusetts Medical School.[14] Less imbued with a Western therapeutic language, Kabat-Zinn is able to articulate the ethos of Zen as a way of life through a language of simplicity and clarity (1990, 1994, 2005). Kabat-Zinn attempts to recuperate what he sees as a core component—mindfulness—in Buddhist teachings without having to carry the baggage of religion. He is one of those who have successfully secularized the notion of mindfulness. He offers innovative methods to connect the body with the mind and a path for cultivating positive affective experiences by reducing stress, depression, anxiety, and tension. His writing is making its way back into East Asia and shaping some therapists' practices there.[15]

A third person who has made a major contribution to the articulation of neuroscience with Zen Buddhism is a Japanese psychiatrist, Tomio Hirai. He believes that the goal of psychotherapy coincides with that of Zen Buddhism—namely, to achieve a tranquil state of mind free of suffering, and that meditation can help reach this state of being by attaining the true self (Hirai 1989). His passion is to validate and demystify the therapeutic effects of intense meditation through what he sees as scientific and positivist methods. His research involved psycho-physiological experiments on forty-eight Zen priests and their trainees in a Japanese temple. For example, his team used electroencephalograms (ECGs) to record brain waves, respiratory functions, galvanic skin reflexes, and other physiological changes before, during, and after meditation. These studies show that the slowing down of ECG patterns during meditation and an absence of habituation together indicate specific changes in consciousness. Hirai, who is heavily influenced by Zen master D. T. Suzuki, suggests that *satori* (the state of enlightenment), the ultimate goal of Zen, is an altered mental state produced through meditation. But it is not a state of disassociation or trance; rather, it is a state of "relaxed awareness accompanied by constant responsiveness" made possible by the so-called "storehouse consciousness" (Hirai 1989: 101).[16] Hirai concludes that Zen meditation proves to have "therapeutic effects on the human mind and mental fitness" (1989: 157).

Today with more advanced technologies, many scientists continue to engage in research on the effects of intensive meditation on mind and body. One of the noteworthy attempts is the Shamatha Project led by Dr. Clifford Saron, a neuroscientist at the University of California–Davis. His team finds that intensive meditation helps sustain attention, regulate emotions, and improve psychological well-being and health-related biomarkers.

But can we fully explain the power of meditation, mindfulness, and other Buddhist practices through science?[17] Kornfield and Kabat-Zinn represent a fusion effort that takes spirituality seriously by recognizing its vital role in healing and well-being without subjugating it to the judgment of science. Their goal is not to test or validate spiritual practices through the notion of science, but to broaden and strengthen the path to well-being and invite us to reflect upon hegemonic Western biomedical claims on health.

This everyday approach based on self-cultivation and mind work articulates well with the effort to indigenize psychotherapy in East Asia. For instance, Hwang and Chang (2011) have pointed out that self-cultivation practices derived from the traditions of Confucianism, Taoism, and Buddhism have been a core component of indigenized forms of psychotherapy in China, Japan, and Korea. Three states of self, advocated by the three traditions—the relational self, the authentic self, and the nonself respectively—have been adopted by therapists to achieve their pragmatic goals of therapy. Two approaches developed in Japan—Morita therapy (*sentian liaofa* 森田疗法) and Naikan therapy (*neiguan liaofa* 内观疗法)—are especially successful in this effort.

Morita therapy was created in the 1920s by a Japanese psychiatrist Shoma Morita, who used Zen principles and practices to alleviate emotional disorders. Morita believed that human beings are motivated by two opposing drives: the desire to live a full and meaning life and the desire to maintain comfort and security. These two desires are often in conflict with one another, as the drive to live a successful life can often lead to anxiety, risk, and uncertainty. Conducted usually in complete social isolation, this therapy aims to teach clients how to accept things as they are ("arugamana") and not suppress or avoid distressing feelings. It focuses on experiencing the present and nature by withholding value judgments (Hwang and Chang 2011: 1012). The aim is to cultivate an authentic self with awareness and mindfulness in harmony with the natural ecology. Strongly influenced by Zen, Morita therapy transcends the mind-body dualism and attends to bodily sensations, thoughts, and action simultaneously.

In this spirit, happiness is not the absence of discomfort but the ability to live a full and meaningful life regardless of one's emotional state of being.

In Japan, another culturally specific therapy, Naikan (meaning "inside looking" or "introspection"), was developed by a Buddhist, Ishin Yashimoto, in the 1940s. Its method focuses on self-reflection, especially one's relationship with significant others (such as the mother). Through the therapy process, one gradually cultivates feelings of gratitude, indebtedness, and loving kindness by realizing how one's life has long been supported by others. This new perspective is often transformative and brings the client closer to parents, relatives, and friends. Naikan has been quite successful in combining secularized religious practices with cognitive psychotherapy. As Ozawa-de Silva's (2010) study shows, Naikan has deep roots in Buddhism and the cultivation of love and compassion is central to Naikan therapy. Its goal is to address suffering on an existential (rather than medical) level by "facilitating a transformation in subjectivity, that is, a change in the manner in which the subject experiences his or her existential circumstances" (159).

Both Morita therapy and Naikan therapy have gradually found their way into other East Asian societies. Some Chinese therapists find them particularly helpful for treating anxiety and obsessive-compulsive disorders among certain clients. Next, I will discuss how the general spirit of fusion approaches has been taken up by some Chinese psy-practitioners and clients.

BRIDGING THE SPIRITUAL AND THE THERAPEUTIC

Lin Liuchen, who conducted ethnographic fieldwork in a private counseling center in Beijing, has observed that four of the therapists there engage in some kind of religious or spiritually oriented activities such as hand-copying Buddhist texts, taking annual pilgrimages to the sacred Putuo Mountain, or participating in fortune-telling using Tarot cards or reading the I Ching (2012: 130–31). During my fieldwork in Kunming, I also noticed that Daoist and Buddhist teachings and practices permeated widely the field of psychotherapy and popular psychology in multiple ways, sometimes subtly and sometimes obviously. Many therapists were influenced to a varying degree by the Daoist worldview and Buddhist approaches to relieving suffering even though they were not necessarily self-identified as Daoist or Buddhist followers. Several spiritual figures became happiness and life gurus with star power among certain educated urban social strata.

Glancing at Chinese bookstores today, it is not difficult to find many books that explore the intersection of religion, therapy, and well-being. For example, *Buddhism and Mental Health* (Shi and Liu 2005), coauthored by a Buddhism scholar and a psychology professor, is a typical one catering to readers interested in applying Buddhist wisdom to psychological health on a rudimentary level. Another current trend is to spread spirituality and happiness talk through popular writings by Tibetan lamas. The most noticeable book today is a national bestseller *Living through Suffering* (2012) by an iconic Tibetan Buddhist figure, Khenpo Sodargye (see also Smyer Yu 2013). His writing has been enthusiastically embraced by many Chinese college students and faculty as well as young professionals who aspire to learn how to live a happier and more meaningful life.

The Chinese translation for psychology is *xinlixue* 心理学, literally meaning the study of the heart (or the psyche). Some Buddhism scholars argue that since the tenets of Buddhist teaching are also about the heart (*xin* 心) and its ultimate goal is to relieve human beings from suffering (*ku* 苦), Buddhist thoughts have much to contribute to modern psychology. For this reason, Khenpo Sodargye is regarded by some Chinese college students as *"xinling de yisheng"* 心灵的医生 ("the doctor of the heart") (Symer Yu 2013). From this perspective, all kinds of distress (depression, stress, anxiety, anguish, and so on) are derived from *xin*, polluted by worldly desires and attachment. Thus, if we can constantly work on the heart, tranquility, clarity, and freedom will naturally arise. As one psychotherapist in Kunming explained to me: "I appropriate everything that is useful in my therapy including Zen (*chanzong*). As ancient folks pointed out, all problems can ultimately be summarized in one word, *ku*. And there are many methods to relieve the *ku*. The approach of Western psychology and psychiatry is more technical (drugs, talk therapy, and other therapeutic techniques), but I think it is more important to focus on the understanding of the person, the self, and the affective experiences from a philosophical and spiritual perspective."

Yet, even those who hope to integrate religious elements in their practice are very careful about how the fusion method is presented and perceived. To understand why, one must not forget the traumatic fate of religion in the Chinese socialist context. As Smyer Yu has argued extensively, religion was largely relegated to the realm of "superstition" and thus lost public legitimacy in the social and political life under Mao (2012).[18] Even in the reform and opening-up years marked by various religious revivals, the specter of this troubled history constantly comes back to haunt people in the age of global modernity. In this context, the desire to use science to validate Buddhist practices in the therapeutic regime is in part a reaction to the social marginalization of religion shaped by socialist modernity. Some hope that the scientific claim can recast Buddhism in a different light.

More than ten years ago, a team of Chinese psychiatrists and mental health workers got together in order to develop what they called "Chinese Taoist cognitive psychotherapy," a distinct approach that sought to "blend empirically validated forms of psychotherapies, especially cognitive therapy, with aspects of Chinese culture that may be therapeutically useful" (Zhang et al. 2002: 116). A total of 143 patients diagnosed with generalized anxiety disorder (GAD) from four mental health centers participated in the study. The premise was that both perceptions of stressors and coping strategies were rooted in one's value system. The treatment was largely based on cognitive therapy yet incorporated some Taoist values such as following natural laws, letting go of excessive control, and a flexible development of personality to help patients regulate their affect and cope with reality. While this study sought to blend Taoist principles with cognitive therapy, its overall language and research method were carefully selected so as to reflect its ultimate scientific orientation. In my view, culture (or Taoism more specifically) is used lightly here, like frosting, and not deeply integrated into the psychotherapeutic practice to transform patients' mood and life.

MEDITATING FOR SUCCESS AND HAPPINESS

Other therapists, such as Mr. Ling, take a more implicit or limited approach in blending different methods. Ling's expertise is to train enterprise employees to foster a positive outlook of work and cultivate a sense of happiness in life. Every year he leads a team of four to five psychotherapists to hold a series of workshops at some fancy resorts, which were well funded by a few large state firms in Yunnan Province. The most popular theme is how to generate *zhichang xingfu* ("workplace happiness"). *Zhichang* is a relatively new, depoliticized term that has appeared over the past fifteen years or so. It differs from the personal and familial realm, yet it is closely tied to one's sense of fulfillment and success. Linking *zhichang* to the notion of happiness is also novel in the Chinese cultural context because "work" under socialism was regarded as part of the larger revolutionary project, rather than a site for personal happiness (Rofel 1999).

The bulk of Ling's teaching consisted of basic ideas in positive psychology and the Satir Model of family therapy. It was presented in modern, scientific terms, although specific examples he used are mostly drawn from contemporary Chinese experiences. His lectures were largely based on Seligman's positive psychology with a focus on three specific aspects: how to create positive emotional experiences, how to acquire positive personal traits, and how to foster a positive organizational environment. Each student was given a study booklet compiled by Ling, with lecture notes and several tests measuring one's emotional state of being, stress levels, and communication styles. He also provided each with a copy of the Chinese translation of Tal Ben-Shahar's wildly popular book, *Happier*—regarded as the "bible" of the science of happiness in China. This book was endorsed by many Chinese politicians, social scientists, artists, entrepreneurs, and celebrities alike. At the same time, the Satir Model of therapy was selectively introduced to help participants foster positive habitual responses to emotions and improve their interpersonal communication skills—as these abilities were touted as a key to professional success and personal happiness. The aim of Ling's training course was to help the clients augment positive emotional experiences and create positive social relationships.

A typical workshop lasted for three days with about thirty participants from a local enterprise. It was designed to be *participatory (canyu)* and *experiential (tiyan)*. It included two short periods of guided meditation in the morning and afternoon. Participants were told that meditation was an effective way to reduce stress and anxiety, enhance cognitive capability, and create a tranquil, joyful personal world. They were also assured that meditation was highly compatible with positive psychology and the Satir Model of therapy, and thus it was a must-learn lesson.[19] Ling made it very clear to his students that the meditation he taught was not religious in nature, but only for modern therapeutic purposes. As a guru of creating a successful personal life and positive enterprise culture, he sought to rescue meditation from the religious domain and endow it with a scientific aura. Much of the breathing technique used in the meditation was inspired by visual imagination and positive associations for physical and mental relaxation. The goal was practical and secular without the intent of engaging a deeper spiritual exploration. Given the increased speed and stress of contemporary Chinese urban life, such meditation practices are refreshing and appealing to many participants. As one young woman explained to me during the break at a workshop: "This is starkly different from the past dull political thought education I attended at my firm. Rather than being lectured by a party cadre, I get to do something with a counseling expert that actually benefits my own body and mind. I can almost feel immediately a positive energy flowing through my body. Meditation gives me a chance to slow down and a space to retreat."

Another participant, a mid-level manager in his thirties, said that regular meditation helped improve his ability to focus and memorize, and thus function at work and home more efficiently.[20] "It is worth ten minutes a day to get the reward of a sharpened mind. I never thought I would do anything like this before—sitting idly with my eyes closed and doing nothing. I am usually an action person, but am persuaded now to slow down a bit in order to work better," he laughed. What attracted him most in this therapeutic exercise was not the potential spiritual healing that meditation promises to bring; rather, it was the newfound benefits of living a more competitive and successful life with the aid of meditation and psychological tools of self-improvement. In this fashion, meditation is being increasingly incorporated into postsocialist everyday urban life for both broader therapeutic and non-therapeutic purposes. In fact, practicing meditation and yoga, among other things, has become a new middle-class marker for some young Chinese urban professionals who aspire to enhance the quality of their life through self-care practices (see also Farquhar and Zhang 2012). Today, although pursuing inner spiritual life has lost its appeal to some urban Chinese, others still find spirituality necessary and powerful in transforming their life, especially when it promises to bring well-being and success in a hyper-materialist world.

REFLECTIONS

The recent proliferation of xingfu discourses and practices is inseparable from the emerging postsocialist urban aspirations for personal success and well-being in an increasingly anxious society. It is also rooted partly in urban professionals' pursuit for a new kind of self, one that is not only successful, but also better able to manage emotional and social life.[21] Although more and more Chinese people have begun to realize that material success does not necessarily lead to a sense of xingfu, their quest for happiness is still largely tied to the commonly held ideal of success. As the chief editor of the Chinese magazine Xinli states in a special issue on xingfu: "Our ultimate goal is to help readers strengthen the twin wings of success and happiness." For this end, positive psychology, Buddhism, Daoism, and other forms of cultural practices can all be mobilized to cultivate "the good life." But what does "the good life" mean for urban Chinese today, and is it simply a mirage? Not many people I spoke to seem to have a clear answer. To achieve this idealized but indefinable mode of life, both psychotherapeutic and spiritual practices have become useful because they *promise* to bring inner transformations for individuals without necessarily changing one's social and economic circumstances. Thus, the selling point of therapeutic technologies in this context is not to treat illness, but to generate good feelings and a sense of well-being through expert intervention and self-initiatives.

The anthropologist Peter van der Veer has argued that the "appropriation of spiritual traditions to cater for the newly emerging middle classes" as seen in India and China is a creative "response to new opportunities and anxieties produced by globalization." (2009: 1117). This insight is helpful in explaining why and how science, religion, and spiritual practices have been appropriated in recent years to shape the new "happiness craze" across Chinese cities and beyond. It is in the context of China's unprecedented urban socioeconomic restructuring and cultural change that psychological experts and lifestyle gurus have come to capitalize on the spreading anxiety and unfulfilled desires created by ruthless market competition and the promise of new possibilities (see also Yang 2013a).[22] Further, my research shows that the happiness project is quite unevenly engaged and has different implications for different people. While some people are able to delve deeply into the fusion approach and acquire an authentic experience of transformation and well-being, in many other cases I observed, spiritual practices are highly commercialized for practical purposes while the notion of science is frequently invoked but without vigorous engagement. In other words, the many versions of xingfu I have observed are far from the vision of "well-being" originally articulated by positive psychology or Buddhist psychology. Rather, they are oriented toward how to foster a sense of feeling good (often fleeting), but lack a further attempt to search for deeper meanings or self-empowerment crucial to the cultivation of a long-lasting form of well-being.

In the broader sociopolitical context, one is not surprised to find that the Chinese state has become increasingly welcoming toward this particular psychological approach to a "happy" self and life for two reasons: First, it is seen as less threatening to the status quo than other therapeutic approaches oriented toward addressing victimization and empowerment. The pursuit of happiness may therefore redirect people's attention to personal matters and coping strategies, instead of challenging the established social order. Second, the "happiness craze" has an element of individualization in that it is unlikely to turn into an organized mass movement. These largely individual-oriented and inward-looking practices are thus depoliticized and even drain potential collective revolutionary energy.

Finally, I am troubled by my observation that few Chinese urbanites I met have expressed serious concerns about whether these diverse cultural traditions and therapeutic orientations are truly compatible with one another, or whether they will eventually lead to the "good life" or enhance the crafting of a new self. It seems that, in a postsocialist world marked by a high degree of eclectic ideologies and practices, everything goes as long as it *promises* a path to a happier and successful life (even though this life might be a mirage). Yet, at the same time, one cannot easily dismiss the power of this promissory lure offered by psychological and spiritual practices, because they produce tangible effects on the shaping of people's lived experience.

CHAPTER 7

Therapeutic Governing

In February of 2004, after an intense quarrel over a card game, a student named Ma Jiajue from a poor rural family brutally killed four of his classmates with a heavy hammer in a dormitory of Yunnan University. He stuffed their bodies in the closet and fled to another province by train. He was soon captured by the Chinese authorities, sentenced, and executed four months later. Ma was reported to have displayed a troubling self-abased mentality and difficulty with his social life. This incident shocked the entire nation and provoked widespread debates on the social and psychological factors that drove Ma to commit this horrific crime. It also brought public attention to the dire situation of mental health services in China. Since then, all Chinese colleges and universities have been required to establish a psychological counseling center and integrate mental health work in managing student life.

On May 12, 2008, a strong earthquake, measured at 8.0 magnitude, jolted Wenchuan country in Sichuan Province, leaving some seventy thousand people dead and nearly four hundred thousand people injured. For the first time in recent Chinese history, teams of psychologists and psychotherapists were sent to the disaster region to help the survivors who suffered from severe posttraumatic stress disorder (PTSD). They also provided counseling to the distressed rescue workers and soldiers who witnessed the horrendous scenes of catastrophic destruction and death.

In 2010, eighteen young Chinese workers employed by a Foxconn factory based in the city of Shenzhen attempted suicide by jumping off the building. Fourteen of them died. Although no one knew for sure what drove these young workers to take their own life, it was widely speculated that the harsh working conditions they had to endure contributed to the tragic act—namely, long working hours, a repetitive job, social isolation, inadequate pay, and a crowded living space. Foxconn received wide criticism from the public, and the company responded by installing suicide-prevention nets, raising wages, and bringing in professional counselors to deal with workers' psychological problems.

The above events were tragic and disturbing in different ways, but they all drew wide public, media, and government attention to the role of psychological well-being and care in managing the population in diverse situations as China undergoes massive and rapid socioeconomic transformations. Although the three events concern very different social groups in quite different situations, they together raise an important question: How and why has psychological intervention, often in the name of *guanai* (loving care), gradually become a valued tool of managing citizens and governing society in postsocialist times? What happened at Foxconn is not an isolated case; it indicates a broader challenge facing many other firms in China today regarding how to create and maintain a stable and productive labor force facing intense market competition.

Recently, the Chinese president, Xi Jinping, has advocated for the so-called "China Dream," in which people's happiness and well-being (not just economic development) have become a core component of this new vision. Chinese psychologists and mental health professionals have quickly linked the significance of their work to the China Dream discourse and articulated psychological health to the official notion of socialist harmony first advocated by former President Hu. It is in this context that *xinli guanai* 心理关爱 (psychological care) is becoming a new and useful tool for Chinese officials and organizational managers in their effort to cultivate a sense of well-being, stability, and social harmony among their constituents beyond the pursuit of material wealth.

As China is undergoing profound changes, ruptures, and social polarization during the economic reform years, there has been a constant search for innovative ways to govern the society. The Chinese party-state has become "flexible" in adopting a wide range of strategies and tailor-made practices in managing differently situated sectors of the population and their emerging problems (see Cho 2013; Tomba 2014; Ong and Zhang 2008). While numerous studies have identified the key changes in the modes of governing from socialist to postsocialist times regarding education, public health, urban residential communities, population, and gender and sexuality (see for example Kipnis

2011; Kleinman et al 2011; Mason 2016; Zhang, Kleinman, and Zhang 2011; Zhang 2011; Greenhalgh and Winckler 2005; Rofel 2007), few have examined experimental practices through what I have called "therapeutic governing" (Zhang 2017), by which psychotherapeutic techniques are appropriated for personnel management in organizations and self-care in everyday life.[1]

In this chapter, I address the following questions through my ethnographic encounters: What does therapeutic governing entail in the context of postsocialist China? What experiments and acts of care are involved and for what purposes? What contradictions and unintended consequences might emerge as new therapeutic methods intersect with socialist rule and ethics? Finally, what does the expansion of a therapeutic culture mean for contemporary Chinese politics and society at large? I argue that psychological counselors and mental health experts are becoming a new form of authority, an indispensable part of creating and managing knowable, stable, and governable subjects for the Chinese military, police, schools, and state-owned enterprises. Individuals, however, are not passive recipients of this new technique of governing; instead, they are active and reflexive agents who choose, reject, and transform its elements depending on their specific circumstances and personal backgrounds. I show that incorporating psychotherapeutic intervention and the language of care into postsocialist governing can simultaneously produce both disciplining and nurturing, repressive and unfettering effects on people's lives.

My ethnographic account focuses on two distinct yet important domains: (1) government agencies under relatively tight state control, especially the police and the military; (2) state-owned enterprises (SOE), which have been undergoing profound commercialization and are profit driven. When I first began my research, I had assumed that the military and the police would be the most conservative units and thus the last ones to embrace psychotherapeutic methods. But I was wrong. There was a growing interest already in pursuing this new line of management. I was surprised by how eager these entities were to incorporate Western psychological techniques in their work to reshape personnel management and create a relatively stable, resilient, and productive workforce. Although the military, the police, and state-owned enterprises have their own rationales, goals, and methods of why or how to incorporate new therapeutics, there are also convergences across these units. We should also keep in mind that what I observe in these specific areas are only part of a much broader trend of psy fever sweeping Chinese cities.

To gain a deeper sense of the on-the-ground practices and challenges, I primarily followed three counselors (Ms. Yang, Ms. Zhou, and Mr. Ling) and their therapeutic work in three different settings (a paramilitary hospital, the municipal police system, and a large state enterprise). I also conducted extensive participant observation at various group-based psychological training workshops designed for enterprise employees. These workshops provided a rich opportunity for me to learn what was taught and how the teaching was received. However, carrying out observation within the military and the police was more difficult due to security concerns and my overseas connection. Thus, I supplemented my observation with interviews of individual officers later and with secondary-source data.

GUAN AI AS THERAPEUTIC GOVERNING

In postsocialist China, it has become more apparent that psychological counselors and other mental health workers are becoming a new form of authority in shaping people's lives, and are an indispensable part of creating and managing knowable and stable subjects for organizations of all kinds—the military, the police, schools, hospitals, firms, factories, and so on.[2] Rather than ruling through domination, coercion, and discipline, the current preferred style of governing is through the mantra of *guan ai* 关爱 (loving care) or *ren ai* 仁爱 (kindheartedness). Sometimes, people invoke a famous saying in an ancient Chinese book called *Shiji* 史记: "If you are kind and loving to your soldiers, they will be eager to die for you." The same goes for an optimal relationship between an emperor and his people: Winning people's hearts is more important and reliable for the ruler. Thus, in official and popular discourses today, a good government is said to guan ai its people; it should be loved instead of feared. As Jie Yang demonstrated in the case of *song wennuan* 送温暖 (sending warmth) to the impoverished people, the Chinese party-state reinserts itself in the lives of the poor by giving them the gift of care and by showing compassion and benevolence (2015: 88). What I seek to show in this chapter is that integrating psychological counseling language and techniques constitutes a critical part of this new soft style of governing that underlines the affective dimension of power. This is not to say that under socialism state power did not work through affects; rather, I argue that while the affective involvement has always been crucial to the state, what is novel for China this time is the incorporation of Western psychological knowledge and methods in order to manage tangled emotions and shape mindsets.

The meshing of therapeutic practices with flexible governing techniques has been received by people with attitudes ranging from enthusiasm to indifference to outright skepticism. Some regard it as a welcome experiment in what has been called "kindly governance," based on the notion of *renxinghua* 人性化 (humanism) in contrast with the past socialist rule largely based on emphasizing class struggle and political coercion.[3] For them, therapeutic governing represents a form of kindly governance marked by care, warmheartedness, and human feelings (*renqing*). At the same time, there are others who are quite skeptical about this shift and see it as a subtle form of manipulation. Under the veil of care and benevolence, they see state power and control at work. Some also point out the danger of psychologizing social and economic problems, implicit in this mode of governing, which might end up bypassing the need to make structural changes by employing temporary and superficial fixes and locating the need for change in the individual rather than in the socioeconomic system.

Unlike Polsky (1991) and Szasz (2001a) who regard the therapeutic state as fundamentally problematic and intrusive, I suggest that the therapeutic state is not a monolithic thing but may take multiple shapes and be embraced by people differently given their varying historical and cultural circumstances. It is also important to note that this trend of fusing psychology in governing practices is still in the very early stage in China; thus, its full potential and effect cannot be easily foreseen and evaluated at this moment. But the trend is gaining momentum and spreading quickly. Rather than rushing to judgment of whether this therapeutic turn in politics is good or bad, I argue that it is more productive to explore what drives the various local authorities to pursue this change, which was seen as dubious just a decade ago, and why some Chinese prefer kindly governance even if it does not realize the promises it makes. Given China's unique path of coalescing economic liberalization, socialist legacies, and global capitalism, it is imperative to understand how therapeutic governing may take on a different character and significance in this country than it has elsewhere. In brief, I maintain that we need to take this new "therapeutic governing" seriously by examining its deployment and diverse actual effects rather than dismissing it simply as a form of false consciousness or psychological manipulation imposed on citizens.

CREATING KNOWABLE AND RESILIENT FORCES

On a July morning in 2009, I visited a newly established psychological counseling office at a paramilitary hospital located near the West Hills on the outskirts of Kunming. The primary function of this hospital is to serve the city's People's Armed Police—a special paramilitary force primarily responsible for domestic security against riots, terrorism, and other emergency situations.[4] This was a midsize hospital with a tranquil setting, tucked in close to nearby green mountains. My friend Mr. Liu, a well-known therapist, came with me so as to introduce me to the counseling office director, Ms. Yang, who had been a longtime friend of his. As we arrived, they greeted each other warmly and then engaged in a quick catching-up conversation. Then, he turned to me and said to her: "This is Dr. Zhang, the friend I mentioned to you on the phone. She is doing research on counseling and mental health in China. She is curious about how you guys handle this in the military. Could you give her some help?"

Yang politely gave me a warm welcome and said: "Of course, it is my pleasure! But we are very new to this domain. I am eager to learn from you too, since you are from America." We shook hands with each other, and then she made green tea for us.

As we just sat down on the black sofa, Liu got up and said, "Actually you two chat. I have to make some phone calls outside." Before he stepped out of the door, he jokingly added: "Don't worry! Li is from America, but she is not a spy. She is originally from Kunming, and I have known her for many years." We all laughed. I intentionally switched from Mandarin to local Kunming dialect to see if she felt more comfortable. "No worries! Mandarin is just fine. I am used to it as our soldiers come from different regions and it is easier to use Mandarin," she explained to me.

Yang, who appeared to be in her early forties, was talkative. She had short hair and wore a white doctor's coat over her uniform. On the wall I noticed a framed poster of medical ethics (*yide*). It was not unusual to find such posters in Chinese hospitals, but another one on counseling protocols was new. It stressed the importance of privacy, mutual respect, openness, and friendliness in counseling relationships. She noticed that I was looking at the posters and explained: "Our soldiers are very new to psychological help and are often worried about their privacy. So I always show these principles to them first and assure them that this is a very different kind of relationship than that under other circumstances."

We had a quick tour of the facilities. The three offices were largely empty, with only an examination bed and several desks and chairs. One of them had a biofeedback machine, but Yang admitted that they had just begun to learn how to use it properly. As we were talking, a young soldier in his early twenties walked in and said he was asked to come for a psychological assessment test. She sent him to the next room and gave him a slightly modified Chinese version of the Eysenck Personality Questionnaire (EPQ).[5] He finished the eighty questions in less than an hour and left quietly. Later, I found out that such standardized tests of assessing one's personality traits had been recently adopted as one of the techniques to screen new soldiers. Soldiers usually had no idea what they would be given before coming to the test or what the test was for. The psychological profile generated would be permanently kept in one's personnel file (dangan 档案). Those who display alarming mental and psychological problems in the test are likely to be expelled from the service. Those with moderate issues are subject to treatment and professional counseling.[6]

Directly incorporating Western-style psychological assessment and intervention into personnel management is novel in China. Its rapid application to the military, paramilitary, and police forces is especially startling given how such practices were perceived as foreign and incompatible with socialist revolutionary causes in even the recent past. But in just a short period of time, psychological education and services have been recognized and promoted by the military and police authorities to strengthen their forces. For example, the Public Security Ministry launched a system-wide campaign in 2008 to expand and improve "psychological training, counseling service, and crisis intervention" for all police officers throughout the nation. The first experimental training center of this kind was established in Guangdong Province to conduct psychological intervention on selected police officers. Then in 2009, the top Chinese military command issued an unprecedented mandate, titled "Of Strengthening Military Psychological Service Work under the New Circumstances," urging local military units to integrate psychological techniques into their work so as to improve combat effectiveness. It also endorsed the establishment of individual psychological profile records for all officers and soldiers. The three major goals of this mandate are: (1) to analyze the impact of major police or military actions on the psyches of the personnel; (2) to predict and understand the changing patterns of their psychological conditions; (3) to enhance the resilience and stability of the forces while reducing the negative impact of stress, especially PTSD. In addition to testing and assessing, newly trained military counselors also engaged in limited individual counseling with soldiers to help "untie the knot of the heart" (*dakai xinjie*) even though many soldiers were guarded as to how much to reveal.[7] These top-down initiatives demonstrate that the Chinese authorities are willing to openly adopt Western psychological techniques in the hope of better managing the armed forces. This change marks a turning point in recent PRC history that the Western clinical/medical gaze has extended into the inner world of soldiers. What matters is not just a strong disciplined body but also a predictable mind and steadfast emotions to better serve the state.

Applying psychological techniques to the military and police forces is not new in other parts of the world. The United States has long been at the forefront of such experiments. During World War II, the US military began to use psychological testing during recruitment to dismiss those who were deemed unfit to endure war trauma. In more recent years, a distinct branch of psychology called "positive psychology" has made its way into the US Army. According to a cover story that appeared in the September 2010 issue of *Harper's Magazine*, Martin Seligman, the past president of the American Psychological Association and the founding father of positive psychology, had been courted by the Pentagon to teach soldiers to learn optimism and gain resilience in order to flourish under harsh combat conditions (Greenberg 2008). The goal of psychology today, as advocated by Seligman, is not to treat mental pathology, but to enhance well-being and build emotional strength (Seligman 1991, 2002). Such close collaborations between the government and the mental health system in advanced liberal societies are controversial. Some see more danger than benefit in adopting psychological intervention in the name of care (see Castel, Castel, and Lovell 1979).[8] Despite the debate on the ethical concerns of psychologists' involvement in military training, it is clear that there has emerged a global trend of embracing therapeutic governing in neoliberal times (see Young 2014; Raikhel 2016). China is still in the early stage of such endeavors.

What makes the Chinese situation even more complicated is the continued effect of socialist political legacies, through which the new therapeutics intersect. This intricate dynamic of different ethics and concerns is well articulated by one of my informants, Ms. Zhou, a police officer and a self-trained counselor in her mid-thirties. When I first met her in 2012, she had already emerged as one of the few well-known psychological health educators in the Kunming police system, even though she had obtained her counseling certificate only four years previously. A mutual friend introduced us at a restaurant over lunch. Zhou, slim and of medium height, showed up in her civilian clothes. She was very modest, but my friend told me later that she was a gifted and popular public speaker with affective power. She was frequently invited to run workshops to train new psy experts among selected police officers and give lectures to local police units in several large city districts on how to manage stress, reduce workplace conflicts, and cultivate balanced mental well-being.

The biggest challenge Zhou faced was to negotiate two points of tension: First, there are diverging demands and expectations from the leaders above and ordinary police officers. On the one hand, party leaders want to get a better sense of the "pulse" of their police unit in order to foresee problems before they arise, thus they mandate regular reports from Zhou based on her counseling work. On the other, individual police officers hope to obtain professional help to deal with their personal problems such as stress, depression, PTSD, and interpersonal conflicts. Reporting would violate the trust between the therapist and the client. But in the military context, the principle of confidentiality in counseling is often not well observed, as it clashes with strict official order and discipline. Given this dilemma, building trust between the therapist and the officers is essential but difficult.

Second, there is a thin line between socialist thought work and therapeutic work.[9] Zhou's dual identity as a Communist Party member and a counselor mean that her professional goals and political loyalty are often in friction with one another. As we were eating, she looked away for a minute as if she was thinking about something. Then, she said to me: "I often feel caught in between. I am grateful for my superiors who support me in my new line of work, but at the same time, they dictate how things should be done and expect me to play an old role with a new face. If I am not careful, I can easily become their instrument of control and lose the trust of the officers." Zhou was genuinely interested in helping police officers improve their quality of life. She cared about their well-being and wanted to teach them how to manage stress, deal with trauma, and articulate their emotional problems. She loved offering individual counseling and collective workshops and regarded this work rewarding in comparison with political thought work. But beneath the lure of the new therapeutics lies sustained pressure to serve the existing power structure and hierarchical rule. This dilemma is widely shared by other counselors I have interviewed. In particular, counselors working in the military and police settings are more constrained in their therapeutic efforts than those working in civilian organizations. There are politically bounded limits to their roles as heart-to-heart listeners and caring healers.

There are also other practical obstacles in this new terrain of therapeutic work. Very few people within the military and the police have had professional training in how to conduct psychological work. They know very little about what psychology and counseling can offer in this highly hierarchical and masculine environment. Even though the higher-level authorities, who also do not know much about the use of psychotherapeutics, have now endorsed the incorporation of psychological tools, most military officers and cadres on the ground remain skeptical about the efficacy of psychology and counseling in improving combat effectiveness and the stability of the armed forces. Thus, there is a big gap between the idealized vision articulated from above and the actual enactment. Local-level authorities are not always willing to provide necessary financial and moral support, but only pay lip service to soldiers' psychological health to meet mandates from their superiors.

Back at the paramilitary hospital, Ms. Yang, told me a story of how pioneer psychological workers like her managed to start from scratch without much institutional support:

> Our psychological branch was created in 2006 under the order of the military authorities above, but it was far from being ready to operate. I was appointed to lead this new department just because I had studied psychology in my spare time and had just obtained my counseling certificate earlier that year. Soon two other people (an old nurse and a young doctor) who had almost zero training in psychology and counseling were assigned to our branch. This is very typical in the military, that you do not ask why but simply carry out the order. I was so scared and confused because I had no idea how to run a place like this and what to do. I was frantically searching on the internet, making phone calls, and visiting civilian counseling offices elsewhere to try to get a sense of what equipment we needed, what our office should look like, what services should be provided. Essentially, we had no guidance and I was on my own to figure everything out.

Her account about how counseling work was implemented in state-owned organizations is very typical. Usually when an official order was issued, people scrambled to put a team together or establish an office to show that they followed the order, but they could hardly engage in any real work. Those who are put in this line of work tend to be under-trained and have few resources to work with. Leaders hope that with its perceived scientific power, the new psychotherapeutic tools can become a means of foreseeing and solving problems. It can also replace the socialist thought work that is losing its appeal among the younger generation. But in general, leaders have no clue about how psychological work is done and whether it works for the military and the police.

A new task assigned to grassroots counselors is to create psychological files for personnel in their work units. The use of *dangan* (personnel files) is not new to China. This practice to keep track of citizens' behavior has a long history in most socialist states (see Verdery 1996, 2014). As a tool of surveillance and control, *dangan* is designed to produce traceable knowledge about each citizen and map out the social landscape for the party-state in power.[10] In the past, dangan usually consisted of comments and evaluations concerning one's personality, communication skills, political attitude and behavior, and social relationship with others. It was usually written by one's supervisors, teachers, or the personnel division director who was usually a party cadre. The content was accumulative and would follow a person from early school years to work units. Most remarks were mundane but occasionally negative notes (such as violating an ethical code of conduct or participating in impermissible activities) could be recorded and would have a significant impact on one's life trajectory. I remember while growing up I was always wondering and at times anxious about what was written in my *dangan*, which I never saw. It remained a mystery to me and served as a powerful mechanism to regulate my social and political behavior at the time.

What is new today is a heightened attention to the psychological and mental aspects of a person. More striking is the desire to incorporate Western testing methods and psychological language in generating such records for personnel. The notion of "scientific method" is particularly invoked to claim validity for creating the psychological dangan of soldiers and officers. The key elements recorded include: (1) personal growth history—covering basic information about the individual and his/her family background and upbringing; (2) individual cognitive abilities—including one's level of awareness, understanding, judgment, and so on, observed by the psy professionals; (3) personality traits—measured by using the Eysenck Personality Questionnaire (EPQ); and (4) an assessment of one's overall psychological state of being, which is often measured by the Minnesota Multiphasic Personality Inventory (MMPI). These aspects together form the psychological quality (*xinli suzhi* 心理素质) of a person. These psychological testing tools, new to most Chinese people, tend to hold mysterious power due to the scientific aura attached to them.[11]

It is not hard to imagine that creating comprehensive psychological files in a work unit of several thousand people is a time-consuming and labor-intensive undertaking. With only a couple of counselors, the task is even more arduous. While military authorities in some areas have begun to utilize such data to evaluate a candidate's qualification for promotion or identify individuals with mental distress for targeted intervention, the majority of files simply sit in the office cabinets gathering dust. Still in the early stage of experiment, the stated potential for managing troops through psychotherapeutics has not yet been fully realized. But things are gradually changing in recent years. When I met Ms. Yang for the first time in 2009, her work was limited to establishing psychological files for some two hundred newly admitted paramilitary soldiers. After the initial screening, two young men were identified as having mental illness and were subsequently dismissed. When I returned to visit Yang two years later, she reported that "psychological fitness" was beginning to be considered as an important factor in the evaluation for promotion.[12] A psychological profile would help determine whether a candidate was capable of handling challenging tasks or had a suitable personality for assuming a leadership role. Since much of this prediction was driven by test results and numbers, I asked her about the reliability of such new testing and profiling. She was quite ambivalent about it but said that if the military leaders decided that the new psychological techniques were better than the old methods, they must follow the order regardless of the actual effectiveness. Yet, it remains highly debatable whether such new measures in the name of science are more objective and reliable than the old-fashioned way of observation by superiors.

During my conversations with Yang, I was curious about what common problems were found among soldiers requiring psychological and administrative interventions. She identified two. First, many of them have trouble handling social relationships and in managing their emotions. Fear, homesickness, anxiety, and stress are common and may intensify after leaving home for military service. Some of them experience depression, anxiety disorders, or restlessness. Yang's explanation is that in recent years the new recruits tend to have been born after the 1990s, and many of them are the single child in the family or come from a divorced family. Thus, they tend to be self-centered and have few communication skills and little experience with material hardship in their life (see also Fong 2006). The sudden transition to a collective lifestyle under rigid military discipline poses a big challenge to them and causes maladaptive behavior.

Second, Chinese military and paramilitary troops are regularly called to perform disaster relief work and other dangerous rescue missions (such as for earthquakes and flooding). The exposure to gruesome scenes and high pressure place them in higher risk for PTSD—a new category of illness that did not exist in China until recent years.[13] "But we are very cautious about making any diagnosis, because mental illness labeling can have serious consequences for the soldiers. Therefore, we try to focus on education and prevention through lectures or collective workshops rather than individual counseling," said Ms. Yang. In general, I find that mental or psychological illnesses are more stigmatized in the military and police than that in the civilian setting. But ironically, due to the demanding and stressful nature of military and police work, its members are more likely to experience traumas and psychological disturbance. It is in this context that positive psychology, which promises to cultivate well-being and resiliency in the broader social context (rather than treating mental illness in a medicalized language), appears very appealing to some military counselors.[14] They must tread lightly to figure out what is socially and politically acceptable and unacceptable in carrying out mental health work.

If the military organizational structure is more hierarchical and driven by official mandate, the civilian setting allows more flexibility but also presents different challenges. Next, we will turn to look at why and how some state-owned enterprises (SOE) embrace therapeutic governing.

ENHANCING PRODUCTIVITY, REDUCING CONFLICTS

The taxi I took was circling around an area dotted by many luxury resorts near beautiful Lake Dian. The driver was a bit lost and frustrated trying to find the particular hotel I wanted to go to. "Too many resorts here! They all look alike and have similar names," he grumbled. Finally, he found the place and dropped me off. I was already late and rushed into the hotel lobby looking for the workshop I was going to attend. It was the summer of 2012. I was very excited that my friend Mr. Ling, a self-fashioned, well-known therapist, invited me to participate in a three-day training workshop whose theme was "Fostering Positive Mindset and Happiness in Workplace." The workshop was specifically designed to enhance human resources development for a large local tobacco firm, Yunda, which paid the entire cost (over 30,000 yuan). Because of his extensive experience in psychologically related training work for many local enterprises, Ling and two of his assistants were invited by Yunda to carry out a series of workshops for its employees. Each time, thirty to forty people were selected by the firm to participate, and this one I joined was the fourth in the series.

Every day we began with twenty minutes of relaxation and meditation practices accompanied by smooth New Age music or nature sounds (such as raindrops falling, birds singing, ocean waves). A female assistant drew the curtains down and guided us with her soft voice: "Take a deep breath. Close your eyes. Let go of all your worries." Then we gradually moved into the instruction part. Mr. Ling stressed in the beginning, "This workshop is very different from any other organized activities you have encountered before. This is participant-centered and experiential (*tiyan*). We observe the following principles—sharing one's experiences and feelings openly, fully accepting others, listening attentively, and being nonjudgmental and egalitarian." In short, he presented the workshop as a safe haven for self-exploration and a reliable path to authentic happiness—an antidote to the confusion and distress caused by recent social and structural changes. He did so not through lecturing but through what Chinese people call "tiyan," which literarily means using your body to experience something.

The core of his teaching was based on Martin Seligman's positive psychology and Satir family therapy with a focus on interpersonal communication skills.[15] He told the audience: "I am not a psychiatrist to treat your mental illness here. I am a therapist whose goal is to help you nurture positive emotions and foster healthy familial and interpersonal relationships. Resilience and happiness can be cultivated if you intend to do so and have the right tool." His tone was upbeat and assuring, as if he could sense the hidden yearning for living a good life among the participants.

As he spoke, I looked around the small conference room, in which thirty-six of us were sitting. Some people looked attentive and hopeful; others appeared to be unsure, checking their smart phones occasionally. Ling noticed that some were drifting, so he added more personal stories and interactive sessions to his lectures. For example, participants were given time to practice attentive listening and being listened to while identifying their own strengths in front of others. After we were all paired up, we each listened to our partner speaking about his or her own background and favorite activities for three minutes, and then we summarized what was said in one minute. Some people started to laugh as they were surprised how much information was missed or misheard in this process. Ling explained that this practice was important because careful listening was not only the first step for communication but also the basis for engineering social recognition. A common complaint SOE workers had was that no one listened to them, and they were the passive recipients of policy changes. Thus, they felt that their worth was not validated and their contribution was not appreciated. Attentive listening practiced here addressed this problem, albeit in a limited way.

Next, we practiced building mutual trust and team spirit through bodily interaction. Five people were grouped together and one of them was asked to lean back completely, letting go of all control, with the others standing behind to catch the person (a "trust fall"). It was a worthy exercise because most of us had never tried such a thing before. Some had difficulty in trusting others and struggled to let go. Ling underscored the centrality of cultivating trust in a workplace and believed in working on clients' affective level rather than their rational thinking. "Trust does not exist naturally or emerge in abstract thinking. It needs to be nurtured through frequent collaboration and it comes from the heart, not the brain," added Ling.

To understand why the talk of happiness, personal fulfillment, and harmony is gaining traction in Chinese state-owned enterprises, one must take into account the profound transformations that the SOEs have gone through and the new challenges facing them during the period of economic reform. After massive privatization of the state-owned enterprises in the late 1990s, the remaining state firms had to dramatically reform their operations to enhance productivity so as to stay competitive in the new market economy. Yunda was one of the few large, lucrative firms in Yunnan Province, as it monopolized the entire tobacco industry—the most important pillar of the regional economy.[16] However, this firm was also under pressure to improve efficiency by adopting new production methods and management styles. These structural changes put workers under greater pressure to perform better and compete with one another for limited material resources in the company. The situation generated grassroots resistance and a great deal of anxiety. Discontent among SOE employees was on the rise. It was telling that at the beginning of the workshop Ling conducted a quick survey in which 90 percent of the participants reported a very low "happiness index"—a popular, imported, well-being measurement guide frequently invoked by Chinese leaders and psychological professionals in recent years. Upper-level managers were deeply

concerned about an alarming culture of complaints among disgruntled workers. Yet they did not know how to curb it effectively.

Every day after the workshop, everyone was treated with a ten-course dinner prepared by the resort in the banquet room. At our last dinner, I happened
to sit next to the head of Yunda's human resource management division, Mr.
Wu, a thin, middle-aged man with a Red Pagoda cigarette in hand. Knowing
that I was Ling's friend and a professor from America, he was very polite to
me. After he poured some red wine in my glass, I thanked him and asked why
he wanted to sponsor this training series for the employees. He took a long
drag on the cigarette and then replied with a big sigh:

> To tell you the truth, it is extremely difficult to do employee work nowadays. They
> appear to be irritable, grumpy, and defiant toward any form of authority. The old
> thought-work method based on political persuasion does not work anymore, while
> the new material-based method based on monetary reward does not seem to work
> either. I have tried everything, but in vain. A friend of mine suggested that I try
> to incorporate psychotherapeutic techniques. So I approached Mr. Ling. After
> the first session, I noticed some positive changes already taking place among the
> participants. They became calmer, more positive, and less confrontational.

Despite many changes brought by the reform, most Chinese state enterprises still require party leaders to perform *zhigong gongzuo* (workers' work),
which usually entails shaping the mindset, attitude, and quality of life of the
employees. The human resources division is typically responsible not only for
hiring and salary, but also this type of "thought work," combined with other
acts of care for employees—a socialist legacy. Yet today most workers have
become deaf to what they deem as dull and formulaic political thought work
devoid of any meaning. Therefore, when they are exposed to new psychologically oriented training like this workshop, they find it quite refreshing and
useful for improving their personal, family, and social life. The depoliticized
language of self-care and the professional guidance for emotional well-being
appear to be liberating and heart-warming, especially to those feeling worn
out and stuck in their workplace.[17]

In this kind of training, proper management of emotions (instead of socioeconomic problems) becomes the focus of therapeutic intervention. As Mr. Wu
succinctly put it, "Our goal is to instill a positive outlook on life among workers
by using positive psychology, while making them realize that even if one cannot
change the reality, one still has control over how to respond. And this realization
is powerful and helpful!" As a mid-level cadre, Wu wanted the workers to feel

more contented, which would make his job easier. For this reason, he was willing to try new approaches like psychological coaching. His bold act was not without risk in the beginning. When he first broached this idea to the top firm leaders a few years ago, they thought he was out of his mind, since it was rare for any SOEs to integrate psychology in personnel management. But he did not give up. When the psy fever spread further and positive psychology became popular, he proposed his idea again and provided evidence of how this new approach worked for other enterprises in Beijing and Shanghai. Finally, Wu successfully persuaded the firm leadership to let him try with sufficient funding. When the first workshop produced desirable results, he contracted Ling's team for a series of six segments aiming to train about two hundred fifty employees.

One can easily launch a criticism of such a therapeutic approach for its inherent risk of interpreting social and economic problems and conflicts in psychological terms. Yet, at the same time, I argue that one cannot easily disregard its impact on Chinese workers. For those I spoke to, the new therapeutic attention to emotions and affects was an appealing alternative to political thought work that had bored or haunted them for years. The personal and visceral transformations they experience through such workshops—feeling happier, being recognized and validated (albeit short-lived in some cases)—should not be simply dismissed as a result of "false consciousness." For example, Xiao Wang, who was in his mid-thirties and held a mid-level technical position in the cigarette production line, was very cynical toward the workshop in the beginning. In his eyes, this was merely a diversion strategy and another subtle way of the authorities brainwashing and controlling them to avoid dealing with the real problems. But since the event was paid for by the firm and there were nice meals offered every day at a luxury resort, he agreed to come. During the first day, he challenged Mr. Ling's teaching frequently and asked tough questions. At times he just fell asleep. However, as time went by, he grew more and more interested in learning the "science of happiness" and theory about personality traits. He even participated in experimenting with the techniques of improving family and interpersonal dynamics from the Satir Model. In the end, he told me that he came to realize this: "What I have learned here turns out to be very helpful to my personal life. Rather than being told how to obey authorities and devote myself to work, this time I am told that it is OK to focus on myself, my feelings, my concerns, and it is OK to foster a relatively open and egalitarian form of communication with my coworkers and bosses. I have come to realize that even if I cannot change the system, it is still possible to create some happiness and retain certain control of my life." His words nicely reveal the complex situation facing Chinese workers like him: On the one hand, he was fully aware of the powerful structural forces shaping his life and his inability to change the newly reformed work system; on the other, he grew more willing to accept therapeutic tools to improve his coping strategies and personal condition.

Thus, unlike the top-down analytics used by Polsky and Szasz, psychology and counseling programs as they are deployed in China serve to govern and heal the population simultaneously. Further, the ways in which this form of therapeutic governing works out in the Chinese context are subtler and more effective. For example, Xiao Wang's shift from cynicism to acceptance was heartfelt, as he sensed some palpable positive impact on his life and well-being. Yet, it is important to point out that Nikolas Rose's (1999) argument about the psy disciplines helping govern through freedom in liberal democratic societies does not work in the same way in China. As my account demonstrates, the notion of freedom is not widely invoked or shared; rather it is the art of managing the complex relationships between the self and sociality, between self-care and social obligations that is central to therapeutic governing.

What we witness in Chinese firms resonates well with what Eva Illouz calls "a new emotional style" of corporate management in postindustrial capitalist societies. In her insightful book *Cold Intimacies*, Illouz makes a compelling argument that the making of capitalism is inextricably intertwined with the making of emotions. She demonstrates how the twentieth-century therapeutic culture has eroded the boundaries between the private and the public, the inner and the outer, by making emotional life central to the workplace (2007: 16). For this reason, she coins the notion, "emotional capitalism," to refer to "a culture in which emotional and economic discourses and practices mutually shape each other" (2007: 5). It is in this context that she argues that psychologists and counselors, armed with special knowledge, have become the experts to improve human relations and increase productivity. She further explains the crux of this shift: "Psychologists seemed to promise nothing less than to increase profits, fight labor unrest, organize manager-worker relationships in a non-confrontational way, and neutralize class struggles by casting them in the benign language of emotions and personality" (Illouz 2007: 17). Yet, as she shows, many workers find this new language of psychology appealing and helpful because it appears to be democratic and personal. The twin goals of equality and cooperation can enable new forms of sociality but also put new constraints on the conduct of social relations. Therefore, they are double-edged swords, and their effect depends on how they are used.

Illouz's incisive analysis is pertinent to my attempt to understand the shift toward making the management of emotional life central to Chinese corporations in recent years. SOEs are now under double pressure: to become more efficient and profitable to survive in a market economy, and to maintain the political stability and social harmony mandated by the party-state. It seems to me that the new psychotherapeutic approach to emotional management and communication style can partially serve to ease the tension between workers and managers by shifting one's focus from structural problems to a subjective realm of personality, emotions, and social recognition. By recognizing, accepting, and validating workers' feelings, personnel managers like Mr. Wu can at least foster a sense of social recognition that workers appreciate and make their managerial job relevant once again in an era of changing values and expectations.

REFLECTION

In this chapter, I have tried to outline an emergent terrain in which psychotherapeutic knowledge and techniques are being gradually incorporated into postsocialist governing through the idiom of guan ai. Although my focus is on the military, the police, and state enterprises, this trend extends into other organizations and social domains. The language of therapeutic care (rather than the language of political control) is deployed to define the logic of this new form of governing based on affective politics.[18] There is a tendency to psychologize various kinds of social and interpersonal problems as Chinese human resource managers creatively incorporate counseling techniques into their work. They do so by using a depoliticized language of therapy (thus bypassing socialist thought work) to reshape workers' affective sphere in the hope of governing better. The expansion of therapeutic techniques beyond the medical setting into work, military, and other social domains is significant because it allows fuller engagement of subjects' minds and bodies in a way that appears to be benign and apolitical.

Further, the impact of this therapeutic turn goes even more deeply than the level of managerial styles because it inevitably entails the remaking of soldiers, police officers, and workers into new subjects through simultaneously being both governed and cared for. It is in this broader sense that I speak of "therapeutic governing" to highlight how the "psy fever" not only reconfigures governing practices but also remakes postsocialist subjects. In light of this, I suggest that the key question we need to ask today is not whether state power is increasing or penetrating further into society but, rather, how a different mode of governing that draws upon the expertise of psychological specialists in the name of therapeutic care is transforming Chinese organizational life, the modality of power, and citizen-subjects from the inside out.

As I have shown, however, this shift toward affective power is not a linear process but one full of contradictions. Most grassroots psy specialists working for the military, the police, and the state enterprises are not callous pawns of the Chinese state, but are genuinely interested in the therapeutic and caring dimension of their work. Yet they are also aware that their efforts can be easily tainted and appropriated by the political authorities for other purposes, causing harm to their clients. Since many of these psy experts inhabit a double identity as professional counselors and a party members, they must cautiously walk a fine line between two different sets of interests and demands from the clients and the party-state. In the emerging postsocialist regime of China, knowing, caring, and regulating is coalescing together beyond conventional boundaries. There exist constant frictions among these divergent efforts, so difficult choices between serving the clients or serving the party must be made from time to time. In the new therapeutic culture, it is increasingly difficult to discern what efforts are intended to increase work efficiency and social stability, and what efforts are intended to enhance individual psychological well-being and emotional outlook. The intertwining of these interests and practices thus further complicates the intricate nature of therapeutic governing in reform-era China.

Finally, much of what I have delineated here is experimental and sometimes controversial in Chinese society. Whether the therapeutic turn will lead to a state of "human flourishing" and create greater resilience among the people as some positive psychologists have envisioned (Seligman 1991) or enable a form of subtle and deeper social control or "kindly power" (Yang 2015) remains to be seen. But for China, the Pandora's box of psychological practices is already wide open. We are likely to encounter an ambiguous period where the new mode of care/governing blends psychology, affective care, and politics together in an attempt to manage rising social distress and potential friction as China continues its postsocialist transformations.

Epilogue

As I was wrapping up my research for this book in September of 2017, the Chinese state made an announcement that stunned everyone in the counseling field: Psychotherapy certification was removed from the existing one hundred forty officially recognized professions. This meant that the national psychotherapist certification program, which was launched in 2002, would cease to exist after being in place for fifteen years. It was estimated that by 2017 between two hundred thousand to six hundred thousand people had acquired certificates through this program.[1] This bombshell decision shook the entire Chinese counseling world and caused widespread confusion, anxiety, and resentment. For several months, the Chinese counseling realm was chaotic. Those who had already been certified thought that their paperwork had become worthless overnight; those who were preparing to take the exam lamented that they might just have missed the last train; the agencies that had profited for years from offering prep courses and testing feared that they would soon be out of business. The clients in treatment were worried that their therapists would simply disappear and leave them helpless.

After the initial shock settled, many professionals and prominent figures in counseling began to contemplate the implications of this dramatic state decision. They came to conclude that this change did not mean that the state would eliminate the counseling profession or suppress psychotherapy; rather, it signaled a move toward decentralization and reconfiguration. For instance, Dr. Lingchun from the Chinese Science Academy explains: "The profession still exists, but the state has decided to withdraw from the business of certification." In other words, in the future local professional psychological organizations and associations, not the central government agencies, will be encouraged to certify practitioners and step up their regulatory roles. Yet, as I write this epilogue, no specific guidelines and plans for how decentralization should be carried out are available.

It has been almost ten years since I began my preliminary research for this book. A lot has happened and changed since then. Psychological counseling has evolved from a novel practice and marginal profession to a widely recognized technology of self-regulation and emotional management for individuals, families, and organizations in Chinese cities. Despite having acquired material comfort, middle-class members, particularly women, are keen to learn new psy tools to manage their emotional and psychological crises. The state has shifted its stand from initial reluctance and skepticism to a more welcoming but selective appropriation of this new intervention in improving the well-being of the population and the productivity of the workforce.

But the recent decision to terminate the certification program was puzzling to many. I spoke to several therapists in Kunming recently and asked for their reactions. They admitted that it took them a few months to process the news, but, in the end, they did not seem overly worried about their practices. They argued that "the need for psychological service is there no matter what; therefore, market demand will guarantee the existence of the profession." They speculated that the government probably realized that the national accreditation program had issued too many certificates and most recipients were unqualified. Thus, it was better to halt it and figure out new ways to regulate this young profession. At this point, it is hard to tell whether this is merely an optimistic interpretation on their part or a true beginning of government efforts to reshape this "Wild West"—like field.

Another significant move by the Chinese party-state took place about a year prior to this cancellation announcement. On October 25, 2016, the central government released the "Healthy China 2030 Blueprint," outlining the principles, rationales, and steps to improve the macro-health of the Chinese population over the next fifteen years.[2] It declares that "human health is an important indication of a prosperous nation and a strong state." Although there had been some health-related campaigns in socialist history, this is the first time that the health and well-being of the nation have been considered of paramount strategic importance and placed on the very top of the government's agenda and long-term planning. As President Xi asserted, "Without the whole population's health, there will be no comprehensive *xiaokang shen-ghuo* 小康生活."[3] From this perspective, population health is one of the cornerstones of the nation's welfare and the very foundation of sustainable development and the ambitious new "China Dream" that Xi has promoted.

In my view, the "Healthy China 2030 Blueprint" is significant because it represents a vital shift in postsocialist governmentality in China. In his essay "The Politics of Health in the Eighteenth Century," Michel Foucault put forward the notion of "noso-politics" (a form of biopolitics based on treating diseases) to highlight the deep-seated linkage between the state of a population's health and the mode of governing.[4] He writes, "No doubt there is no society which does not practice some kind of 'noso-politics': the eighteenth century didn't invent this. But it prescribed new rules, and above all transposed the practice on to an explicit, concerted level of analysis such as had been previously unknown. At this point the age is entered not so much of social medicine as of a considered noso-politics" (1980: 167). Thus, noso-politics foregrounds disease control and the health of the population as a key problematic of contemporary government.

I find that Foucault's notion, "noso-politics," nicely captures the essence of what is happening in China today. This is the first time in the history of the People's Republic of China that the health and physical/mental well-being of the entire population is underscored as an essential objective of political power. And this shift is consistent with what Foucault has characterized as modern governmentality. In contrast with sovereignty, the ultimate goal of government is to optimize "the welfare of the population, the improvement of its condition, the increase of its wealth, longevity, health, etc." (1991: 100). Several China scholars such as Susan Greenhalgh, Edwin Winckler, and Everett Zhang have demonstrated how the population became a central concern of governing for modern Chinese state over the past several decades (see also Kohrman 2004; Mason 2016; Cho 2013 on Chinese biopolitics). For Greenhalgh and Winckler, it is through what they call "the governmentalization of the population" (2005) that took place in the decades since 1980; for Zhang, it is through the combination of Western influence and the homegrown Chinese notion of *minsheng* (民生), the idea that the livelihood of every living being in the population is presented as the objective of post-Mao governmentality (2011).

While the concerns for health and the use of medical intervention to improve the well-being of the population were part of the transformations these researchers illustrated, never before were they made so explicitly, so central, and so detailed as the "Healthy China 2030 Blueprint" does. This plan accentuates two big aims: (1) promoting "*da jiankang* 大健康" (macro-health), which refers to a long-term, holistic approach to the health of the people/masses (*renmin qunzhong*), not just individuals; (2) focusing on "*jibing zhiliao* 疾病治疗" (treatment of diseases), which targets major illnesses afflicting the Chinese population, such as cancers, heart diseases, diabetes, tuberculosis, HIV/AIDS, and other infectious diseases. The plan also calls for the enhancement of health education, health care service, and preventive medicine for the entire Chinese society.

The general reaction of the public to the "Healthy China" plan is positive so far, but many have serious doubts about its real effects. Past experiences point to a familiar pattern, in which state initiatives like this one tend to make a lot of noise in the beginning but fall short in practice, and they tend to promise far more than what they can accomplish. Chinese health care professionals are particularly concerned that this national project will become another hollow political campaign that pressures them to meet unrealistic quotas and make a big show of busy activity without producing any meaningful impact on people's lives.

Indeed, soon after the blueprint was released, the Chinese State Council launched a national program called "Poverty Relief through Health" (*jiankang fupin* 健康扶贫). Urban doctors, nurses, and psychologists are pressed to visit rural villages and poor areas and offer free health education, treatment, psychological counseling, and other services. These efforts have become part of a top-down political mandate to be fulfilled, much like the kind of state projects Jie Yang (2013c) has documented as "*song wennuan*" ("sending warmth") to the unemployed workers. Reading the official documents and interpretations, one cannot help but notice that the language used in them is strikingly familiar to the ones used in previous socialist political campaigns—it is full of exaggerated numbers and unrealistic goals. When I visited Kunming this summer in 2018, a psychological counselor I worked with at the provincial health institute told me how she saw this state project: "When you watch the actual practice on the ground, you would know it is hopeless and ridiculous. All that local government and state agencies care about is to produce some impressive numbers such as the scale and coverage ratio (*fugai mian*) of service. We were told to just train a few people in each village through a couple of lessons and send them out to help others in psychological distress. This way, the coverage of service percentage would shoot up. But how is it possible to train a counselor in a day or two? This is totally ignorant and irresponsible! I do not know if I should cry or laugh." She was shaking her head as she let out a big sigh. But then she added, "I suppose having a plan and an objective is better than nothing. At least now physical and psychological health is on the radar screen of the government."

This book is largely based on my years of ethnographic fieldwork in one Chinese city—Kunming, a midsized metropolitan area located in China's borderland. This place has its advantages (under less strict political scrutiny, more space for experimentation with new ideas) and disadvantages (slower pace of change and less global exposure) in the development of psychological counseling. Yet, the affective experiences, therapeutic politics, and sweeping changes in subjectivity and sociality I document through my research resonate well with those of other Chinese cities (for example, Beijing and Shanghai as studied by anthropologists Jie Yang and Huang Hsuan-Ying). It is not my intention to generalize what I have learned from Kunming to urban China as a whole, but I hope that this study can offer a window into a changing world in which affects, sociality, and politics become deeply entangled with one another and mediated by a new therapeutic culture.

In the years to come, as Chinese society moves into a new era envisioned by the Xi regime as a "Healthy China" and the "China Dream," the inner revolution I trace in this book will continue to expand and intensify. Today, what is most fascinating, in my view, is the application of human and health sciences to Chinese people's interior lives—their hearts and minds, and the extent to which psychological science in particular is seen as vital for individuals and families to flourish and achieve the good life. Psychotherapeutic intervention in a variety of forms will thus play an even more important role in reconfiguring the personal, social, and political realms of an anxious society that is undergoing unprecedented structural and cultural transformations while still aspiring for the fantasy of the good life.

NOTES

INTRODUCTION

1. All the names of my informants in this book are pseudonyms. I have also altered some aspects of their lives in order to disguise their identity. The woman I call "Hongnan" is comfortable with the way I presented her story here and has in recent years shared her experience with her friends and become very vocal about mental health awareness.

2. Sing Lee has demonstrated that "social change in China has real social consequences in the mental health arena," particularly with regard to the rising prevalence of depression (2011:178). See also Emily Ng's research (2009).

3. See "100 Million People Suffer Depression in China," *China Daily*, November 28, 2016, http://www.chinadaily.com.cn/china/2016-11/28/content_27501518.htm.

4. The number of people seeking such help is increasing steadily according to various reports and my interviews with therapists. The Chinese Psychological Society and the Chinese Psychotherapy Networks all claim that the demand is increasing rapidly. My interviews with the therapists in Kunming also indicate that they have more clients every year. Some have doubled or tripled the number of clients over the past five years. I have tried to research on this issue, but there are no reliable data available at this point on the actual number of help seekers.

5. This statement may be a bit too sweeping, since part of traditional Chinese culture (such as Confucianism) also encouraged self-cultivation, but the point is that this focus on personal emotional conditions represents a significant shift in recent Chinese history.

6. I use the term *postsocialist* to refer to a unique condition, under which China has largely embraced global market capitalism while the legacies of socialist values and practices remain salient in many social and political domains.

7. A Chinese therapist and writer provocatively called this phenomenon "a psychological revolution" (*xinli geming*) to highlight its scale and impact (Liu 2011).

8. Such popular self-help projects are sometimes lumped in the genre called *xinling jitang* 心灵鸡汤 (the chicken soup for the soul); this framing is less stigmatized and more accessible (see Zhang, Y. 2014; Bunkenborg 2014).

9. Although it is difficult to identify a direct causal relationship between recent societal transformations and the rising popularity of psychological care and mental health in China, it is clear that this is the context in which the new counseling movement is unfolding. I am inspired by newer phenomenological approaches seeking to link subjective and intersubjective experiences to broader political, social, and structural forces (Desjarlais and Throop 2011).

10. Jie Yang cites Chinese sociologist Zhou Xiaohong, who regards anxiety as "an epochal syndrome of the rapidly changing Chinese society" (2018: 39). Yang uses another phrase, "the heart of China's economy" (2015) to describe the emotional consequences of the economic reform and emphasize the importance of the psychological dimension in understanding Chinese society. I prefer the word *pulse* because it is commonly used in traditional Chinese medicine and adopted by ordinary people in their everyday language.

11. A team of Chinese researchers have recently completed a cross-sectional epidemiological survey of more than thirty-two thousand people in China and found that anxiety disorders were the most common problems among them (Huang et al. 2019). They attribute the rising psychological pressure and stress to China's rapid social change.

12. Some forty years ago, the poet W. H. Auden published a long six-part poem "The Age of Anxiety" describing what he saw as the troubling human condition. Writer Alex Williams suggests that today this condition has become a shared cultural experience that "metastasizes through social media" (2017).

13. I thank Junko Kitanaka for bringing this important difference to my attention.

14. I am inspired by the concept "governing through science," developed by Susan Greenhalgh in her recent writing (2020).

15. This phenomenon is similar to what Tomas Matza (2018) has termed "psychosociality" formed in the context of Russian psychological practices.

16. Ativan is a brand name of a generic antianxiety drug called lorazepam, which belongs to a group of drugs called benzodiazepines. It affects chemicals in the brain that may be responsible for balancing anxiety. It is widely used in the United States.

17. In this book, I have tried to include some of my own personal and family's lived experiences. I will leave it to the readers to judge whether the incorporation of such self-narratives in my ethnographic account is effective and suitable.

18. According to a 2009 survey by Michael Philips et al. (cited in Cyranoski 2010), 17.5 percent of Chinese have some form of mental illness. Yet, the mental-health infrastructure is severely underdeveloped. The ratio of psychiatrists to the population is 1.5 per 100,000 people (Cyranoski 2010), and the ratio for counselors to the population is 2.4 per 1 million people (Lim et al. 2010). Michael Philips, Huaqing Liu, and Yanping Zhang (1999) suggest that China's suicide rate (largely among rural women) is one of

the highest in the world today and one of the reasons might be the lack of treatment for persons with depressive illness, although they also point to other important social factors that contribute to the high suicide rate.

19. See Sing Lee's (2011) account of the recent expansion of Big Pharma and the commercialization of depression in China. Yet there exists a strong aversion toward psychotropic drugs among Chinese for cultural reasons (see Ng 2009).

20. There was a significant change in 2017 regarding state policy of issuing certificates, which I discuss in detail in the epilogue.

21. Due to privacy concerns and the sensitivity of conducting any surveys in China, especially in the realm of mental health and personal problems, I chose to rely on qualitative materials—narratives and accounts provided by my informants.

22. Although the concept of "assemblage" has been largely associated with the work of Deleuze and Guattari (1987), in this book, I draw more specifically from the analysis of "global assemblages" developed by Collier and Ong (2005) and emphasize its ability "to speak of emergence, heterogeneity, the decentered and the ephemeral in nonetheless ordered social life" (Marcus and Saka 2006: 101).

23. Arthur Kleinman defines "somatization" as "the substitution of somatic reoccupation for dysphoric affect in the form of complaints of physical symptoms and even illness" (1980: 149).

24. Susan Brownell (1995) develops a different notion of somatization: Chinese people are often caught in a web of social interdependency, which is often expressed in conceptions of the body.

25. See also Cristiana Giordano's discussion of translation and difference in the context of making migrant subjectivities and citizenship in Italy (2008). She notes "To translate is simultaneously to betray and to be faithful to an original meaning; it produces both understanding and misunderstanding" (2014: 42).

26. Another dimension of this uneven power relations is the role of gender in counseling. See Yang (2013b).

27. The Chinese notion of self often contains three layers of meaning: spiritual, physical, and material (Huang 2005: 367).

28. Lawrence Kirmayer's work (2007) provides a useful starting point to think about the intimate interplay between psychotherapeutic techniques and cultural concepts of the person across different times and places.

29. In her study of bipolar disorder in China, Emily Ng (2009) points to the rise of a multifaceted individualism by analyzing generational difference in the location of agency. By contrast, Yunxiang Yan (2010) has argued that the individualization of Chinese society is the antithesis of individualism (see also Beck 1992). He insists that the two concepts are different: Individualism refers to a personal attitude or preference; individualization alludes to a macro-sociological phenomenon, which may or may not result in changes in personal attitudes.

30. My previous research on Chinese gated communities, for example, shows that real estate developers and property management agencies have become an important form of local authorities shaping and regulating urban community life (2010).

CHAPTER I. PSY FEVER

I. Emily Baum (2018) shows that the police administered the asylum in the early days and arrested vagrant and lunatics, which led to the association of mad people with a deviant identity (See also Chen 2003: 126).

2. Zhiying Ma points out that the Chinese family was often regarded by missionaries as an "iron cage" that chained the insane inside to protect the family's face (2014).

3. The book was translated into German in 1882, and then into English from German in 1891. Wang's translation was based on the English version. Hoggding incorporated many new developments in chemistry, physics, and biology into his account of psychology.

4. The dark side of psychiatry as a form of political control, torture, and punishment is also manifested in the Soviet Union's methods to deter dissidents and in the so-called "enhanced interrogation techniques" authorized by the Bush administration.

5. This is based on Chinese researchers' observations and no specific numbers are available. In the countryside, the need is there too but has not caught enough official and public attention.

6. By 2017 some rough estimates suggest the total number nationwide has exceeded three hundred thousand, but no reliable survey data are available.

7. Moreover, some recent research show that the national obsession with quality has extended from the social and cultural level to the biological and cellular level in reproductive health—sperm bank quality control (see Wahlberg 2018) and maternal serum screening for high-quality births (Zhu 2013).

8. Some Chinese universities reportedly asked their students to sign a contract waiving the university's responsibility in the event of student suicide, rather than strengthening counseling service (Grenoble 2013).

9. In China, there are two terms commonly used to refer to those practicing psychological counseling: *zixun shi* 咨询师 (counselors) and *zhiliao shi* 治疗师 (therapists). Although the latter carries slightly more medical weight than the former, they are not clearly differentiated and often used interchangeably in everyday conversations among Chinese people.

10. The exchange rate in the 2010s was roughly US$1 to ¥6.8.

11. In China Western medicines, especially psychotropic drugs are not allowed to be advertised on TV or radio. Thus, direct marketing and word of mouth are the common way of recruiting consumers.

12. Much of the information in this section is provided by a series of essays (author unknown) posted online at https://www.douban.com/group/topic/19622398/ in 2011, which detailed the historical development of early Sino-German engagement.

13. This quote is from Zhao Xudong's 2006 biography on the World Psychiatric Association-Transcultural Psychiatry Section website.

14. Later Zhao was promoted and moved to Shanghai to lead one of China's top medical universities, Tongji University.

CHAPTER 2. *BENTUHUA*: CULTURING PSYCHOTHERAPY

1. Compare Amy Borovoy's fascinating study of Japanese psychiatrist Takeo Doi's early attempt to develop an "indigenous" form of Japanese cultural psychology that can bridge ideas of relationalism and individualism, Japanese particularism and Western humanism (2012). See also Rong-Bang Peng's investigation into the indigenous psychology movement in Taiwan (2012).

2. Throughout this book, I mostly use the term "clients" (*zike* or *laifangzhe*) rather than "patients" (*bingren*) to refer to those who seek counseling and therapy from practitioners outside the hospital setting because this is how they are called in China due to the strong stigma attached to mental patients.

3. I translated all the documents and the application for this firm and thus had the opportunity to gain deeper knowledge of how this process worked and what motivated Chinese therapists to engage in the Satir Model. A more detailed account can be found in chapter 4.

4. To be sure, there are many different family therapy schools available, but the Satir Model has emerged as the most influential one in China today (see Chen 2015).

5. Internet addiction (*wang yin* 网隐) has been an officially recognized pathological category in the Chinese version of DSM since 2013.

6. For example, the American Psychiatric Association Practice Guidelines (April 2000) suggests that CBT is one of the most effective treatments for major depressive disorder.

7. For more analysis of affective practices in therapeutic intervention among the poor in China, see Jie Yang's insightful work on "the affective state" (2013c).

8. One of the most compelling pieces of evidence is a collection of Jung's writing translated by R. F. C. Hull, titled *Psychology and the East* (1978). See also Jung (1969).

9. See Thomas Kirsch's insightful analysis in his foreword to *Rongge yu fenxi xinlixue* (Jung and analytical psychology) (Shen 2004).

10. Cai admitted that this case was unusual with regard to the close connection made between the client and the therapist due to their prior friendship and common love of poetry. Also, it was long-term based unlike most other cases.

11. Art therapy can include painting, drawing, dance, music, pottery, and other forms of engagement. In this chapter I focus on painting and drawing because it is the commonly used method of the therapists I worked with.

12. The house-tree-person test was first developed by an American psychologist, J. N. Buck in 1948 and adopted widely in the 1950s and 1960s. Originally it was designed for a personality test and later was used commonly in art therapy for assessing trauma and for free expression.

CHAPTER 3. THERAPEUTIC RELATIONSHIPS WITH CHINESE CHARACTERISTICS?

1. One example given with regard to cultural sensitivity is this: "Western therapists sometimes express their empathy through hugs, touches, and even kisses, but Chinese

culture does not allow such behaviors, especially between the two opposite genders" (*National Occupational Qualification Training Textbook: Psychological Counselor Level III* 2005: 61).

2. Even though this is a false distinction, as many researchers have shown, it is widely regarded as valid by most Chinese people.

3. A similar pattern in which clients looking up to an authority figure in therapeutic settings is found also in Vietnamese society (Paterson 2006).

4. While privacy awareness has been increasing in recent decades (see Yan 2003), young children and frail seniors who need care from others do not enjoy privacy in the family as much as other family members.

5. In her study on psychiatric reform in Greece, Elizabeth Davis shows that what has emerged there as a therapeutic norm between the therapist and the patient are collaborative relationships quite different from psychoanalysis. This kind of therapeutic relationship is "conditioned by his or her growing awareness of a responsibility to self-care, and an increasing competence at achieving it" (2012: 15). This is in contrast with the situation in China I have described.

CHAPTER 4. BRANDING THE SATIR MODEL

1. Compare Christopher Harding's (2009) account of the de facto franchising of Freud's psychoanalysis in Japan and India during the 1920s and 1930s (2009).

2. Sanzi Jing 三字经 is a famous classical Chinese text created approximately in the Song Dynasty. It embodies basic Confucians ideas used to teach especially children.

3. All the information presented here is based on the PowerPoint presentation slides Liu shared with me.

4. There is a certain resemblance between this franchising model and early multilevel marketing described by Lyn Jeffery in the 1990s (2001).

5. I did not pay any fees because Liu waived them. I was also aware that my appearance—a professor and researcher from an American university—brought him a certain amount of prestige. And he never failed to introduce me to the participants.

6. In more recent years, some anthropologists have begun to pay more attention to the role of affect in psychotherapy. For example, Samuele Collu sees affect as a type of "atmospheric" forces capable of possessing the clients in a therapeutic milieu (2019).

7. This phenomenon is prevalent particularly in the martial arts world and the early qigong fever in China (see Chen 2003). Such masters often became public figures and exude a high level of charisma.

8. All the information used here is from the handbooks, pamphlets, and workshop advertisements I collected during my fieldwork with the permission to use from Liu.

9. I do not mean to suggest that Liu made up these facts and numbers, but rather I intend to show how certain aspects of Satir's life and her impact were selected and put together in order to create an aura.

10. Cited by Douglas Todd in his interview with Banmen (2010).

CHAPTER 5. CRAFTING A THERAPEUTIC SELF

1. For more detailed discussion on the complexity of the middle classes, see *In Search of Paradise* (Zhang 2010). See also *The Global Middle Classes* (Heiman, Freeman, and Liechty 2012).

2. The reconfiguration of the self takes place in a variety forms and domains (see Zhang and Ong 2008), but the therapeutic turn is relatively new and unique in that it focuses on the possibility of healing with the help of psy experts.

3. In another article (Zhang 2017), I explicitly address the relationship between therapeutic works and modes of governing and state efforts to incorporate positive psychology in the management of the military, the police, and state enterprises.

4. Zhu's trip to Tibet is not uncommon and can be seen as part of the popular trend among some Chinese urbanites in search of spirituality and enlightenment through modern pilgrimages (Palmer and Seigler 2017; Smyer Yu 2012).

5. A famous Zen Buddhist expression of a high state of being is *xin ru mingjingtai* 心如明镜台: "When one's heart is as lucid as a dustless mirror, one will be able to see things clearly and comprehend life."

6. Zhiying Ma (2012) argues that despite the influence of the holistic language of Chinese medicine, psychiatric discourse in China still largely produces a separation between the body and the mind, the biological and the sociopolitical. However, in the counseling world this is not quite the case; there is much more fusion effort.

7. Based on his experience of training Chinese therapists, Antje Haag suggests that in a close-knit society like China, shame and the concern of losing face, which often manifest in Chinese counseling, are important correctives in the social order. Thus, Chinese clients often seek conformity and do not like to challenge the therapist (2018: 24).

8. See also Pritzker's (2016) analysis of inner-child emotion pedagogies in China, which reveals how Chinese people have a distinct understanding of an intricate relationship between the inner and outer self.

9. Talk therapy is used by mental health professionals in the medical setting, but the general trend is that many people embrace the mass training programs for purposes other than medical treatment (see Huang 2014). Concerns about mental illness rarely enter such training sessions, in contrast to hospital settings.

10. This search for the good life in my view is very different from what Zhang et al. (2011) call "the quest for an adequate life" based on the notion of *minsheng* (livelihood of the people). For middle-class Chinese, the notion of the good life promises much more than an adequate life (see Borovoy and Zhang 2016).

11. This article appears in http://blog.sina.com.cn/u/3164664704, September 18, 2014.

12. Jie Yang's recent research shows that the urban poor are also drawn into what she calls "the psycho-politics" that attempts to turn them into happy subjects who can realize their own potential (2013a, 2013b). This psychologization project is primarily a government-initiated process, which is quite different from the middle-class project of the self I examine here. The latter is largely grass-roots initiated and profit driven.

13. *The Psychiatric Society* shows that psychiatry and its allied activities (such as psychoanalysis, group therapy, and counseling) have always had important political and social implications. One of its explicit tasks is to help achieve consensus and social integration through controlling and standardizing human beings (Castel, Castel, and Lovell 1982: xxii).

14. This is one of the questions raised by journalist Evan Osnos (2011) in his thinking about the relationship between psychoanalysis and an authoritarian state.

CHAPTER 6. CULTIVATING HAPPINESS

1. Jie Yang's recent research shows that underprivileged people in China also are called to pursue happiness by engaging in psychological self-help to unlock their positive potential (2013a).

2. The two terms *happiness* and *well-being* are used interchangeably in this chapter because the Chinese translation of "well-being" (*xingfu gan*) is almost identical with that of "happiness" (*xingfu*). "Well-being" also conveys a sense of health in addition to feeling well.

3. Tracing the history of xingfu in the Chinese context, Lang Chen shows that in classical Chinese the concept of happiness was frequently expressed through the word *fu*, and later evolved into the term *xingfu* via Japan in late nineteenth century (2019).

4. Becky Hsu identifies three strands of the happiness pursuit in Chinese society: the happy and prosperous family, the greater good, and individual fulfillment (2019: 10–15). She argues that the search for happiness is very much tied to how they construct their versions of the good life.

5. Compare Foucault's study of the proliferation of discourses on sexuality and the rise of psycho-medical disciplines in French history as positive mechanisms that produced knowledge, generated power, and constituted new subjects for regulation (1990).

6. Along with this "happiness fever" is a related craze on "positive energy," which is widely applied to the personal, interpersonal, and national political spheres (see Du 2014).

7. Horizon is a reputable research firm based in Beijing and specializes in conducting large surveys for domestic and international researchers.

8. A few exceptions include Jie Yang's work (2013) and some recent books such as *Deep China* (Kleinman et al. 2011) and *Chinese Modernity and the Individual Psyche* (Kipnis 2012).

9. This form of popular leisure activities is called "nongjia le" ("seeking happiness in the peasant family life") that offers rural landscapes, natural organic food, and relaxation away from the city.

10. See *Beijing Review* at bjreview.com.cn. December 4, 2014.

11. Robert Emmons, a psychology professor at UC Davis and the chief editor of the *Journal of Positive Psychology*, works on the science of gratitude and received a major grant of $5.6 million from the John Templeton Foundation to study how to cultivate gratitude to improve human life.

12. Seligman has been invited to speak to the United States military, teaching soldiers how to resist torture, evade interrogation, handle trauma, and endure battlefield stress (Greenberg 2008).

13. There has also been a global traffic of Buddhist literature into China in recent years. The most influential books on how to live a happy, wise, and enlightened life include the Chinese translations of works by Pema Chodron, Thich Nhat Hanh, and Sogyal Rinpoche.

14. Kabat-Zinn obtained his PhD in molecular biology from MIT in 1971 and was also trained as a Zen Buddhist student with a passion for meditation and yoga.

15. It is interesting to note that both Kornfield and Kabat-Zinn draw heavily from Buddhism and Daosim and their teachings are traveling back from North America to China. This is a phenomenon similar to what Palmer and Seigler describe in their book *Dream Trippers* (2017)—a Westernized version of Daoism is going full circle, traveling from America to influence Daoism in China.

16. Storehouse consciousness is the eighth and most fundamental one of the eight consciousnesses in the Yogacara school of Buddhism. It is regarded as ripening consciousness or root consciousness with transformative power (see Jiang 2004).

17. See also Mingyur Rinpoche (2005).

18. Even though today Buddhism is officially classified as one of the five state-recognized religions in China, it does not, in practice, completely escape the shadow of superstition.

19. There are several terms corresponding to the form of meditation practiced: *jingxin, jingzuo, dazuo,* or *mingxiang*. It is quite different from the widespread qigong meditation of the 1990s as document by Nancy Chen (2003).

20. The irony of using meditation for competitive advantages has been noted by DeSteno: "Gaining competitive advantage on exams and increasing creativity in business weren't of the utmost concern to Buddha and other early meditation teachers." (2013).

21. See Nikolas Rose's extensive analysis of the relationship between psychology, power, and the remaking of the self (1990, 1996).

22. The connection between spiritual and religious pursuits with rapid urbanization and rising urban anomie is also discussed by Harkness (2015) in the context of South Korea. Fisher (2015) also shows how public religious spaces become an alternative expression of hopes and fears of the uncertain future in post-reform Beijing.

CHAPTER 7. THERAPEUTIC GOVERNING

1. One of the few exceptions is Jie Yang's book (2015), but the focus there is on how therapeutic governance is applied to the destitute and marginal social sectors. Another volume, edited by Andrew Kipnis, examines the relationship between the individual psyche and Chinese modernity, but the question of governing through therapeutics is not the central concern (Kipnis 2012). Vanessa Pupavac was first to use the term *therapeutic governance* to describe psychosocial intervention in risk management by Western states to reduce politics to administration (2001).

2. Tomas Matza finds a similar trend in postsocialist Russia, where "psychological education" and psy experts are widely incorporated in practices of neoliberal governmentality (2012).

3. The notions of "kindly power" have become popular in the study of China today (see Yang 2010). They point to the possibility of rule that appears benevolent to the masses. Comparing it with the use of caring forms of surveillance in the digital age (Bauman and Lyon 2013), the Chinese case is more of a bottom-up movement largely aimed at self-help and self-care.

4. The People's Armed Police is considered an armed force with its own uniform. It differs from but often works with the People's Liberation Army, the public security police, and fire fighters in many emergency circumstances.

5. EPQ was originally devised by German/British psychologists Hans Jürgen Eysenck and his wife, Sybil B. G. Eysenck, and has since traveled to North America and other parts of the world. A group of Chinese psychologists based at Peking University revised its short scale for the Chinese population. It is one of the most popular personality testing tools used in China today.

6. The Chinese military and paramilitary had long screened soldiers by using medical exams, but the focus in the past was primarily on the physical aspects, not so much on mental and psychological health through systematic evaluations.

7. *Dakai xinjie* 打开心结 is a common Chinese saying that means solving one's emotional and psychological problems by undoing the knot in the heart.

8. Psychological intervention disguised in the form of care has also been widely adopted by other neoliberal states as a technology for managing poor and the marginal groups. See, for example, Clara Han's account on Chile (2012).

9. For more detailed discussion on the similarities and conflicts between the two approaches, see Zhang (2014).

10. Although dangan cannot usually be reviewed by the subject person, it is different from what Verdery calls "secret files" kept by the secret police in the case of Romania (2014). The latter is targeted at certain citizens in question and is more secretive and detailed than the former.

11. Other evaluation tools are used as well in China, but these two (EPQ and MMPI) are most popular because the questionnaires tend to be shorter and thus quicker to finish.

12. "Psychological fitness" (roughly translated into Chinese as *xinli jiankang* or *xinli suzhi*) is a relatively new term that began to surface in more recent years, yet it is articulated with the Chinese notion of *suzhi*, which refers to human quality. It is largely believed in China that although one's psychological fitness" can be trained and improved, it is partially pre-determined. And it includes both the social and the inner dimensions of the self.

13. Similarly, some scholars have argued that depression as a medical category did not exist in China until recent years (Lee 2011); it was conceived as the stagnation of qi in traditional Chinese medicine (Zhang 2007) or as somatic experiences and was expressed very differently through a culturally specific category—neurasthenia—that

was popular under socialism (Kleinman 1982). Thus, it would be interesting to explore how traumatic experiences and impacts were conceived and expressed prior to the arrival of the language of PTSD.

14. Kitanaka shows a similar trend of utilizing mental health screening and prevention efforts in the Japanese workplace (2014).

15. The Satir family therapy model was developed by an American psychotherapist, Virginia Satir (1916–1988). It focuses on improving interpersonal communication and family dynamics.

16. The production and sale of cigarettes is the most important industry in tobacco-rich Yunnan. This industry is owned and regulated by the government, bringing in $119 billion in profits and tax receipts in 2011 (see Kohrman 2017).

17. The responses, however, are not necessarily uniform. As Jie Yang (2015) points out, some marginalized urban workers have also expressed a nostalgia about certain previous forms of communist thought work based on intimate interactions (such as *cuxi tanxin*—heart-to-heart talk with one's knees facing against another's knees). In other words, professional counseling and thought work are not opposite to one another; both require intimacy and psychological knowledge of different kinds. I wish to thank the anonymous reviewer who shared this insight with me.

18. See also Sandra Hyde's (2017) study of addiction care and Nicholas Bartlett's (2016) research on the therapeutic value of compulsory labor among recovering drug users in southwest China.

EPILOGUE

1. See, for example, a Chinese doctor's November 6, 2017, blog post at http://blog.sina.com.cn/congzhong.

2. See http://www.xinhuanet.com//politics/2016-10/25/c_1119785867.htm.

3. *Xiaokang*, is a term that was used by the Deng Xiaoping regime to refer to a relatively comfortable living condition that exceeds the basic survival needs for food and clothing. It has been widely adopted in the official and popular discourses in China and is regarded as signifying the goal for Chinese society by about 2021.

4. The word *noso* comes from the Greek word *nasoa*, which means "disease."

REFERENCES

Anagnost, Ann. 2004. "The Corporeal Politics of Quality (Suzhi)." *Public Culture* 16 (2):189–208.

Asad, Talal. 1986. "The Concept of Cultural Translation in British Social Anthropology." In *Writing Culture: The Poetics and Politics of Ethnography*. Edited by James Clifford and George Marcus, 141–64. Berkeley: University of California Press.

Bakhtin, M. M. 1981. *The Dialogic Imagination*. Austin: University of Texas Press.

Banmen, John. 2008. *In Her Own Words—Virginia Satir*. Phoenix: Zeig, Tucker & Theisen, Inc.

Bartlett, Nicholas. 2018. "Idling in Mao's Shadow: Heroin Addiction and the Contested Therapeutic Value of Socialist Traditions of Laboring." *Culture, Medicine, and Psychiatry*. 42 (1): 49–68.

Baum, Emily. 2018. The Invention of Madness: State, Society, and the Insane in Modern China. Chicago: University of Chicago Press.

Bauman, Zygmunt, and David Lyon. 2013. *Liquid Surveillance: A Conversation*. Cambridge, UK: Polity.

Beck, Aaron. 1993. *Cognitive Therapy and the Emotional Disorder*. New York: Penguin.

Beck, Ulrich. 1992. *Risk Society: Towards a New Modernity*. Translated by M. Ritter. London: Sage.

Benjamin, Walter. 1969. *Illuminations: Essays and Reflections*. Translated by Harry Zohn. New York: Schocken Books.

Biehl, Joao. 2005. *Vita: Life in a Zone of a Social Abandonment*. Berkeley: University of California Press.

Blum, Nava, and Elizabeth Fee. 2008. "The First Mental Hospital in China." *American Journal of Public Health* 98 (9): 1593.

Borneman, John, and Abdellah Hammoudi. 2009. *Being There: The Ethnographic Encounter and the Making of Truth*. Berkeley: University of California Press.

Borovoy, Amy. 2012. "Doi Takeo and the Rehabilitation of Particularism in Postwar Japan." *Journal of Japanese Studies* 38 (2): 263–95.

Borovoy, Amy, and Li Zhang. 2016. "Between Biopolitical Governance and Care: Rethinking Health, Selfhood, and Social Welfare in East Asia." *Medical Anthropology* 36 (1): 1–5.

Bregnbaek, Susanne. 2016. *Fragile Elite: The Dilemmas of China's Top University Students.* Stanford, CA: Stanford University Press.

Brownell, Susan. 1995. *Training the Body for China: Sports in the Moral Order of the People's Republic.* Chicago: University of Chicago Press.

Bruce, Shadra. 2010. "China Embraces Positive Psychology." *Mental Health News.* http://mentalhealthnews.org/tag/shadra-bruce/.

Bunkenborg, M. 2014 "Subhealth: Questioning the Quality of Bodies in Contemporary China." *Medical Anthropology* 33 (2): 128–43.

Caplan, Eric. 1998. *Mind Game: American Culture and the Birth of Psychotherapy.* Berkeley: University of California Press.

Castel, Robert, Francoise Castel, and Anne Lovell. 1979. *The Psychiatric Society.* Translated by Arthur Goldhammer. New York: Columbia University Press.

Chang, Doris, Huiqi Tong, Qijia Shi, and Qifeng Zeng. 2005. "Letting a Hundred Flowers Bloom: Counseling and Psychotherapy in the People's Republic of China." *Journal of Mental Health Counseling* 27 (2): 104–16.

Chen, Lang. 2019. "The Changing Notion of Happiness: A History of Xingfu." In *The Chinese Pursuit of Happiness: Anxieties, Hopes, and Moral Tensions in Everyday Life.* Edited by Becky Hsu and Richard Madsen, 19–41. Berkeley: University of California Press.

Chen, Nancy. 2003. *Breathing Space: Qigong, Psychiatry, and Healing in China.* New York: Columbia University Press.

Cheng, Louis Yang-ching, Fanny M. C. Cheung, and Char-Nie Chen, eds. 1993. *Psychotherapy for the Chinese.* Hong Kong: Chinese University of Hong Kong.

Cho, Mun Young. 2013. *The Specter of "the People": Urban Poverty in Northeast China.* Ithaca, NY: Cornell University Press.

Chua, Jocelyn Lim. 2014. *In Pursuit of the Good Life: Aspiration and Suicide in Globalizing South India.* Berkeley: University of California Press.

Clough, Patricia Ticineto, and Jean Halley, eds. 2007. *The Affective Turn: Theorizing the Social.* Durham, NC: Duke University Press.

Cohn, Lawrence. 1998. *No Aging in India: Alzheimer's, the Bad Family, and Other Modern Things.* Berkeley: University of California Press.

Collier, Stephen J., and Aihwa Ong. 2005. "Global Assemblages, Anthropological Problems." In *Global Assemblages: Technology, Politics and Ethics as Anthropological Problems.* Edited by Aihwa Ong and Stephen J. Collier, 1–21. Malden, MA: Blackwell.

Collu, Samuele. 2019. "Refracting Affects: Affect, Psychotherapy, and Spirit Dis-Possession." *Culture, Medicine, Psychiatry* 43: 290–314.

Crapanzano, Vincent. 1981. *The Hamadsha: A Study in Moroccan Ethnopsychiatry.* Berkeley: University of California Press.

Cruikshank, Barbara. 1996. "Revolutions within: Self-Government and Self-Esteem." In *Foucault and Political Reason: Liberalism, Neo-liberalism and Rationalities of Government*. Edited by Andrew Barry, Thomas Osborne, and Nikolas Rose, 231–51. Chicago: University of Chicago Press.

Csordas, Thomas, and Arthur Kleinman. 1990. "The Therapeutic Process." In *Medical Anthropology: A Handbook of Theory and Method*. Santa Barbara: Greenwood Press.

Cyranoski, David. 2010. "China Tackles Surge in Mental Illness." *Nature*, November 10. https://www.nature.com/articles/468145a.

Davis, Elizabeth. 2012. *Bad Souls: Madness and Responsibility in Modern Greece*. Durham, NC: Duke University Press.

Deleuze, Gilles, and Felix Guattari. 1987. *A Thousand Plateaus: Capitalism and Schizophrenia*. Minneapolis: University of Minnesota Press.

Desjarlais, Robert, and Jason Throop. 2011. "Phenomenological Approaches in Anthropology." *Annual Review of Anthropology* 40: 87–102.

DeSteno, David. 2013. "The Morality of Meditation." *New York Times*, July 5, 2013.

Du, Shanshan. 2014. "Social Media and the Transformation of 'Chinese Nationalism.'" *Anthropology Today* 30 (1): 5–8.

Dumit, Joseph. 2003. *Picturing Personhood: Brain Scans and Biomedical Identity*. Princeton, NJ: Princeton University Press.

Duncan, Whitney. 2018. *Transforming Therapy: Mental Health Practice and Cultural Change in Mexico*. Nashville, TN: Vanderbilt University Press.

Ehrenreich, Barbara. 1983. *The Hearts of Men: American Dreams and the Flight from Commitment*. Garden City, NY: Anchor Books.

Ellis, Albert. 2001. *Overcoming Destructive Beliefs, Feelings, and Behaviors: New Directions for Rational Emotive Behavior Therapy*. Amherst, NY: Prometheus Books.

Engebretsen, Elizabeth. 2009. "Intimate Practices, Conjugal Ideals: Affective Ties and Relationship Strategies among Lala ("Lesbian") Women in Contemporary Beijing." *Sexuality Research and Social Policy*. 6 (3): 3–14.

Farquhar, Judith. 1996. *Knowing Practice: The Clinical Encounter of Chinese Medicine*. Boulder, CO: Westview Press.

Farquhar, Judith, and Qicheng Zhang. 2012. *Ten Thousand Things: Nurturing Life in Contemporary Beijing*. New York: Zone Books.

Fisher, Gareth. 2015. "The Flexibility of Religion: Buddhist Temples as Multiaspirational Sites in Contemporary Beijing." In *Handbook of Religion and the Asian City: Aspiration and Urbanization in the Twenty-First Century*. Edited by Peter van der Veer, 299–314. Oakland: University of California Press.

Fong, Vanessa. 2006. *Only Hope: Coming of Age under China's One-Child Policy*. Stanford, CA: Stanford University Press.

Foucault, Michel. 1980. "The Politics of Health in the Eighteenth Century." In *Power/Knowledge: Selected Interviews and Other Writings 1972–1977*. Edited by Colin Gordon, 166–82. New York: Pantheon Books.

———. 1988. "Technologies of the Self." In *Technologies of the Self: A Seminar with Michel Foucault*. Edited by L. H. Martin, 16–49. London: Tavistock.

————. 1990. *The History of Sexuality: An Introduction. Volume 1.* Translated by Robert Hurley. New York: Vintage Books.

————. 1991. "Governmentality." In *The Foucault Effect: Studies in Governmentality.* Edited by Graham Burchell, Colin Gordon, and Peter Miller, 87–104. London: Harvester/ Wheatsheaf.

————. 2006. *Psychiatric Power.* London: Palgrave Macmillan.

Frammolino, Ralph. 2004. "China Discovers the Couch." *Los Angeles Times,* September 17, 2004.

Fromm, Erich. 1960. "Psychoanalysis and Zen Buddhism." In *Zen Buddhism and Psychoanalysis.* Edited by D. T. Suzuki, Erich Fromm, and Richard De Martino, 77–141. New York: Grove Press, Inc.

Gao, Juefu. 1985. *Zhongguo xinlixue shi* [The history of Chinese psychology]. Beijing: People's Education Publishing House.

Gao, Zhipeng. 2013. "The Emergence of Modern Psychology in China, 1876–1929" *Annual Review of Critical Psychology:* 293–307.

————. 2015. "Pavlovianism in China: Politics and Differentiation across Scientific Disciplines in the Maoist Era" *History of Science* 53 (1): 57–85.

Giordano, Cristiana. 2008. "Practices of Translation and the Making of Migrant Subjectivities in Contemporary Italy." *American Ethnologist* 35 (4): 1–19.

————. 2014. *Migrants in Translation: Caring and the Logics of Difference in Contemporary Italy.* Berkeley: University of California Press.

Goldstein, Jan. 2005. *The Post-Revolutionary Self: Politics and Psyche in France, 1750–1850.* Cambridge, MA: Harvard University Press.

Good, Mary-Jo DelVecchio, Sandra Hyde, Sarah Pinto, and Byron Good, eds. 2008. *Postcolonial Disorders.* Berkeley: University of California Press.

Greenberg, Gary. 2008. "The War on Unhappiness: Goodbye Freud, Hello Positive Thinking." *Harper's Magazine,* June, 2008.

Greenhalgh, Susan. 2020. "Governing through Science: The Anthropology of Science and Technology in Contemporary China." In *Can Science and Technology Save China?* Edited by Susan Greenhalgh and Li Zhang, Ithaca, NY: Cornell University Press.

Greenhalgh, Susan, and Edwin A. Winckler. 2005. *Governing China's Population: From Leninist to Neoliberal Biopolitics.* Stanford, CA: Stanford University Press.

Grenoble, Ryan. 2013. "Chinese Students Sign 'Suicide Waivers' before Starting College." *Huffington Post,* September 18, 2013.

Haag, Antje. 2018. "Psychoanalytically Oriented Psychotherapy and the Chinese Self." In *Psychoanalysis in China.* Edited by David Scharff and Sverre Varvin, 21–32. London: Routledge.

Han, Buxin, and Kan Zhang. 2007. "Psychology in China." *The Psychologist* 20: 734–36.

Han, Clara. 2012. *Life in Debt: Times of Care and Violence in Neoliberal Chile.* Berkeley: University of California Press.

Harding, Christopher. 2009. "Sigmund's Asian Fan-Club? The Freud Franchise and Independence of Mind in India and Japan." In *Celebrity Colonialism: Fame, Power and Representation in Colonial and Postcolonial Cultures*. Edited by Robert Clarke, 73–87. Newcastle upon Tyne, UK: Cambridge Scholars Publishing.

Harkness, Nicholas. 2015. "Other Christians as Christian Others: Signs of New Christian Populations and the Urban Expansion of Seoul." In *Handbook of Religion and the Asian City: Aspiration and Urbanization in the Twenty-First Century*. Edited by Peter van der Veer, 333–50. Oakland: University of California Press.

Heiman, Rachel, Carla Freeman, and Mark Liechty, eds. 2012. *The Global Middle Classes: Theorizing through Ethnography*. Santa Fe, NM: SAR Press.

Herman, Ellen. 1995. *The Romance of American Psychology: Political Culture in the Age of Experts*. Berkeley: University of California Press.

Hirai, Tomio. 1989. *Zen Meditation and Psychotherapy*. Tokyo: Japan Publications.

Honig, Emily. 2000. "Iron Girls Revisited: Gender and the Politics of Work in the Cultural Revolution," In *Re-Drawing the Boundaries of Work, Households, and Gender*. Edited by Barbara Gutwisle and Gail Henderson. Berkeley: University of California Press.

Hsing, You-Tien. 2012. *The Great Urban Transformation: Politics of Land and Property in China*. Oxford: Oxford University Press.

Hsu, Becky Yang. 2019. "Introduction." In *The Chinese Pursuit of Happiness: Anxieties, Hopes, and Moral Tensions in Everyday Life*. Edited by Becky Hsu and Richard Madsen, 1–18. Berkeley: University of California Press.

Hsu, Becky Yang, and Richard Madsen, eds. 2019. *The Chinese Pursuit of Happiness: Anxieties, Hopes, and Moral Tensions in Everyday Life*. Berkeley: University of California Press.

Huang, Hsuan Ying. 2014. "The Emergence of the Psycho-Boom in Contemporary Urban China." In *Psychiatry and Chinese History*. Edited by Howard Chiang, 183–204. London: Pickering & Chatto.

Huang, Yueqin, et al. 2019. "Prevalence of Mental Disorders in China: A Cross-Sectional Epidemiological Study." *Lancet Psychiatry* 6: 211–24.

Hwang, Kwang-Kuo. 2005. "The Idea of the Face in Chinese Society." In *Huaren bentu xinlixue* [Chinese indigenous psychology]. Edited by Yang Guoshu, Huang Guangguo, and Yang Zhongfang, 354–94. Chongqing: Chongqing University Press.

Hwang, Kwang-Kuo, and Jeffrey Chang. 2011. "Self-Cultivation: Culturally Sensitive Psychotherapies in Confucian Societies." *Counseling Psychologist* 37 (7): 1010–32.

Hyde, Sandra. 2017. " 'Spending My Own Money, Harming My Own Body': Addiction Care in a Chinese Therapeutic Community." *Medical Anthropology* 36 (1): 61–76.

Illouz, Eva. 2007. *Cold Intimacies: The Making of Emotional Capitalism*. Cambridge, UK: Polity Press.

Jeffery, Lyn. 2001. "Placing Practices: Transnational Network Marketing in Mainland China." In *China Urban: Ethnographies of Contemporary Culture*. Edited by Nancy Chen, Constance Clark, Suzanne Gottschang, and Lyn Jeffery, 23–42. Durham, NC: Duke University Press.

Jenkins, Janis. 1998. "Diagnostic Criteria for Schizophrenia and Related Psychotic Disorders: Integration and Suppression of Cultural Evidence in DSM-IV." *Transcultural Psychiatry* 35: 357–76.

Jenkins, Janis, and Robert Barrett. 2004. "Introduction." In *Schizophrenia, Culture, and Subjectivity.* Edited by Janis Jenkins and Robert Barrett, 1–25. Cambridge: Cambridge University Press.

Jenkins, Janis, Arthur Kleinman, and Byron Good. 1991. "Cross-Cultural Studies of Depression." In *Psychosocial Aspects of Depression.* Edited by Joseph Baker and Arthur Kleinman, 67–99, Hillsdale, NJ: Erlbaum.

Jiang, Chengcheng. 2011. "Chinese Flock to Free Lectures on Happiness, Justice." *Time,* August 25, 2011.

Jiang, Tao. 2004. "Storehouse Consciousness and the Unconscious: A Comparative Study of Xuan Zang and Freud on the Subliminal Mind." *Journal of the American Academy of Religion* 72 (1): 119–39.

Jung, Carl. 1959. *The Archetypes and the Collective Unconscious.* Princeton, NJ: Princeton University Press.

———. 1961. *Memories, Dreams, Reflections.* New York: Vintage Book.

———. 1969. *Man and His Symbols.* New York: Dell Publishing.

———. 1978. *Psychology and the East.* Translated by R. F. C. Hull. Princeton, NJ: Princeton University Press.

Kabat-Zinn, Jon. 1990. *Full Catastrophe Living: Using the Wisdom of Your Body and Mind to Face Stress, Pain, and Illness.* New York: Bantam Dell.

———. 1994. *Wherever You Go There You Are: Mindfulness Meditation in Everyday Life.* New York: Hyperion.

———. 2005. *Coming to Our Senses: Healing Ourselves and the World Through Mindfulness.* New York: Hyperion.

Kalff, Dora. 1980. *Sandplay: A Psychotherapeutic Approach to the Psyche.* Boston: Sigo Press.

———. 1991. "Introduction to Sandplay Therapy." *Journal of Sandplay Therapy* 1 (1). Online, https://www.sandplay.org/product/volume-01-number-1/.

Katie, B., with S. Mitchell. 2002. *Loving What Is: Four Questions That Can Change Your Life.* Nevada City, CA: Harmony Books.

Kipnis, Andrew. 2011. *Governing Educational Desire: Culture, Politics, and Schooling in China.* Chicago: University of Chicago Press.

———., ed. 2012. *Chinese Modernity and the Individual Psyche.* New York: Palgrave Macmillan.

Kirmayer, Laurence. 2005. "Culture, Context and Experience in Psychiatric Diagnosis." *Psychotherapy* 38: 192–96.

———. 2007. "Psychotherapy and the Cultural Concept of the Person." *Transcultural Psychiatry* 44 (2): 232–57.

Kirmayer, Laurence, and Eugene Raikhel. 2009. "From Amrita to Substance D: Psychopharmacology, Political Economy, and Technologies of the Self." *Transcultural Psychiatry* 46 (1): 5–15.

Kitanaka, Junko. 2012. *Depression in Japan: Psychiatric Cures for a Society in Distress.* Princeton, NJ: Princeton University Press.

———. 2014. "Work, Stress, and Depression: The Emerging Psychiatric Science of Work in Contemporary Japan." In *Stress, Shock and Adaptation in the Twentieth Century.* Edited by David Cantor and Edmund Ramsden, 222–37. Rochester, NY: University of Rochester Press.

Kleinman, Arthur. 1980. *Patients and Healers in the Context of Culture.* Berkeley: University of California Press.

———. 1982. "Neurasthenia and Depression: A Study of Somatization and Culture in China." *Culture, Medicine and Psychiatry* 6 (2): 117–90.

———. 1986. *Social Origins of Distress and Disease: Depression, Neurasthenia, and Pain in Modern China.* New Haven, CT: Yale University Press.

———. 1991. *Rethinking Psychiatry: From Cultural Category to Personal Experience.* New York: Free Press.

———. 2000. *Narrative and the Cultural Construction of Illness and Healing.* Berkeley: University of California Press.

———. 2010. "The Art of Medicine. Remaking the Moral Person in China: Implications for Health." *The Lancet* 375 (9720): 1074–75.

Kleinman, Arthur, and Byron Good. 1985. "Introduction: Culture and Depression." In *Culture and Depression.* Edited by Arthur Kleinman and Byron Good, 1–33. Berkeley: University of California Press.

Kleinman, Arthur, Yunxiang Yan, Jing Jun, Sing Lee, Everett Zhang, Pan Tianshu, Wu Fei, and Guo Jinhua. 2011. *Deep China: The Moral Life of the Person.* Berkeley: University of California Press.

Kohrman, Matthew. 2004. Body of Difference: Experiences of Disability and Institutional Advocacy in the Making of Modern China. Berkeley: University of California Press.

———. 2017. "Curating Employee Ethics: Self-Glory amidst Slow Violence at the China Tobacco Museum." *Medical Anthropology* 36 (1): 47–60.

Kornfield, Jack. 1993. *A Path with Heart: A Guide through the Perils and Promises of Spiritual Life.* New York: Bantam Books.

Kuan, Teresa. 2015. *Love's Uncertainty: The Politics and Ethics of Child Rearing in Contemporary China.* Oakland: University of California Press.

Larson, Wendy. 2009. *From Ah Q to Lei Feng: Freud and Revolutionary Spirit in 20th Century China.* Stanford, CA: Stanford University Press.

Lawrence, Dune. 2008. "As Stress Grows, Chinese Turn to Western Psychotherapy." *International Herald Tribune*, October 21, 2008.

Lee, Haiyan. 2010. *Revolution of the Heart: Genealogy of the Love in China, 1900–1950.* Stanford, CA: Stanford University Press.

Lee, Sing. 2011. "Depression: Coming of Age in China." In *Deep China.* Coauthored by Arthur Kleinman, Yunxiang Yan, Jing Jun, Sing Lee, Everett Zhang, Pan Tianshu, Wu Fei, and Guo Jinhua, 177–212. Berkeley: University of California Press.

Lewis, Bradley. 2013. 'What to Do with the Psychiatry's Biomedical Model? In *Krankheirskonstruktionen und Krankheitstreiberei.* Edited by Michael Dellwing and Martin Harbusch, 389–410. Wiesbaden, Germany: Springer VS.

Li, Mei-ge, and Guan Liang-rong. 1987. "Brief Introduction of the Chinese Psychological Society." *International Journal of Psychology* 22: 479–82.

Li, Shaokun. 2007. *Zhongguo de xinlixuejie* [China's psychology world]. Beijing: Shangwu Publishing House.

Li, Xiaohong. 2012. "On Chinese College Students' Suicide: Characteristics, Prevention and Crisis Intervention." *International Journal of Higher Education* 1 (2): 103–7.

Lim, Soh-Leong, Ben Kock Hong Lim, Rand Michael, Rainbow Cai, and Cheryle K. Schock. 2010. "The Trajectory of Counseling in China: Past, Present, and Future Trends." *Journal of Counseling & Development* 88: 4–8.

Lin, Liuchen. 2012. "An Ethnography of a Private Psychological Counseling Center: Transformations of the Chinese Psyche in the early Twenty-First Century." Master's thesis, Central Minzu University, China.

Liu, Lydia. 1995. *Translingual Practice: Literature, National Culture, and Translated Modernity—China, 1900–1937.* Stanford, CA: Stanford University Press.

Liu, Tianli, and Xiaoying Zheng. 2016. "Cultural Revolution and Onset of Schizophrenia in China." *Schizophrenia Research* 170 (1): 232–33.

Liu, Xin. 2002. *The Otherness of Self: A Genealogy of the Self in Contemporary China.* Ann Arbor: University of Michigan Press.

Liu, Yaochen. 2011. *Xinli geming* [Psychological revolution]. Beijing: The Overseas Chinese Publisher.

Lock, Margaret. 1995. *Encounters with Aging: Mythologies of Menopause in Japan and North America.* Berkeley: University of California Press.

Luhrmann, T. M. 2000. *Of Two Minds: An Anthropologist Looks at American Psychiatry.* New York: Vintage Books.

Ma, Zhiying. 2012. "When Love Meets Drugs: Pharmaceuticalizing Ambivalence in Post-socialist China." *Culture, Medicine, Psychiatry* 36: 51–77.

———. 2014. "An Iron Cage of Civilization? Missionary Psychiatry, the Chinese Family and a Colonial Dialect of Enlightenment." In *Psychiatry and Chinese History.* Edited by Howard Chiang, 91–110. London: Pickering & Chatto.

Marcus, George E., and Erkan Saka. 2006. "Assemblage." *Theory, Culture & Society* 23 (2–3): 101–9.

Martin, Emily. 2007. *Bipolar Expeditions: Mania and Depression in American Culture.* Princeton, NJ: Princeton University Press.

Maslow, Abraham. 1954. *Motivation and Personality.* New York: Harper.

Mason, Katherine. 2016. *Infectious Change: Reinventing Chinese Public Health after an Epidemic.* Stanford, CA: Stanford University Press.

Massumi, Brian. 2002. *Parables for the Virtual: Movement, Affect, Sensation.* Durham, NC: Duke University Press.

Matza, Tomas. 2009. "Moscow's Echo: Technologies of the Self, Publics and Politics on the Russian Talk Show." *Cultural Anthropology* 24 (3): 489–522.

———. 2012. "'Good Individualism'? Psychology, Ethics, and Neoliberalism in Post-socialist Russia." *American Ethnologist* 39 (4): 805–19.

———. 2018. *Shock Therapy: Psychology, Precarity, and Well-Being in Postsocialist Russia*. Durham, NC: Duke University Press.

Mezzich, Juan E., L. J. Kirmayer, A. Kleinman, H. Fabrega Jr., D. L. Parron, B. J. Good K. M. Lin and S. M. Manson. 1999. "The Place of Culture in DSM-IV." *Journal of Nervous and Mental Disease* 187 (8): 457–64.

Mingyur Rinpoche, Yongey. 2007. *The Joy of Living: Unlocking the Secret and Science of Happiness*. New York: Harmony Books.

Moore, Malcolm. 2009. "China Has 100 Million People with Mental Illness." *Telegraph*, April 28, 2009.

National Occupational Qualification Training Textbook: Psychological Counselor Level III. 2005. Beijing: Minzu Publisher.

Ng, Emily. 2009. "Headache of the State, Enemy of the Self: Bipolar Disorder and Cultural Change in Urban China." *Culture, Medicine, and Psychiatry* 33: 421–50.

Nolan, James. 1998. *The Therapeutic State: Justifying Government at Century's End*. New York: New York University Press.

Ong, Aihwa, and Li Zhang. 2008. "Introduction: Privatizing China: Powers of the Self, Socialism from Afar." In *Privatizing China, Socialism from Afar*. Edited by Li Zhang and Aihwa Ong, 1–19. Ithaca, NY: Cornell University Press.

Osnos, Evan. 2011. "Meet Dr. Freud: Does Psychoanalysis Have a Future in an Authoritarian State?" *New Yorker*, January 10, 2011.

Ozawa-de Silva, Chikako. 2010. "Secularizing Religious Practices: A Study of Subjectivity and Existential Transformation in Naikan Therapy." *Journal for the Scientific Study of Religion* 49 (1): 147–61.

Pai, Sung-Yun. 1989. "Neurasthenia in China: Pavlovian Theory, Knowledge-Power, and the Birth of the Chinese Field of Psychiatry." Master's thesis, Harvard University.

Palmer, David. 2007. *Qigong Fever: Body, Science, and Utopia in China*. New York: Columbia University Press.

Palmer, David, and Elijah Seigler. 2017. *Dream Trippers: Global Daoism and the Predicament of Modern Spirituality*. Chicago: Chicago University Press.

Pandolfo, Stefania. 2000. "The Thin Line of Modernity: Some Moroccan Debates on Subjectivity. In *Questions of Modernity, Vol. 11: Contradictions of Modernity*. Edited by Timothy Mitchell, 115–47. Minneapolis: University of Minnesota Press.

Paterson, Jim. 2006. "When East Meets West." *Counseling Today*. January 7.

Pellow, Deborah. 1996. "Intimate Boundaries: A Chinese Puzzle." In *Setting Boundaries: the Anthropology of Spatial and Social Organization*. Edited by Deborah Pellow, 111–36 Westport, CT: Bergin & Garvey.

Peng, Rong-Bang. 2012. "Decolonizing Psychic Space: Remembering the Indigenous Psychology Movement in Taiwan." PhD dissertation, Duquesne University.

Petryna, Adriana. 2003. *Life Exposed: Biological Citizens after Chernobyl*. Princeton, NJ: Princeton University Press.

Phillips, Michael R. 1998. "The Transformation of China's Mental Health Services." *China Journal* 39: 1–36.

Philips, Michael R., Huaqing Liu, and Yanping Zhang. 1999. "Suicide and Social Change in China." *Culture, Medicine and Psychiatry* 23: 25–50.

Plotkin, Mariano Ben. 2001. *Freud in the Pampas: The Emergence and Development of a Psychoanalytical Culture in Argentina*. Stanford, CA: Stanford University Press.

Polsky, Andrew. 1991. *The Rise of the Therapeutic State*. Princeton, NJ: Princeton University Press.

Pritzker, Sonya. 2011. "The Part of Me That Wants to Grab: Embodied Experience and Living Translation in U.S. Chinese Medical Education." *Ethos* 39 (3): 395–413.

———. 2016. "New Age with Chinese Characteristics? Translating Inner Child Emotion Pedagogies in Contemporary China." *Ethos* 44 (2): 150–70.

Pupavac, Vanessa. 2001. "Therapeutic Governance: Psycho-social Intervention and Trauma Risk Management." *Disasters* 24 (4): 358–72.

Qian, Mingyi. 1994. *Xinli zixun yu xinli zhiliao* [Psychological counseling and psychological therapy]. Beijing: Beijing University Press.

Qian, Mingyi, Craig W. Smith, Zhonggeng Chen, and Guohua Xia. 2002. "Psychotherapy in China: A Review of Its History and Contemporary Directions." *International Journal of Mental Health* 30 (4): 49–68.

Raikhel, Eugene. 2016. *Governing Habits: Treating Alcoholism in the Post-Soviet Clinic*. Ithaca, NY: Cornell University Press.

Rieff, Philip. 1966. *The Triumph of the Therapeutic: Uses of Faith after Freud*. New York: Harper & Row.

Rofel, Lisa. 1999. *Other Modernities: Gendered Yearnings in China after Socialism*. Berkeley: University of California Press.

———. 2007. *Desiring China: Experiments in Neoliberalism, Sexuality, and Public Culture*. Durham, NC: Duke University Press.

Rogers, Carl. 1951. *Client-Centered Therapy: Its Current Practice, Implications and Theory*. London: Constable.

Rose, Nikolas. 1985. *The Psychological Complex: Psychology, Politics and Society in England, 1869–1939*. London: Routledge & Kegan Paul.

———. 1990. *Governing the Soul: The Shaping of the Private Self*. London: Routledge.

———. 1996. *Inventing Our Selves: Psychology, Power, and Personhood*. Cambridge: Cambridge University Press.

———. 1999. *Powers of Freedom: Reframing Political Thought*. Cambridge: Cambridge University Press.

Sampson, E. E. 1988. "The Debate on Individualism: Indigenous Psychologies of the Individual and Their Role in Personal and Societal Functioning." *American Psychologist* 1: 15–22.

Santiago-Irizarry, Vilma. 2001. *Medicalizing Ethnicity: The Construction of Latino Identity in a Psychiatric Setting*. Ithaca, NY: Cornell University Press.

Sargent, Carolyn, and Thomas M. Johnson. 1996. *Medical Anthropology: Contemporary Theory and Method*. Westport, CT: Praeger.

Satir, Virginia, John Banmen, Jane Gerber, and Maria Gomori. 1991. *The Satir Model: Family Therapy and Beyond*. Palo Alto, CA: Science and Behavior Books, Inc.

Scheid, Volker. 2013. "Constraint as a Window on Approaches to Emotion-Related Disorders in East Asian Medicine." *Culture, Medicine, and Psychiatry* 37: 2–7.

Sebag-Montefiore, Clarissa. 2013. "The Chinese Dream." *New York Times*, May 3, 2013.

Seligman, Martin. 1991. *Learned Optimism: How to Change Your Mind and Your Life*. New York: Knopf.

———. 2002. *Authentic Happiness: Using the New Positive Psychology to Realize Your Potential for Lasting Fulfillment*. New York: Free Press.

Seligman, Martin, and Mihaly Csikszentmihalyi. 2000. "Positive Psychology: An Introduction." *American Psychologist* 55 (1): 5–14.

Shen, Heyong. 2004. *Rongge yu fenxi xinlixue* [Jung and analytical psychology]. Guangzhou: Guangdong Higher Education Publisher.

———. 2009. "C. G. Jung and China: A Continued Dialogue." *Jung Journal: Culture & Psyche*. 3 (2): 5–14.

Shen, Heyong, and Gao Lan. 2004. *Shapan youxi: Lilun yu shijian* [Sandplay therapy: Theory and practice]. Guangzhou: Guangdong Higher Education Publisher.

Shi, Chunfa, and Liu Fengzhen. 2005. *Buddhism and Mental Health*. Kunming: Yunnan Minority Nationalities Publisher.

Skultans, Vieda. 2004. "Authority, Dialogue and Polyphony in Psychiatric Consultations: A Latvian Case Study." *Transcultural Psychiatry* 41 (3): 337–59.

Smyer Yu, Dan. 2012. *The Spread of Tibetan Buddhism in China: Charisma, Money, Enlightenment*. London: Routledge.

———. 2013. "Fieldworking with Khenpo Sodargye: The Charismatic Mind of a Modern Buddhist Thinker" [Blog] February 2013. http://www.mmg.mpg.de/special-output/blogs/.

Snyder, Elise. 2018. "The Shibboleth of Cross-Cultural Issues in Psychoanalytic Treatment." In *Psychoanalysis in China*. Edited by David Scharff, 91–98. London: Routledge.

Sodargye, Khenpo. 2012. *Ku Caishi Rensheng (Living through Suffering)*. Lanzhou: Gansu People's Fine Art Publisher.

Sundararajan, Louise. 2005. Happiness Donut: A Confucian Critique of Positive Psychology. *Journal of Theoretical and Philosophical Psychology* 25 (1): 35–60.

Szasz, Thomas. 2001a. "The Therapeutic State: The Tyranny of Pharmacracy." *The Independent Review* 5 (4): 485–521.

———. 2001b. *Pharmacracy: Medicine and Politics in America*. New York: Greenwood.

Szto, Peter. 2014. "Psychiatric Space and Design Antecedents: The John G. Kerr Refuge for the Insane." In *Psychiatry and Chinese History*. Edited by Howard Chiang, 71–90. London: Pickering & Chatto.

Szymanski, Jeff. 2012. "Mental Healthcare in China." *Psychology Today* (online): https://www.psychologytoday.com/us/blog/the-perfectionists-handbook/201201/mental-healthcare-in-china.

Todd, Douglas. 2010. "In China, Vancouver Psychologist Is Famous 'Master.'" *Vancouver Sun*, August 28, 2010.

Tomba, Luigi. 2014. *The Neighborhood Consensus*. Ithaca, NY: Cornell University Press.

Tseng, Wen-Shing. 1999. "Culture and Psychotherapy: Review and Practical Guidelines." *Transcultural Psychiatry* 36: 131–79.

Tsing, Anna. 2004. *Friction: An Ethnography of Global Connection*. Princeton, NJ: Princeton University Press.

Tu, Weiming. 1985. "Selfhood and Otherness in Confucian Thought." In *Culture and Self: Asian and Western Perspectives*. Edited by Anthony Marsella, George Devos, and Francis L. K. Hsu, 231–25. New York: Tavistock.

van der Veer, Peter. 2009. "Spirituality in Modern Society." *Social Research* 76 (4): 1097–120.

Verdery, Kathrine. 1996. *What Was Socialism, and What Comes Next?* Princeton, NJ: Princeton University Press.

———. 2014. *Secrets and Truth: Ethnography in the Archive of Romania's Secret Police*. Budapest: Central European University Press.

Wahlberg, Ayo. 2018. *Good Quality: The Routinization of Sperm Banking in China*. Oakland: University of California Press.

Wang, Fengyan, and Hong Zhen. 2005. *Zhongguo wenhua xinlixue* [Chinese cultural psychology]. Jinan: Jinan University Press.

Watters, Ethan. 2010. *Crazy Like Us: The Globalization of the American Psyche*. New York: Free Press.

Williams, Alex. 2017. "Prozac Nation Is Now the United States of Xanax." *New York Times*, June 10, 2017.

Xu, Jing. 2017. *The Good Child: Moral Development in a Chinese Preschool*. Stanford, CA: Stanford University Press.

Xu, Jinsheng. 2008. *Tong xin* [Empathy]. Beijing: Beijing Astronomy University Press.

Yalom, Irvin D. 1989. *Love's Executioner: And Other Tales of Psychotherapy*. New York: Basic Books.

———. 2015. *Creatures of a Day: And Other Tales of Psychotherapy*. New York: Basic Books.

Yan, Yunxiang. 1996. *The Flow of Gifts: Reciprocity and Social Networks in a Chinese Village*. Stanford, CA: Stanford University Press.

———. 2003. *Private Life under Socialism: Love, Intimacy, and Family Change in a Chinese Village 1949–1999*. Stanford, CA: Stanford University Press.

———. 2010. *The Individualization of Chinese Society*. Oxford, UK: Berg Publishers.

Yang, Guoshu, Huang Guangguo, and Yang Zhongfang. 2008. *Huaren bentu xinlixue* [Chinese indigenous psychology]. Chongqing: Chongqing University Press.

Yang, Jie. 2010. The Crisis of Masculinity: Class, Gender, and Kindly Power in China. *American Ethnologist* 37 (3): 550–62.

———. 2013a. "'Fake Happiness': Counseling, Potentiality, and Psycho-Politics in China." *Ethos* 41 (3): 291–311.

————. 2013b. *"Peiliao*: Gender, Psychologization and Psychological Labor in China." *Social Analysis* 57 (2): 41–58.

————. 2013c. "Song Wennuan, 'Sending Warmth': Unemployment, New Urban Poverty, and the Affective State in China." *Ethnography* 14: 104–25.

————. 2015. *Unknotting the Heart: Unemployment and Therapeutic Governance in China*. Ithaca, NY: Cornell University Press.

————. 2018. *Mental Health in China*. Cambridge, UK: Polity Press.

Yang, Li, and Vivian Lou. 2013. "Applying the Satir Model of Counseling in Mainland China: Illustrated with 20 Case Sessions." *Satir Journal of Counseling and Family Therapy* 1: 18–39.

Yang, Mayfair. 1994. *Gifts, Favors and Banquets: The Art of Social Relationships in China*. Ithaca, NY: Cornell University Press.

Young, Allan. 1982. "The Anthropologies of Illness and Sickness." *Annual Review of Anthropology* 11: 257–85.

————. 2014. "Resilience for All by the Year 20." In *Stress, Shock and Adaption in the Twentieth Century*. Edited by David Cantor and Edmund Ramsden, 73–95. Rochester, NY: University of Rochester Press.

Yue, Xiaodong. 2004. *Dengtian de ganjue* [Feeling like in heaven]. Shanghai: Shanghai People's Publishing House.

Zhan, Mei. 2009. *Other-Worldly: Making Chinese Medicine through Transnational Frames*. Durham, NC: Duke University Press.

Zhang, Everett. 2011. "Introduction: Governmentality in China." In *Governance of Life in Chinese Moral Experience: The Quest for an Adequate Life*. Edited by Everett Zhang, Arthur Kleinman, and Tu Weiming, 1–30. London: Routledge.

Zhang, Everett, Arthur Kleinman, and Tu Weiming Zhang, eds. 2011. *Governance of Life in Chinese Moral Experience: The Quest for an Adequate Life*. London: Routledge.

Zhang, Li. 2010. *In Search of Paradise: Middle-Class Living in a Chinese Metropolis*. Ithaca, NY: Cornell University Press.

————. 2014. "Bentuhua: Culturing Psychotherapy in Postsocialist China." *Culture, Medicine, and Psychiatry* 38 (2): 283–305.

————. 2015. "Cultivating Happiness: Psychotherapy, Spirituality, and Well-Being in a Transforming Urban China." In *Handbook of Religion and the Asian City*. Edited by Peter van der Veer, 315–32. Berkeley: University of California Press.

————. 2017. "The Rise of Therapeutic Governing in Postsocialist China." *Medical Anthropology* 36 (1): 6–18.

————. 2020. "Embracing Psychological Science for the Good Life?" In *Can Science and Technology Save China?* Edited by Susan Greenhalgh and Li Zhang. Ithaca, NY: Cornell University Press.

Zhang, Li, and Aihwa Ong, eds. 2008. *Privatizing China, Socialism from Afar*. Ithaca, NY: Cornell University Press.

Zhang, Yalin, Derson Young, Sing Lee, Honggen Zhang, Zeping Xiao, Wei Hao, Yongmin Feng, Hongxiang Zhou, and Doris F. Chang. 2002. "Chinese Taoist

Cognitive Psychotherapy in the Treatment of Generalized Anxiety Disorder in Contemporary China." *Transcultural Psychiatry* 30 (1): 115–29.

Zhang, Yanhua. 2007. *Transforming Emotions with Chinese Medicine: An Ethnographic Account from Contemporary China*. Albany: State University of New York Press.

———. 2014. "Crafting Confucian Remedies for Happiness in Contemporary China: Unraveling the Yu Dan Phenomenon." In *The Political Economy of Affect and Emotion in East Asia*. Edited by Jie Yang, 31–44. London: Routledge.

Zhu, Jianfeng. 2013. "Projecting Potentiality: Understanding Maternal Serum Screening in Contemporary China." *Current Anthropology* 54 (S7): S36–44.

Zhu, Jianjun. 2008. *Laizi dongfang de xinli zhiliaofa* [The psychotherapy from the Orient]. Hefei: Anhui People's Publishing House.

INDEX

Jung Institute (Zurich), 59
Jungian psychology, 47; influence of on
  sandplay therapy, 58–69

Kabat-Zinn, Jon, 141, 142, 183nn14–15
Kaiping Peng, 138–39
Kalff, Dora, 59
Kerr, John G., 23–24
Khenpo Sodargye, 144
Kipnis, Andrew, 18, 183n1
Kirmayer, Lawrence, 177n28
Kleinman, Arthur, 12, 27, 117, 177n23
knowledge: constitutive nature of, 14;
  psychological, 14
Kongzi, 23
Kornfield, Jack, 140–41, 142, 183nn15
Kunming, 22, 41, 48, 174; economic reform in,
  10; growth of, 9; lack of mental health
  facilities in, 9
Kunming Municipal Industry and Commerce
  Bureau, 98
Kunming Saibaiwei Vocational School, 32–33

Lan, Marie, 95
Laozi, 23
Lao Zi, 62
Lewis, Bradley, 130
lingxing ("spirit" or "wisdom"), 60
Lin Liuchen, 143
Li Shaokun, 23
Liu Hui, 136–37
Liu Kun, 93–94, 99–100, 108–9
Liu Zhen, 49–52, 53
Living through Suffering (Sodargye), 144
Li Yang, 95–96
Li Zhang, 1–2; affiliation of with the Yunnan
  Provincial Health Education Institute,
  10; counseling sessions with Shuyu, 78–81;
  panic attack of, 7–8; physical and
  psychological problems of her mother,
  87–91; ties of with the Xinlin internship
  center, 10
Li Zixun, 31, 35
Lou, Vivian, 96–97
Love's Executioner: And Other Tales of
  Psychotherapy (Yalom), 91
Lu Minxin, 122–24, 127
Lu Zhiwei, 25

Ma Jiajue, 150
Makun, 71–72

Malaysia, 95
Mao Zedong, 27, 42, 107, 144; death of, 29;
  post-Mao era, 17, 172
Marxism, 96
Maslow, Abraham, 120
Matza, Tomas, 130, 184n2
May Fourth Movement, 16
meditation, 140–43, 183nn19–20; Daoist
  meditation, 58; incorporation of in
  cognitive behavioral therapy (CBT),
  57–58; success and happiness as a goal of,
  145–47; workplace happiness (zhicjang
  xingfu), 145; workshops concerning,
  146–47; Zen meditation, 58
Meiyue, 83–85
mental illness, 176–77n18; association of
  with "madness" in China, 27; number
  of Chinese suffering from, 3; treatments
  for, 27
Mental Philosophy: Including the Intellect,
  Sensibilities, and Will (Haven), 24
mindfulness, 57–58, 140–43
Minnesota Multiphasic Personality Inventory
  (MMPI), 160
mood disorders, 4, 9, 27
Morita, Shoma, 142
Morita therapy, 142–43
Mozi, 23
Mr. Ling, 145–46, 153, 163–64
Mr. Wu, 165–66
Mr. Xiao, 117–18
Mr. Yuan, 29
Ms. Yang, 153, 155–56, 159, 161–62
Ms. Zhou, 82–85, 153, 157–60

Naikan therapy, 142; roots of in Buddhism,
  143
Nanjing Advanced Normal University, 25
National Center for Mental Health
  (China), 3
National Vocational Standards for Psycho-
  logical Counselors, 34
neurasthenia, 27–28, 29; in Chinese society, 12
New Peoplemaking, The (Satir), 48
Ng, Emily, 177n29
Nolan, James, 20–21
Northwest Satir Institute, 95
"noso-politics," 172, 185n4
Novak, Sandy, 95
Nu xinlishi (The female psychological counse-
  lor [Shumin]), 35

Founded in 1893,
UNIVERSITY OF CALIFORNIA PRESS
publishes bold, progressive books and journals
on topics in the arts, humanities, social sciences,
and natural sciences—with a focus on social
justice issues—that inspire thought and action
among readers worldwide.

The UC PRESS FOUNDATION
raises funds to uphold the press's vital role
as an independent, nonprofit publisher, and
receives philanthropic support from a wide
range of individuals and institutions—and from
committed readers like you. To learn more, visit
ucpress.edu/supportus.